The Future of the Electronic Marketplace

The Future of the Electronic Marketplace

edited by Derek Leebaert

The MIT Press
Cambridge, Massachusetts
London, England

Second Printing, 1999
© 1998 Massachusetts Institute of Technology

Set in Sabon by Wellington Graphics.
Printed and bound in the United States of America.

Library of Congress Cataloging-in-Publication Data

The future of the electronic marketplace / edited by Derek Leebaert.
    p. cm.
  Includes bibliographical references and index.
  ISBN 0-262-12209-X (hard : alk. paper)
  1. Electronic commerce. I. Leebaert, Derek.
HF5548.32.F87 1998
658.8′00285—dc21   97-46856
                                                                    CIP

Contents

Acknowledgements

Donna Farmer, Esq., serving as Counsel for the Technology Subcommittee of the Science Committee of the US House of Representatives, was an invaluable guide through the worlds of finance, technology, and public policy. She is a worthy advisor to America's lawmakers and business leaders. Michael Peterson, software engineer, industry executive, and technology visionary, continues to be a patient tutor. Spencer Brittain Bradley of the Advisory Board Company keeps offering provocative insights into the capabilities of natural language processing.

Timothy Dickinson, of the *Paris Review* and of innumerable consultancies in banking, business analysis, and economic forecasting, is the ultimate and friendliest critic for anyone lucky enough to work with him. Peter Schilling offered his own contribution at a vital moment. So too did management strategists John May and Douglas Miscoll.

Scott Behnke, Senior Internetworking Consultant at Linguateq, Inc., was grossly underemployed in handling the logistics of the manuscript. And Norman Ball of CalNet used a lucid pen as well as practical business experience to catalyze the overall effort. Finally, Ed Stephenson, Maurice Zilber, and Estelle Moeri kindly offered encouragement and wisdom.

The Future of the Electronic Marketplace

Present at the Creation

Derek Leebaert

Until very recently, it would have been easy to say that all of us who enter a market are to some degree "present at the creation." From generation to generation, markets were always re-creating themselves. But now, in the information age, the very idea of what a market is tends to change seemingly by the minute.

The essays in this volume have been written by some of the principal navigators of the high winds of electronic commerce. They explain their activities and visions as re-creation presses hard upon re-creation. There are people still alive who were born before the discovery of radio: most adults can remember a world without modems and personal computers. Now the logic of these familiar tools, the logic of choices and outreaches barely imaginable only 20 years ago, has to be put to a million tasks that entrepreneurs are offering the world with the speed of magicians, with the power won from mathematics, money, and silicon.

Today, we no longer need a coffeehouse like Lloyd's or a buttonwood such as sheltered the first brokers of the New York Stock Exchange to make a market. Anyone with access to electricity can make a market at will. And the market is making new buyers, sellers, and even intermediaries out of the sheer richness of its possibilities.

An electronic marketplace, whatever it may sell, brokers knowledge of a previously unorderable magnitude. It therefore deals in a previously unorganizable possibility. The duration of a transaction shrinks from the months taken by Columbus, or from the maddening intervals of literally pushed paper, to a pulse of electricity. The market's prime task, which is to go beyond choiceless exchanges between neighbors to creative gatherings with wide-open possibilities, becomes ever more achievable at the same time that it furthers (in the words of Norbert Wiener, one of the pioneers of the computer era) "the human use of human beings."

The means may be electronic, but the marketplace is intensely human. Communication technologies join with information to free us from previously exhausting intervening processes.

Responses are becoming ever denser and more usefully intricate, whether called up by a car collector specifying the seventeen criteria that a 1963 Cadillac must meet for him to buy it or by a graduate student in the life sciences establishing the cost of originating a cross-species gene.

The electronic marketplace opens doors from Wall Street to Khartoum to downtown Tokyo, making them no more distant than if they were around the corner. We hear the hum of new commerce, but most of us have not walked in. We are still cautiously lumbering from store to store to buy a new shirt or visiting multiple dealers to haggle over a new Buick.

The marketplaces we mainly frequent still possess the old built-in inequalities and compulsions. Producers and distributors still have the advantage that comes from controlling the main spigots of information—print and broadcasting. Consumers have yet to acquire the sense that technology enables them to gain real-time feedback, to better compare any two or more things seeking their dollars, and to work toward a real partnership with the manufacturer in creating the products they use.

The participants in the electronic marketplace of 2008, however, will stand or fall by the test of a steadily increasing "reciprocity of communication." Minds are no longer meeting just in a coffeehouse or a car lot; they are beginning to meet in the whole electronic world, finding doors open to choice where blank walls stood only yesterday.

Even those of us who are in the middle of creating this market (or, rather, its first great iteration) understand that ours are only the first improvements of this new space. Certainly the changes ahead are equal to those brought on by the coming of literacy and powered transportation. The authors in this volume admit that they can see only the earliest outlines of this force, even as it sweeps them up. But they are well positioned to offer imaginative opinions on what may lie ahead: the procedures, tools, and consequences that will radiate into the wider society. They seek to ask the right questions and thus to draw upon their individual experiences in a cross-section of the industries that are moving ever further into this marketplace: communications, retailing, manufacturing, energy, banking, accounting, transportation.

It is impossible to include insights from every form of endeavor that these initiatives are facilitating. Some additional fields (advertising and health care, for instance) would be exciting topics for entire volumes. But one of the commanding characteristics of the new marketplace is that once-contrasting industries and professions are ever more naturally melding: e.g., education with entertainment, retailing with manufacturing and advertising, and communications with energy utilities and medicine. They are all connected by finance and accounting—disciplines which themselves are changing rapidly.

One way to begin gaining a perspective of 5 or 10 years is to share the thoughts of those business leaders who are actually fighting their way to market. Moreover, the authors in this book tend to have large and healthily contrasting stakes in the outcomes.

Dean Acheson used the phrase "present at the creation" to make sense of his experiences as US Secretary of State when the world had to be rebuilt after history's greatest war. Now these essays seek to map the tremendously creative destruction of the greatest peaceful revolution to date through the eyes of several of its foremost expert dreamers.

The microchip helped bring down Communism and end the Cold War. Communication technologies that the chip makes possible are now pushing the sense of individual initiative not as something risky or luxurious but as a birthright for all. Centralizing authorities, public and private, are too heavy and slow to meet challenges to grow and adapt at the speed of newly informed consumers and garage entrepreneurs. Kenneth Boulding, economist and poet, saw a world in which the utility of the Coca-Cola Corporation outlasted that of the US government. Perhaps we are now able to see just that possibility unfolding.

The other authors and I emphasize "the electronic marketplace" in contrast to (say) "digital commerce" because the marketplace has always been a space in which to meet and argue and bargain over things—a place of freedom and newness, offering reciprocities not thought of until encountered. It is a place to criticize and to confront criticism, imposing efficiencies on its participants and giving opportunity to creation. It is the place, real or notional, of reasoned discussion between buyer and seller. Once one rode a mule to the market; now one rides the Internet. The electronic marketplace gathers the "what ifs" and answers them with "so thens." It says that nothing is perfect, but that most things are useful once each finds its price. "Digital commerce," on the other hand, is an administrator's vision: predictable, functional, unenergizing, and lacking the blood, sweat, and (their cousin) excitement of the constant, sleepless electronic market.

Electronic commerce has been building up for several decades through money transfers between banks and through the modestly efficient trans-actions between vendor and supplier made possible by electronic data interchange (EDI). But the marketplace as it is now taking shape is pushing outward from big routinizing institutions toward individual consumers, endlessly compounding the numbers and types of trans-actions.

Who comes to this marketplace, with what intent, and who reaps most advantage? There is no telling. Advantage teeters on a breathtakingly shifting balance, with virtually everyone likely to gain at various points. But Gregg Zachary of the *Wall Street Journal* has reported cogently about a stark trend toward inequality, and others have done likewise.

"The most important product of mining," said the French sociologist Frederic LePlay, "is miners." By the same token, but even more pro-foundly and much more humanely, we are beginning to see that the most important product of the electronic marketplace is the electronic work-force. And everyone who comes into this marketplace is part of that workforce, for so much of the work done there is working for oneself by buying just the right thing.

These essays set out to envision the flexibility and expansion of the marketplace over the next decade, some of its instruments to this end, some of the pitfalls, and some of the questions of how to set price and value upon these changes. We know that many things are being gained. We don't necessarily know what, where, or how much is being gained, or by whom, and what the effects might be, but the authors at least are scattering some ideas which they hope may begin offering answers.

Most businesspeople today tend to assume the existence of many technological accomplishments that have not in fact yet arrived—for instance, data interoperability, a sizable speed bump on the road to market. Such inexact assumptions may be called the "reading edge" of technology: seeing articles in *Forbes* and *Fortune,* or in *Communications of the ACM* or *IEEE Spectrum,* readers assume that the next miracle has already arrived, or is at least nearly at hand, and they are often jolted to learn that it is still a few years away. But despite delays, we are all in the vortex of what Gerald Piel—not the least of its catalysts—called "the acceleration of history."

Everyone is being accelerated away from the triumphalist ukase of early-twentieth-century industrialism that the customer can "have any color so long as it's black." All of us come not just to buy and sell but (more consciously than earlier visitors to dustier marketplaces) to deliberately alter—to reshape products, services, and ways of doing business. The concept of mass customization has by now become pretty familiar, however close on the "reading edge." Less examined have been the implications for decision and control, for continuous adaptation, for vigilance, for pricing, and for branding.

Should we also be weighing the dangers of unreflective instantaneous response and the pitfalls of easy access? (The communication systems of the 1920s, after all, pulled hordes of unprepared new investors into the money centers, to the grief and disaster of many.) Might we consider just how financial derivatives embody the expansion of choice in the electronic marketplace, while keeping before our eyes just what that did for Orange County? For better or worse, ever more complicated choices are going to have to be made, and steadily faster. The more efficient the entry mechanism, the easier entry is; however, exit is often handled not electronically but by the law of contracts—a much trickier turnstile to swing.

What kind of institutional markets can survive instantaneous communications? To what extent can central banks even stabilize currencies? Will interest-rate controls be trampled to pieces under the international dance of capital? What might be the nature of a stock exchange if stocks can be traded anywhere? Must there be radical new ways to monitor these ghostly transactions? What might the existence of new markets suggest for legal authority and for enforcement? It can be tricky to try to answer these questions, but it would be fatuous not to ask them. Absent vigilance, marketplaces do not survive. The new world of commerce requires reasonably clear, just, and enforceable regulations, if only to impose some degree of honest disclosure.

The right to open a marketplace was once a jealously guarded sovereign privilege. When people do not need a geographical meeting place, they confront all sorts of not-fully-thought-through contingencies, not least the questions of vigilance. The power of this marketplace, however, lies in part in its ability to take advantage of the absence of fixed locations, of habit, and of regulation by those who got there first. If it is not to deliver itself to the anarchy of ruinous fraud or desperate private reprisal, this marketplace has to rediscover old prudences but also to invent new forms of answerability.

Aside from the arguments over whether such new gifts empower the weak or reinforce the strong, it will be interesting to see what sorts of temperaments excel in it—what curious analogies will arise, say, to today's currency traders. What yet more extraordinary futures will emerge? What new ways to package risk will be imagined? What properties will be disaggregated and securitized, as have thoroughbred horses, Chilean earthquake risks, and collateralized car-loan pools?

Much of the preservative energy of civilization still goes into telling people what they don't know or can't do. But now ever more people can set out to define ever more jobs. They can draw on their own skills without getting permission to take every initiative and without having their every competence assessed at demoralizing length from above. The task is proposed, the solution is left to those responsible, and (as George Patton said of his troops while blasting into Germany) the result is likely to be astounding. In fact, the real task is created only after being assigned as an idea.

Does any sensible manager know what an objective's exact requirements should be, or how to pursue them, until he encounters the imaginations of those charged with achieving it? When Franklin Delano Roosevelt had to get an atomic bomb—never before made—produced at greater speed than a new generation of something familiar, such as battleships, he commissioned a few good people and told them the money was there, rightly believing that this would prove enough. No one wrote equations on his desk; he would not have understood them anyway. There is increasingly a place for such confident flexibility when presuming to manage innovation.

People in the Marketplace

Thus, we begin with people. Earlier generations proved smart enough to handle each of the previous upheavals, from agriculture to corporations, with less help from precedent than we will have this time. But all this speed of communication means that our own professional skills quickly become outdated. The result is more challenging, less boring, and never free of the need to retrain (if you're a pessimist), and it provides a continuous incentive to enlarge oneself (if you're an optimist).

Some argue that, at least in the short run, there will be a substitution of technology for lower-paid, lower-skilled workers, and that the automation of service is an important influence behind wage stagnation and income inequality—and indeed such seems to be a first consequence of all mechanizations of basic processes. But the Java programmer was emancipated by the cotton gin, to paraphrase Robert Heinlein. What we are actually seeing is an unprecedented electronically driven worldwide audit of repetitive and previously fixed activities—whether those of a factory heretofore anchored outside Detroit or Toulon or those of an insurance company with six layers of procedures. Distance keeps being flattened institutionally no less than it is being killed geographically.

In the era of repetitive, mind-killing jobs, those in authority regarded the workforce with suspicion verging on contempt. Now there is a chance for everyone to get more done with more interest and more personalization. The worldwide scope and the transactional complexity of the tasks ahead mean that they will be best accomplished by people with self-respect and plain committed interest who are not merely following orders.

Meanwhile, we see and feel the subversive power of knowledge as particular occupations become obsolescent and as many work functions (such as the higher levels of nursing and lab work) become de facto liberal professions. We see it in the confident attitudes of skilled practitioners. Hospital managements, for instance, are always behind in their awareness of what their physicians are prescribing and what procedures their surgeons are adopting. It will not be long before managements in all sorts of other organizations have similar problems of assimilating what is actually going on. Along the way, new forms of perceived self-interest will arise as individuals are less beholden to institutions.

We in the United States broke out of the Ford-through-IBM era not under pressure from foreign competition—which is anyway grossly exaggerated (cheaper foreign factor costs bring down our internal prices and enhance our flexibility)—but under pressure from an awareness that work procedures were simply becoming outdated in relation to opportunities. Practices that came into being in the same way as the QWERTY keyboard (designed to be inefficient so as not to be jammed by fast typists) are still wearyingly obstructive. They are certain to be axed for the crime of irrationality; we just don't know when. In the new marketplace, voices (as usual) are raised against the often-stern adaptations enforced by competition. They resonate with the anticipated pains of learning and the even greater anticipated agony of having to unlearn.

We should worry about such change, but we are unlikely to regret it in the long run—especially when the old labor market is giving way to a receptive electronic market in which individuals no longer have to move to where the jobs are. Now people will prepare themselves for work they can sink their teeth into. At present, nearly all individuals spend their lives at jobs well below their abilities—just watch most people's true competencies as they play poker, talk politics, handle baseball statistics, use their home computers, and so on.

And a job does not have to last a lifetime. People grow, and jobs that stifle growth are blessings only to those who fear that otherwise they may go hungry. Furthermore, people know that the unchanging job is a thing of the past. It might, in fact, be hoped that many jobs do die. There are all too few worth preserving. Why should certain people be locked into being telephone operators, baggage checkers, or coal miners?

Will the electronic marketplace diminish work or elevate it? Will most people have more routinized or more intellectually demanding jobs? Will they even have jobs at all? Many argue that, as the new automation makes its way into category after category that seemed irreducibly human, we can no longer assume that technological advances will either create more jobs or make what jobs remain more satisfying, as was the case (reckoning from generation to generation) in the industrial past. Some see this marketplace as characterized by sterile, clerkless stores and peopleless service centers.

Technology has long been blamed for exacerbating unemployment. During the 1930s, Charles Beard and other intellectuals insisted that when goods could be produced too easily labor became dispensable. In the 1960s, the young Woody Allen had a comedy routine about a talking elevator that took his father's job. In 1963 the AFL-CIO published a report showing that it required four times the capital of a decade before to "endow" a new job. Somehow, the 1960s boomed in spite of this.

With the use of automated voice recognition, the number of telephone operators has fallen from 250,000 in 1956 to barely 50,000 today. Similar replacement has hit bank tellers (and vice presidents), mobile workers such as utility meter readers (fast being replaced by transmitters), and account managers for (e.g.) Goodyear stores. Is this a Darwinian transformation? Is it sweeping with equal indifference through information-rich jobs such as those of the highly trained engineers presiding over help desks (who now may merely be overseeing a smart network that allows customers to handle their own problems)?

Some see a bifurcation of work as the main consequence of the information technology revolution, with the electronic marketplace dividing its suppliers uneasily into those with dull, routinized, insecure jobs and those with loosely defined, intense, improvisational skills—all of which is said to exacerbate an unpleasant distinction of class, caste, and function between implicit "geniuses" and "morons."

By 2008, work, leisure, and consumption will be feeding into one another in curious ways, and they will be undergoing further transformation by intelligent networks. Consumption will be increasingly easy, efficient, and individuated. Appetites not only highly specified but also clarified by opportunity will demand customization of products and services. Leisure is almost inescapably a form of consumption, so the concentration of work time will give people a broad spectrum of ways to spend their hours more creatively and meaningfully.

Most talent is wasted, said Eric Hoffer, matter-of-factly rather than angrily. Most ideas—even good ones—are not even heard, let alone acted upon. But this is not necessarily so anymore. For instance, the US venture capital industry (which invested more than $12 billion yearly in young companies during the late 1990s) has fueled innovation for more than a generation. The process by which concepts and entrepreneurs are selected for institutional financing is still strikingly inefficient, however, with seminal technologies often neglected as candidates for commercialization. In the marketplace of 2008, it might be hoped, early-stage investing will be far less arbitrary as matches between individual innovators and individual investors (as well as specifically concerned companies) become ever wider and better informed.

Buying, Selling, and Specializing

All advances are unfamiliar to the generation during which they come into general use, only to become unfamiliar again as they are replaced. A mother who tells her whining child "You sound like a broken record" is asked "What's a record?" A teacher who encourages her third graders to become pen pals with kids in a developing country is asked "What is pen pals?"—but then a voice pipes up from the back of the classroom: "It's like email, only you use pencil and paper."

For several years, pundits had only to invoke "virtual shopping" to feel elevated above the common horizon. Now the Internet has already jerked what was largely thought to be an airy concept into increasingly profitable buying and selling. As the practical visionary Walter Forbes explains, the "virtual store" can expand at the special speed conferred by not having to meet rent, inventory, and most overhead. Its challenge to mall-bound "brick-and-mortar" commerce should provide one of the heavyweight battles of the early twenty-first century.

Virtual stores not only do without many material things; they also draw on many new and impalpable strengths—prodigies of shared product information, a range of comparisons directly available for customers who would wear themselves out reviewing so many showcases in the real world. As in all changes of such magnitude, individual habits will reshape themselves at least as rapidly as will the processes of offering, ordering, and delivering goods.

Department stores and "megastores" have succeeded so far by offering diversity rather than concentrating on the most profitable items, by being able to turn goods over steadily at low markups (economies of time due to a common location being worth some economies of price), and by providing entertainment in addition to goods. Virtual stores will offer all this, and much more, deploying their own forms of secure transactions, effective advertising, and steady alertness to new products.

The sheer range of information and customized services can be troubling to shoppers, writers, and travelers using the Internet, which is a sort of superb catalogue published in non-alphabetical order and seemingly designed for people with time to kill. But time is a peculiarly precious commodity, and there is no point in saving time that would be spent driving from store to store only to lose it staring at a screen.

How can all the information now available be organized and made quickly interrogable? This is what several authors get excited about: electronic agents, or avatars, that go substantially beyond what is discussed even on the "reading edge," being in effect meta-agents (roughly, "agents using agents") that give each user what Denos Gazis calls his or her "personal application specificity." The creation of such agents will probably entail an interweaving of neural networks and a reassessment of past promises of artificial intelligence. Initially, agents will make it easier to sort through the daunting masses of product offerings and travel conditions; eventually, hyperintelligent agents will serve as guides through the whole body of human knowledge. By about the year 2005, PASHAs—personal application-specific hyper-intelligent agents—will be able to become expert assistants to humans, able to escort them through complex tasks, from managing their finances to coping with the vagaries of traveling through congested urban networks. Businesses will find in PASHAs a convenient army of intelligent assistants able to optimize many processes around the clock, from regulating energy consumption to tracking and improving the movement of inventories and shipments.

Gazis, as well as Forbes, has examined some of the implicit possibilities. He has, in fact, helped bring the book down to earth by dispersing the clouds of bits and bytes to hold these processes to the test of how all the sweaters, Web TVs, cars, and garden tools accessible through Forbes's electronic gateway will actually arrive at the doorstep or the loading dock—the fundamental issue of literal traffic management far too often overlooked in babble about "the information highway." Here we have another reminder that no revolution has ever fully been able to dispense with its predecessors.

Advertising—that is, conveying a good's particular desirability—clearly cannot be jettisoned. In the existing marketplace, the amount of worthwhile information available to most buyers is still relatively small. There is only so much time and space for print and broadcast advertising, bought by the sellers for their single purposes. Tomorrow's advertising will be valuable to the extent that it can assume substantive feedback from the people to whom it is aimed.

The electronic marketplace is, at one end, a new overall broadcasting tool, the ultimate town crier. At the other end are to be found tremendous opportunities for targeting highly defined groups. This new marketplace rewards the capacity to mine sophisticated databases in order to identify buying patterns, demographic data, credit ratings, popular Internet chat rooms, zip code correlations, and voting habits. Both focused and inter-active, it commits the seller and the buyer to a dialogue. Companies can move from mass marketing to direct marketing, from selling to everyone to selling to an ever more refinable slice of the market. And with this comes great immediacy. An issue of a magazine might close to advertisers 90 days ahead of the publication date. TV spots have to be in 2 weeks before broadcast time. On the Web, information is posted daily, and customer surveys, advertising, and sales are rolled into one electronic interface.

Companies are increasingly searching for ways to fund entertainment and information services on the Web. While some Web sites have resorted to subscription schemes, others have begun to sell advertising space within their sites. As advertising on the Internet grows, more interesting content will likely become available, which will, in turn, attract new viewers to this medium and therefore attract more advertisers.

However, the first attempts, using simple banners rotated through a Web site, have not provided advertisers the results that they sought: this paradigm appeals largely to advertisers of computer technology products. Other approaches, such as the use of browser meta-data (basic geographic and domain name information) for targeting and the use of inference engines to tailor messages, have not fared any better. None of these approaches provides the capability to access information about a person's activities and affinities beyond the Web. The key for marketers will be to integrate traditional direct and database marketing techniques with their interactive activities.

What is likely to become commonplace by 2003 is targeted, interactive advertising and direct marketing that use information gleaned from external sources of information (e.g., third-party databases, customer information systems) and thus reflect ever more details about an individual's offline lifestyle and purchasing habits. Promotions and advertising can then be tightly coordinated, and a direct communication channel with the customer can be established and maintained.

Such an approach, now being explored by Intelligent Interactions Corp., makes it possible to examine customers' habits over time. Affinity groups can be built and test marketing conducted in an efficient and cost-effective manner. By 2001, through the integration of new media and traditional broadcasting technologies, targeted promotions and advertisements will be delivered during regular television programs. All this can be realized provided there is a mechanism to target and interact with the consumer, using familiar sources of information.

To convey their desires more effectively, buyers themselves are increasingly likely to work their way behind brand definitions. The really rich already draw on a range of services and providers not known to them by name, which they obtain (usually through intermediaries) for specific objectives, not lifetime familiarity. In fact, most brands offer comfort of habit and uncomplicated choice, not unique advantage. But the faster the market moves, the more deeply its offerings are subject to scrutiny. The shapeless advantages of a brand might therefore be less likely to keep their psychic beachheads.

At present, most sellers have at their disposal relatively raw information, not very sophisticatedly accessible, about buyers. The valuable insights that such information unquestionably contains are still pretty deeply buried. But not for much longer.

What is now called "relationship management" involves the statistical projection of how people respond to products and services, to overtures, and to other people with the same interests. Analyses such as those performed at Carnegie Mellon University for Bell Atlantic offer far deeper and more specific understandings of behavior in the marketplace than ever before—with predictive capabilities likely to leave all previous techniques in the dust by, say, 2005.

The power to profile the customer is progressing from something akin to the shadow outlines of radar to something more like the images of faces seen on television. Using highly intelligent agents to edit all this data will assure increasingly precise portraits. The exactness of profiling raises not only questions of privacy but also questions of what is proprietary and what is secure.

The propensity to buy products and services has as much to do with the purchaser's feelings about who or what is doing the selling as with price, quality, and accessibility. Trust is part of the commodity. What affinity groups will be targeted? What memberships will be offered to consumers, with the more or less ulterior purpose of selling to them?

The market is preparing a firing squad for middlemen, insurance salespeople, investment bankers, travel agents, car dealers, and other delegated influencers of buyers' judgment. We now go to the source. The purge has already torn great gaps in the ranks. Wal-Mart, still America's largest retailer, enjoyed a short period of greatness—it genuinely represented another iteration of the acceleration of history, owing in part to its early adoption of EDI and other innovative tools for inventory management and distribution. But even the best companies run through their cycles of triumphant assertion and counter-challenge much faster, and are easier to emulate in all but the most secret processes. They are much more subject to well-aimed slice competition if they cannot be challenged head-on by their rivals.

Despite the excitement about communication technologies' throwing open the perfect market, middlemen (or, more likely, middlemachines) may nonetheless still be necessary to give form and depth to choice. Databases indeed carry more options, and are less impolitely told to move on to a better offer, than weary human go-betweens.

The fixed price, an innovation of truth-bound Quakers in the seventeenth century, was a forward step, allowing better planning of supplies and better management of time. No longer did 15 people have to wait in line while two argued over the price of an apple. But over the long haul it was somewhat of a step back, in that it standardized only one factor in the exchange relationship. A customer who would not buy without free delivery might keep prices down by increasing economy of scale, but was really always a bit of a freeloader.

What happens when a highly calibrated marketplace can be established whose visitors can insist that they wish to buy a box of cereal 28 days from now, discounted 8 percent for the slow season? At Oxford, in the early 1960s, a minor scandal ensued when some American students offered to pay more than the going rate for typing if it could be done quicker. Whereas queuing offers advantage to those for whom a need is not urgent, the electronic marketplace short-circuits the notion that the reward of patience (i.e., the willingness to invest time, to incur opportunity cost) is cheapness.

Products and services will be increasingly shaped by individual desire rather than by standard form—often at the initiative of a supplier excited by opportunity. Meanwhile, it is possible to minimize the routine input and perhaps to shift labor to the interesting and specific—the creative segments of production. The "human use" indeed, soaring above the rote labor of Chaplin's *Modern Times*.

As speed of production reduces direct cost, the capital carry costs shrink. But speed is nothing without sales power and flow control. (The faster you make what is not wanted, the faster you go bust.) Continuous adaptation to the world's demand and its propensity to consume—that is, mastery of information—lies at the heart of longevity. The manufacturer can deliver the customized widget at the point of request. The more savings, the better the position to improve the product.

Capacities to customize keep arriving in various industries, increasingly maximizing the pre-production dialectic between consumer and producer. Each new section of a production line can be more specialized than the last, as long as the seller has the power to dissolve the overall portrait of the buying public into more focused "pixels" of particular demands.

The market today—even the market over the Internet—is still a place in which to choose among products already created and services already running. There are, however, no longer any reasons why the individual consumer cannot propose his or her desires as to what should exist while engaging in the dialogue of technological possibility and economy of scale. Consumers can really be present at the creation of a product, helping to build the prototype. Buyers with enormous clout (usually, as is true of the government, due to their freedom from ordinary economic prudence) have always been able to do this. By 2008, wider and wider circles of consumers should enjoy similar clout and interaction when buying anything from harbor dredges to letterhead stationery. Manufacturing merges with service as the roles of consumers and producers converge.

Factories are changing before our eyes, and so may our notions of labor. To be provocative but by no means unrealistic, imagine 12-year-old children coming electronically to work in a distant factory—not the gray-faced waifs enslaved to the looms of the nineteenth century but, rather, children putting in some skill-forming hours on line from home or school. The task might involve writing code or operating a machine. (In the 1980s, Alan Kay showed fascinating videos of what 2-year-old girls could already create on a desktop computer in their first imitative ventures into skill.)

As each new good passes into the flow of trade, its users develop new perspectives on how to use it further, and indeed to reconfigure it. These have often been perspectives not envisaged by the designer: a fireman's outfit turned into a diving suit, for example, or a gun turret used as a mount for a radio telescope. The time required to assess a good's strengths and vulnerabilities and the richness of that assessment do much to determine the good's chances in any marketplace. A product is not viable until it is used—ask the designers of the Edsel.

It is also easier to become an entrepreneur than ever before. One can draw on new capacities to create and target advertising, to find buyers and sellers, and to raise capital from a larger pool of potential investors. Ever more individual enterprise radiates greater energy throughout the economic system. The fundamental ability to bring the critical pieces together is never confined to companies of any given size. The bigger and more stolid a corporation is now, the more it will be compelled to examine itself with a deconstructing eye, "intrapreneuring" its brittle parts with one another and the outside world.

For instance, the steady, downright-encouraged-to-be somnolent utility behemoths are undergoing the advent of what William Bandt calls "smart energy." They will no longer confine themselves to delivering voltage and gas molecules. Instead, they must increasingly offer (through their mighty infrastructure, built for quite other purposes) communication services, automated trading, perhaps movies, and conceivably educational software as they spring forward to become national and international competitors. The consequent regulatory revolution, and the snowstorm of new services, will surpass in their impact the creative destruction of the Bell System.

All this electronic efflorescence—virtual shopping, video banking, intelligent transportation—is growing out of rapidly evolving technologies: PC communications services, the new efficiencies of instant data interoperability that MCI has pioneered, the host of satellites that Irving Goldstein foresees. Ironically, they will also permit so much more to endure.

Dante sighed at how the greatest painters had had their day and been forgotten. Today, 700 years later, art scholarship has produced a multiplex world of appreciation which does not require one epoch of greatness to fall into obscurity to make room for the next. As recently as the 1950s, excellent Victorian art was being thrown out. A hundred years ago, Queen Anne churches were regarded as particularly ugly and were being torn down. Now there are journals and collectors for every period of Western art in at least seven centuries. There is no decade without a large literature, exhibitions, and passionate buyers. Now only 20 or 30 years pass before there is a society for the preservation of a style of architecture.

This largeness of view is the mark not just of abundance but also of the range of thoughtful acceptance that abundance makes possible— acceptance that sustains growth on all fronts, as it should. Fashion, in contrast, is the mark of scarcity of information—something has to go out of fashion for something else to come in. Human inventiveness is too rich for fashion.

Value, Money, and Security

Central to the development of the electronic marketplace is the future of money—how to define it, how to access it, and how to protect transactions.

It has long been true that the right information about money is worth more than money, and certainly there is nothing unique about this in the age of *Being Digital.*

Rational allocation of capital is a never-ending process. If we all had access to the same information, insights, and interpretations as, say, the investor George Soros, we still probably would not be as rich as he. He would still be George Soros, not a learnable condition. But the bands of difference between Mr. Soros and the followers he might not want would grow narrower. Such unique advantages will have to fight harder to assert themselves in a much more nearly instantaneous world.

The electronic marketplace is going to subject the amorphous family of notions loosely called "assets" to much stiffer and more systematic auditing, with new ways, no doubt, of depreciating such ever more impalpable valuables as software and insurance. As Dan Keegan demonstrates in his essay, the most serious judgments will still be made ever faster, but will also be shaped by timeless wisdom.

The less you must spend on what you need to have done for you, the more you can back your particular competencies. Entrepreneurs can focus their resources on what they hope are specific contributions, rather than smearing them over general areas that others are supposed to know about. One result is likely to be ever more dynamism.

Cash, already almost archaic, is remorselessly being displaced by credit, and its velocity in the greater part of economic life keeps dropping. It is ever less useful except in emergencies. The "demonetization" of transactions has become a commonplace, much like the newspaper's ceasing to be an instrument of hot news.

In the electronic marketplace, "demonetization" marches arm in arm with "delocalization" and "decentralization." At the financial level, speed of transaction makes it possible to create all sorts of new financial instruments, such as options to sell interest-rate swaps. New types of rating agencies spring up, to suffer, no doubt, their own encounters with market weeding. But new efficiences also arrive.

A money center bank such as Ed Horowitz's expects to service tens of millions more people in more and more ways previously accessible only to those with private bankers. Video banking is just an early taste of what lies ahead as such services reach into lower-income areas and into emerging markets overseas almost in parallel with the blowing away of old-time "full service" branches.

Not only do new means of access present themselves, to create their own new constituencies as well as to service old ones, but "dead time" actually does die at the mechanical hands of instant-response automation. Time is money; so is overhead.

Twenty years ago, as Martin Mayer recounts in *The Bankers,* General Motors was pleased with itself when the procedures of its Acceptance Corporation gave it "$20 million to play with overnight." That windfall glee is seemingly from another epoch. Saint Augustine said that he knew what "time" meant until he was asked to explain it. A huge body of futures fall into much the same category. Information technologies and their users are getting much more sophisticated than the combinations that produced the current mind-bending financial products.

How safely the vital impalpables, from life savings to psychiatric records, can navigate the electronic ocean is a question that gets more urgent every year. To realize the full potential of the electronic market-place requires that security be real and believed in. It is in this area of brief privilege and intensity that arguments over encryption bring government stomping forward with heavy and fundamentally irrelevant concern about the criminal potential of impenetrable communication.

A provably secure system will never be possible. Encryption can never fully be traversed by technical means, one reason being that cryptographic material can be dissolved within other material. For instance, it is not possible to tell whether one is looking at a message encrypted in an artistic reproduction—for instance, where the Mona Lisa stops and the proprietary technoinformation begins.

More than a few lawmakers and government agencies are short-sightedly trying to stop encryption technologies from being used to make electronic communications secure, thereby undermining many of the efficiencies of electronic commerce. The ongoing controversies over encryption embody the potential, the pitfalls, and the confusion of the electronic marketplace.

Of course, encryption has considerable criminal possibilities, which will energetically be seized upon. Crime is so far an ineradicable aspect of human enterprise. Every great advance has been pressed into the service of wrongdoing. But all these innovations survive and prosper, as will the commercial uses of the most sophisticated encryption, because they offer more positive transformations than damaging ones. Millions of people want encryption capabilities now, and perhaps hundreds of millions will 10 years hence. Restricting commercial encryption may be Washington's big unintended contribution to the international economy as valuable intangibles whisper away from America in search of safer havens.

Encryption will become more sophisticated and more accessible, like any other widely used technology. The sensible thing is to brace for the downside consequences in advance. That is the meaning of serious social change. Critics can always suggest several marked improvements, but we do not ever get all of them.

The efficiencies of using the Internet in business can easily be jeopardized by official restraints on encryption, and such restraints would force users into primitive but highly effective subterfuges. Think of that digitized picture of the Mona Lisa, in full 24-bit color. A low-order bit could bear an encrypted message, although at the visual level it would appear to be meaningless noise. Government will not be able to stay ahead of individual creativity.

To what extent might considerations of general security detract from the economic efficiency of the systems that are to be protected? On what terms, properly vigilant or bureaucratically absolutist, shall we confront encryption? James Woolsey, one of the most thoughtful recent directors of the Central Intelligence Agency, is still astounded that essentially no business leader in the US information technology industries trusts Washington, and particularly the national-security bureaucracy, to have either the professional competence or the unchallengable trustworthiness to justify putting power over electronic privacy into the hands of the government.

Education and Entertainment

Many market forecasters see software and interactive multimedia of all sorts in the service of liberal education and skills training as the biggest new booth in the electronic marketplace in the first decade of the new century. Possibly. Billions have already been sunk into all sorts of supposedly educational technologies, with only minimal returns. Much of what has passed for "educational technology" (or even "edutainment") has merely strengthened the user's mouse finger. Yet the promise remains vast. We know how much more people can take in, we are skeptical of present approaches in the hands of the people who today are the most likely to apply them, and some of us remember (maybe from Marine Corps training films) what happens when a subject is made exciting to learn.

How might electronics be used to enhance the many forms of an individual's intelligence? Surely interactive multimedia approaches can be used to increase cognitive abilities, as they already have been in several schools, boosting standardized test scores. The interested learn, however their interest is first caught.

Pilot projects at the Federal Aviation Administration, at the US Naval Academy, and at blighted elementary schools in Washington hint enticingly at the effectiveness of new tools for assessing every human being's multiple intelligences (static ability or "IQ" being increasingly discredited). Software of this sort will ever more be finding the areas in which children and adults are particularly adept and those in which they are relatively weak. An entertaining interactive assessment, for instance, can direct its users toward customized interactive exercises intended to reinforce cognitive strengths and to shore up weaknesses. There is a potential for helping people become more intellectually adept than ever before. This can give to all instruction far greater opportunities to arouse capacities, not by improving class atmosphere and grade averages but by getting individual talents racing down unpredictable paths.

Teaching as an industry and learning as an experience will increasingly come under the cold eye of times that offer more and demand more. Whether failure shows as glazed expressions in the classroom or as clicking remote controls in the living room, education and entertainment have at least one thing in common: attention.

As the electronic marketplace evolves, people will want to make sense of the competence of strangers and of the rights conferred by previously unencountered certification authorities such as, say, an architectural institute in Laos. They will want to do their own certification in ways that go beyond the most sympathetic subjective approaches. For instance, a school board's or even a nation's educational standards are likely to be overshadowed by the arrival of international standards for math and science.

The education required to sustain the electronic marketplace cannot be limited to a calendar fitted to the agricultural year, drowsy expositions, and bricks-and-mortar fortresses. This is not a call to robotize the deeply human process of discovery; it is an assertion that electronic reinforcements will find their places throughout the whole lifelong course of education, enhancing rather than sacrificing the role of the great teacher in the process. How could the universe or the history of the human race be made as dull as they have been in most American schools?

If a tenth of the energy and talent annually invested in sitcoms were to be applied to any half-dozen eighth-grade courses, what a difference it would make! People are getting fed up with stale education even more than they did with lazy banking. Great lecturers in the tradition of Isaac Asimov and Arthur Schlesinger are expository entertainment, waiting for the electronic marketplace to call them to bigger challenges.

This raises questions of networking the schools and of how to obtain maximum access to high-quality educators. Home schooling, ever more popular, might not be so impressive if the otherwise often intellectually barren high school were supplemented by electronic interactive group commentary on *Anthony and Cleopatra* (e.g., on-screen questions from a class) or by software games related to calculus.

What about the qualifications to teach? Parents and employers of recent graduates are in a steadily stronger position to audit the services provided by teachers. How do the results that got your child his high school diploma stack up against respected standards established by, say, Fudan University in Shanghai? In the 1950s, it was not unknown for an individual to sneak into the Sorbonne and set up teaching as a small business. Any expansion of opportunity benefits swindlers and cranks along with the sensible and applied. We are going to get a lot of Velikovskian geology and Zen genetics, and it should do little harm. But there is still the need to hold courses that we had all better get right, such as where to place the decimal in a morphine prescription. How do we "accredit" in a marketplace that is ever more functionally unpoliceable?

Electronic access, barely out of its infancy, already has one huge scalp on its belt: the corporate hierarchy of the smokestack age. Are we ready for the flattening of other irrelevant qualifications? In Robert Hutchins's day at the University of Chicago, when respected bachelor's degrees were far rarer and more valuable than PhDs are now, a student could sit for a BA after a single semester if he thought himself prepared. This idea is ready to come around again. Tremendous pressure will be exerted on the choke points of qualification and status, and most of it is likely to be salutary. It is irrelevant to the national reputation of a leading software engineer, for instance, that she might be a dropout from a backwater college, and who would ever want to think of Bill Gates as "a Harvard man" (a phrase that, happily, is becoming archaic).

Skills can be "tested" and "certified" not only more precisely but also more efficiently in—as the commercials say—the privacy of your own home. You will be able to test your skills as a lawyer, an undertaker, a gardener, or a physician, finding out whether your understanding of your discipline is literally up to speed. Are you gathering the skills necessary to really be at home in your calling's next iteration of achievement?

Education, however defined, will be accessible anywhere and in ever more modular form. Electronic education in its present stage of development has two particularly promising applications: enhancing the transfer of specific, highly organized presentations of maps, mathematical relationships, molecular structures, metabolic pathways, trade relationships, etc., and representing unfolding processes (for instance, illuminating how we think and imagine our way through various problems).

Schoolteachers dread the possibility that star educators will take over their pupils' attention via educational networks, software, CDs, and Internet group tutorials, leaving them to serve as mere classroom monitors and paperwork checkers. Density of experience is what counts, however, and on-screen excitement calls for comparable quality in flesh-and-blood teaching. The more students see in Virgil or selection theory, the more responsive interest they require. Most of us never knew how much we needed English teachers until we actually saw *Anthony and Cleopatra* and were left bursting with unanswered questions. The great electronic educators will almost certainly leave plenty of tantalizing questions open, knowing that a good argument after a lecture fixes ideas and stretches mental muscles more than the most rapt passive attention.

High-quality, universally accessible educational technology can also serve to lower the age at which children are first exposed to foreign languages and to mathematics. It might be just as simple and far more productive to start 5-year-olds on basic group theory as on addition. The earlier the introduction, the less possibility drained away.

Education, presented as *education,* has a way of being boring, but efforts to present it as entertainment often result in triviality. The challenge is to improve the level of the entertainment. C. S. Peirce's father, an eminent professor at Harvard, kept his 14-year-old son up playing cards until 4 A.M. and urged him to analyze each mistake in detail in order to make him a better applied mathematician. Benjamin Constant's tutor taught him a "secret language," which proved to be Latin. US Army officers have been assigned to Wall Street currency trading rooms to intensify their quick-decision skills.

The most effective education (e.g., reading Samuel Butler's *Hudibras* or seeing the Fibonacci series unfold in snail-shell curves) is often hard to distinguish from entertainment. The distinction between the immediately real and the next fantastic possibilities opening out of it dynamizes the imaginations of all ages. Education and entertainment, learning and imagining, yet further interpenetrate, a pivotal preparation for even stranger futures. TV weather forecasts are now supposed to be "entertaining"; if so, then atmospheric physics, properly presented, will be riveting. There is already a playful Buckminster Fuller web site for geometry.

We will see the intangible become ever more real, and look for the profit in such "realism." The flight simulators developed by the psychologist J. P. Guilford (who pioneered multiple intelligences theory for teaching and training) were only the start. All sorts of incomparably more advanced simulations will lift participants out of their homes, schools, and businesses. Anything truly well done has artistic, and therefore entertaining and edifying, quality.

Thirty years ago, Arthur Clarke prophesied, and dead accurately, that one of the great changes to unfold by the century's end would be an enormous expansion of entertainment. We still have barely begun this expansion, and we show no signs of exhausting the possibilities as interactive media intensify their power to become tools of dramatic organization, inserting passages or indeed whole roles, perhaps played by actors dead or never given such parts in real life. Spontaneous interventions will be edited and reedited as the auditor becomes an equal player with the work of art.

Each her own producer, each his own cameraman. Why not Jack Kennedy in *Henry V*? All sorts of barely controllable initiatives arise, many involving intellectual property. Pornography is, unhappily, the first initiative that comes to mind, but that is only because it is already around. What is truly new we have not thought of yet.

Play rests biologically on unthreatening imitation and experiment, controllable before we go out to meet the saber-tooth tiger or the clan over the hill. Given the huge resources for gaining and reinforcing attention, how do we bring high entertainment back to the heart of learning? The interpenetration of art forms is increasing exponentially. For example, think of the soundtrack as an autonomous serious musical form—and even of Berlioz, who scored for an artillery battery in an early example of multi-media entertainment.

Anything that raises our level of attention has more to offer our long-term development than the most admirable things if taken for granted. "Strike the twos and strike the threes / The Sieve of Eratosthenes," chant the children with the dancing, on-screen numbers in Frederick Pohl's *Drunkard's Walk*. "When the multiples SUBLIME / The numbers that are left are PRIME." Lewis Carroll, an Oxford mathematician, propounded a series of math problems in his novel *A Tangled Tale*. There are going to be many more ways to entertain, and therefore many more ways to learn.

The survival of the movie industry 40 years after television was to have killed it is a reminder that the electronic revolution has widened the spectrum of entertainment, not produced a master form. What new modalities carrying sensory inputs (perhaps heat or pressure) will create interactive audiences as people in some version of a movie theater respond to their fellow watchers as well as to the main drama?

Entire volumes will no doubt be written on these matters. This book can really only try to describe parts of tomorrow's busy marketplace. Other authors will go further as this new world keeps remaking itself like a kaleidoscope.

Business Possibilities

Two significant technological developments are likely to be commonplace by, say, 2003, bringing profound new efficiencies to the emerging electronic marketplace. The first is the ability to simulate business processes on the desk-top, akin to the way that computerized spreadsheets became taken for granted in the early '80s. This capability is increasingly attractive because it is the business of a marketplace to be full of tradeoffs—the more tradeoffs the better. And perhaps the sign of real success in the electronic marketplace is that the tradeoffs are too complex for any single person to understand.

The second development arises from the breakthrough in the capability of computer systems to connect and to exchange information. Most computer users who spend their time on the "reading edge" assume that systems already efficiently communicate with each other. In fact companies increasingly incur staggering costs and delays because their information systems cannot evolve rapidly enough to meet changed business conditions such as the introduction of a new product or service, the latest arrangement with a new distributor, or the sudden need to implement a merger or acquisition.

As for simulation, knowledge is power only if we can exercise power over knowledge. Any business is likely to benefit from both better understanding the interdependence among its activities and from involving additional knowledgeable participants in key decisions. To that end, existing workflow tools—such as Lotus Domino or products from Action Technology—are poised to be turbo-charged by adding on dynamic simulation models that elevate the content of these tools and differentiate them.

How can the perspectives, second-nature techniques, and efficiencies of companies that were information-based to begin with be applied to other companies that wish to flourish in the electronic marketplace?

Sophisticated desktop simulations—made possible by the ever greater powers of graphics, databases, storage capacities, speed, and interfaces— will likely be deployed first in project management, and then in business segments such as sales and human resources, and in industries ranging from banking, to electric utilities, to restaurants.

A construction or a trucking company, for instance, can be as "high tech" (and valuable) as, say, an Internet retailer to the extent that it marshals these new powers of simulation to examine its habits and procedures, detail by detail. Precisely appropriate modeling capacities and databases might be combined with workflow tools to help various enterprises become more competitive. Computer-generated simulations have already proved rewarding to large-corporations: it was through such practices, for example, that MasterCard first introduced co-branded credit cards. In the millennium's first decade, however, sophisticated simulations can devolve to the laptop. A manager even when traveling will be able to access an interactive simulator that has assimilated his company's business conditions, markets, suppliers, and operations, and to ask for its "take" on the "issue of the day" (or month, or year). Every decision or condition will be weighable against perhaps a dozen contingencies—ten reasonable ones and a couple of "wild cards."

Consider being able to anticipate, direct, and measure a truly representative and constantly renewed sample of the individualized "transactions" within a company. (Harold Langworthy touched on the prospects in *Technology 2001*.) Made real by a sense of how things are or might be, decisions can be augmented by using a menu to see how a particular decision will affect all other aspects of the business. Managers can better understand how extensively to delegate decisions, and how to anticipate the extent of rework in product development. Scenarios will be able to succeed one another, and will respond to particular actions that a manager might take in the simulation. Choices will swing into view, not in a random bubbling but according to the initiator's sense of the situation as illuminated by all the otherwise undetectable connections arising from the simulation. Such "simulation modeling" will bring underestimated phenomena (and, of course, plenty of dismissable ones too) front and center to be matched with the company's existing map of its critical path.

One could select the simulation tests that best deal with a problem and circulate them electronically among one's colleagues, who could then use them in their own simulations and planning. Key indicators and deviations will be automatically flagged for the sake of decision-making. Actions, policies, and instructively "failed" experiments will be storable in a "management trainer system." These can be used as the basis for creating additional simulations—for displaying "what-might-have-beens" in looking back at corporate operations. Unique training exercises can result along the way—ones which can be used by managers or, in fact, anyone involved in improving the company's performance.

Simulation, like the electronic marketplace's overall evolution, combines science fiction, available tools, and—ultimately—the practical integration of technologies. All these visions of choice, outreach, and higher productivity presume a degree of interconnectedness getting closer to that of neurons in a brain than that of mere parts in a machine. However, so many assumptions about tomorrow's marketplace too easily assume that chronically stubborn obstacles do not exist.

The second development that is worth noting is the arrival of systems interoperability, meaning the ability of computer systems to talk to each other. In reality, the introduction of new electronic products and services is still plagued by delays and costs. For instance, after introducing the Spectrum Personal Communication Service in the mid '90s, Sprint found itself unable to send correct bills for more than a year because the new technology was supported by a new type of digital switch—one that produced information about calls in a new format while the back office billing systems wanted it in an earlier format. Complicated and expensive incompatibilities of this sort occur constantly in telecommunications, financial services, health care, and energy utilities.

Today's business information systems use just about every computer language, operating system, and hardware platform known. Each system works with unique data formats to execute its programmed function; communication "standards," such as "HL7" in health care or "EDI 811" in telecommunications, are in fact more like guidelines rather than standards. As the formats of records coming into a company change due to a merger (such as Bell Atlantic and NYNEX) or the introduction of a new service such as Spectrum, the computer systems which handle the information must be upgraded in order to recognize the new format. The need for these chronic upgrades eviscerates the real-time efficiencies that might be expected when filing insurance claims, buying a camcorder on the Internet, using a digital phone, or managing heating bills. Labor-intensive corporate back offices now handle these cumbersome problems by one-time solutions which are more tactical than strategic.

One of today's great trends in communication technology—one that offers hopes of resolving all this—is the concept of distributed objects. Executives responsible for their companies' information systems will decide between Microsoft's vision of the solution (DCOM) and the one backed by most everyone else (CORBA). The information, the processes, and the underlying intelligence in the network are of the same origin, but two great commercial forces have different ideas about how to implement the concept.

In theory, distributed objects should be able to talk with any other processes, because everyone in the computing universe will adopt the same set of communication and interchange definitions. If you want to get a debit card validated, you will simply send off a message to the appropriate validation process; it will understand your message regardless of what language you wrote it in, because you will have used the common definition language. The "object request broker" will find the routing information in the definition language and will send the message (or "transaction") to the next appropriate process (station) which will then start a defined set of processes much as happens on an assembly line.

These theories have great promise, according to the software engineer Michael Peterson, but the companies in this marketplace find as much competitive advantage in the uniqueness of their internal processing as they do in accepting open systems. Each of the tough competitors believes that it has a better approach; there is no sense that if they share all their toys they will be rewarded handsomely.

The tantalizing possibility that distributed objects will permit market activities such as ordering and fulfillment to be done in tandem in real time will not be widely achieved anytime soon. No trend will sweep the electronic marketplace so completely that every programmer will be able to support a single approach, let alone to rewrite every line of code. Think of the sunk investment in mainframe legacy systems. The likelihood that one seamlessly harmonious way to communicate will characterize the electronic marketplace is a beguiling theory, but is unrealistic in the real world. In fact, the increasing diversity, competition, creativity, and improvement in the marketplace will work against any uniform theory, language or product.

However, solutions will become commonplace by 2003 which will transcend these unachievable (and undesirable) notions of "standards" while making real-time interoperability possible irrespective of the data's complexity. In their essay here, Ray Smith and his co-authors dismiss the costly and slow process of building one-time conversion routines, as well as the notion that this marketplace will be standardized in its electronic processes.

The alternative on which I have worked is Linguateq's interface management system. It performs in various milieus, from traditional back-office, batch-based billing applications to the real-time operational environment of mediation devices that translate between network switches and telecommunication carrier auditing systems. Such an interface management system combines a fast, real-time flow engine with a flexible interface programming approach. The IMS resides in a network environment: as information leaves one computer system, it can be interpreted, reformatted if necessary, and forwarded to another. Interoperability is thereby achieved by manipulating the information, not the hardware.

The IMS innovation combines the best elements of a network solution and an application solution by joining real-time network benefits with function-specific programming. Rather than taking the risk of disrupting the entire computer system (as a result of new products, new technologies, or new corporate relationships), such a management approach allows a company's technical staff to quickly install new interfaces without having to expensively and slowly modify existing equipment.

Within typical corporate back offices, an interface management system will drastically reduce the cost of converting data formats, thereby removing a source of costly delay in the electronic marketplace. The arrival of real-time interoperability builds on the middle ground between the sterile uniformity predicted by enthusiasts of standardization and the realities of market-driven cultures that are jostling through the randomness of what often looks more like a bazaar than an ordered market.

Conclusion

In a cartoon published in *The New Yorker* in the 1950s, several Muscovites are watching their first TV commercial. Once the announcer says "Rush right out and buy this," they all frantically put on their coats and race for the door. Today, not only has Big Brother fallen, but sellers and advertisers know that they are about to play on a level field with even the smallest of buyers.

Everywhere, we see new opportunities pushing aside old and heavy encumbrances: the state intervention that has a way of turning into high-minded cartelization, the crowding at privileged locations that smothers any original advantage and drives prices up, and (above all) the discouraging sense of how much time something takes—a deterrent that can prevent us from pursuing better approaches in favor of what is tolerably at hand.

Markets have been part of human behavior for centuries. But each level of civilization has enlarged the power to exchange by increasing its outreach across time and space, and by various other means, concrete and abstract: roads, contracts, insurance, telephones, and so on. The electronic marketplace is strengthening purchasers' powers, not only by boosting their abilities to buy in the present (e.g., by making it possible to review a thousand tenders across a dozen countries where before it was hard to check a dozen offers in a single city) but also by giving consumers the ability to go "uptime" and shape a good or a service not yet available. This market enables sellers to better understand the populations within it, to target the narrowest sectors of vivid interest, and to anticipate or even mold such interest.

"The arch never sleeps," say the architects: it adjusts to redistribute the pressure of every shift in the whole building, and the land on which it stands. The economies already industrialized before 1980 are modernizing on the lines mentioned here, and are acting as the main centers of capital and expertise. These modern markets help to alleviate the strain of the changes that all this commercial upheaval imposes on the rest of the world (say, guaranteeing a loan to Mexico or Indonesia). For the moment, they find themselves in the role of the arch. But the marketplace of 2008 is certain to determine the relative prospects of countries as profoundly as it does those of companies.

The essence of this marketplace experience is that, instead of working outward from relatively few centers (such as Manchester, Pittsburgh, and Osaka in the late nineteenth century), it pulls whole continents into the electronic loop, spreading a film of transactions like oil over a flattening planetary surface. Throughout this book, the authors show how this new marketplace seeks to delegate to machines the separating and constricting specializations of the division of labor, which powered earlier industrialization but which Adam Smith rightly dreaded as capable of reducing humans to mere machine tenders. Such delegation in fact acts to raise the demandingness, and with it the level of reward, of human work.

In the United States, the field of information technology—defined as both computing and telecommunications—has become the nation's largest industry. This sector (which does not even include semiconductor manufacturing machines and electronic games) is ahead of construction, food products, and automobile manufacturing. The new wealth, new work practices, and ultimately the new means of commerce which information technology generates are expanding segments of a new world economy, and a planetary marketplace.

We already take it for granted that business can be done anywhere on the planet immediately. And the most exciting aspect of the electronic marketplace may be the prospect of dealing with the billions of individual talents about to arrive.

As is evident from the "Baywatch" T-shirts seen in Borneo and from the currency trading in Cairo, electronic marketplaces are sweeping the world. In terms of formal high culture, something may be lacking amid the speed and pressure, but in terms of a determination to transcend poverty and to overcome obstacles, the overall force is impressive.

But so much of what is required to do business can remain impalpable, while entering distant markets is enticingly easy. Lloyd's of London, which knew America well enough to recruit clients there, proved to know too little about the US courts and the US economy while underwriting such things as real estate liability—and this after its computer and fire insurance debacles in the US. Rigorous routine diligence, even if offered in a specialized software package, might have saved Lloyd's billions. Such diligence is even more necessary for the rest of us.

Once it was difficult to get accurate information about the values of companies in emerging markets. Now, electronic trading systems are becoming widespread, providing real-time information and thereby increasing volume and liquidity. Employment patterns are being transformed, with work of ever higher sophistication and value being done in the emerging markets (often stimulated by that outsourcing in the first place) and then heading back to the developed countries. Consumer demand rises. Adam Smith's great wheel turns in new waters. The Indian software industry, for instance, grew at 35 percent a year through the 1990s. The difference between Bangalore and LA may be 10 years in terms of access to cars, 30 years in percentage of college-educated inhabitants, but only 3 months (if that) in terms of software—indeed, Bangalore may be ahead in software. Clearly, emerging markets no longer must follow the paths of their predecessors. Japan showed that a century ago. The newer industrial societies know what not to do, whether in patterns of city growth or in layers of transportation. Their heritage lies in the future and in things not yet tried. But in the electronic perspective, all countries, places, and people might as well be regarded as in the developing world.

I

Getting Up Closer: Talents and Choices Multiply

1

The Once and Future Craftsman Culture

Les Alberthal

I do not know which of us two is writing this page.
—Jorge Luis Borges

By now we know the revolution will never abate. In the next 10 years, we will witness one of history's greatest technological transformations, in which the world's geographic markets morph into one dynamic, complex organism. As broader application of intelligent systems and advances in digital communications and virtual reality interfaces emancipate customers all over the world from the tyranny of producer-controlled supply chains, we can formulate an interesting scenario. The more technology changes the way products are developed, manufactured, and integrated with the environment, the closer we will come to recapturing the essence of the intimate, village-based craftsman culture of yesteryear, in which the cobbler and the customer convened and conspired together under one roof.

The epigraph from Borges hints at the ongoing and reciprocal nature of writing. By positioning the reader and writer on equal footing, engaged in the regenerative process of composition, reading, and revision, Borges depicts the creative act not as a finite event but rather as an ongoing dialogue of limitless meaning and potential. The written work merely serves as a fluid channel through which the writer and the reader continuously converse.

By substituting "producer" for "writer," "product" for "writing," and "customer" for "reader," we can change the quote to read "I do not know whether the producer or the customer is creating the product." This suggests the continuous interaction and exchange of knowledge that will occur among producers and customers in the virtual global village of the future as products are jointly conceived, developed, made, and remade on an ever-spinning wheel of innovation.

A Virtual Global Village

Before exploring how products will be created in the future, I'd like to envision tomorrow's virtual global village—the playing field on which this revolution will occur. The term "virtual" suggests several things to me when I imagine an electronic marketplace 10 years or so from now. Continued advances in the circuit density of computer chips and the transmission speeds of optical fibers, as well as the subsequent decline in the unit cost of computer power, will allow digital content and human knowledge to be distributed to all parts of the world in the blink of an eye.

Future videoconferencing technology will no doubt improve the collaborative capabilities of teams all over the world. But today, the greatest limitation in collaborating over the Internet is the capacity of the communications lines required to deal with the massive amounts of data involved in large-scale design and development efforts. In the future, a combination of hardwire networks and wireless communications will facilitate real-time collaboration on complex product designs, scientific simulations, marketing plans, and mathematical models. As a result, all aspects of product development—including design, analysis, manufacturing, services, and marketing—will be performed collaboratively and concurrently across departments, enterprises, industries, and countries.

The various groups participating in product development will collaborate with one another in extended virtual environments where a full and exact representation of each product and its associated data will be created, tested, detailed, simulated, and finally manufactured from a digital model rather than a physical one. This digital model will represent a virtual product that "exists" long before it is manufactured. It will possess all the properties and characteristics of what it represents. It will provide unambiguous visualization, stimulation, and response, thus making concurrent design and analysis, supplier and partner communication, and customer evaluation possible. Furthermore, these human networks will enjoy the ability to "build and break" products in a virtual state. As every participant will be working concurrently with the appropriate model of the product, enormous amounts of redundancy and error and enormous engineering costs will be eliminated. In this way, the digital model is analogous to the malleable shoe mold with which craftsmen of the past shaped customized products to conform to individuals' changing needs. As a result of these virtual characteristics, the means of production for producers will shift conclusively from the physical plant floor into the innovative minds of geographically dispersed craftsmen, professionals, and agile work cells.

The word "global" implies that engineers and other professionals will incorporate best thinking, practices, and research from around the world into their product designs.

At the same time, in an electronic marketplace on which the entire intellectual and material resources of India, China, and Brazil (just for starters) are unleashed, the number of product possibilities will multiply exponentially. It is at least as likely that product innovation will originate on the banks of the Ganges, outside a Mongolian marketplace, or in the fevered frenzy of Maracana Stadium as in the sanitized design studio of a posh office building in New York. Many new products will be invented by billions of customers as they consciously or unconsciously articulate their needs and preferences in the course of their daily lives.

The unique "voices" of these individuals will find expression in many forms: the psychographic pattern left in the wake of a person's wanderings among home decorating home pages on the World Wide Web; a surgeon's cardiac activity while performing a liver transplant in a simulated virtual environment, the retinal movements of a young girl as she peruses the myriad delectable offerings in the food building at the Texas State Fair, and so on. Because these "voices" will resonate along a continuous communications loop connecting producers, products, customers, and their physical environments, even the most commonplace events will give rise to new products. As a result, only those enterprises with eyes to see and ears to hear the most physically remote individuals will flourish.

Perhaps the most compelling characteristic of tomorrow's electronic marketplace will be its "village-based" aspect. In the past, before the age of mass production, a craftsman and a customer living in proximity to one another could engage in a highly personal discussion about the world. Through this ongoing dialogue, craftsmen and customers gained knowledge of humankind's potential to use natural resources to better advantage. And each participant benefited. The customer benefited from being able to apply the new product to its intended purpose and thus improve his performance. In addition to receiving pay for his services, the craftsman enjoyed the opportunity to refine the tools of his trade, improve his methods, expand his offerings, and perfect his craft.

In the future, a symbiotic convergence of tactile, stereovision, and voice technologies will produce interactive interfaces tailored to the user's culture. By recreating the intimate dialogue of the village using familiar stimuli of vision, touch, and sound, these virtual reality interfaces will allow individuals to converse fluidly and transparently with the world of information. In the context of product development, these interfaces will serve simply as interactive points at which customers and producers, seeing and manipulating virtual products concurrently, will carry on an unimpeded dialogue. This capability will ensure that final product designs meet and exceed customers' expectations before production begins.

Dismantling the Fordian Complex

The mass manufacturing techniques and corresponding vocabulary introduced by Henry Ford and other early industrial pioneers embodied a set of cultural assumptions about who should perform what work, what their capabilities were, how their lives should be arranged, and how their jobs should be structured. Implicit in these assumptions was the producer's view of the universe. In many ways, the methods by which products are developed and manufactured today still reflects Fordian cultural biases. In sharp contrast, the older craftsman culture viewed the world through the eyes of the customer.

Referring to the difficulty any minority group has wielding the concepts and the words used by dominant institutions to oppress them, the African-American poet Audre Lorde stated that "the master's tools will never dismantle the master's house."[1] As this quote intimates, a high-tech rebirth of the craftsman culture in the future will require first dismantling the prevailing concepts and vocabulary of modern manufacturing.

On today's assembly line and on today's supply chain, work occurs within a physically and temporally constrained context. The supply chain, for example, is an intentionally ordered structure whose purpose is to normalize relations among producers, suppliers, distributors, retailers, and customers. In most instances, the customer is situated pretty far downstream. A more appropriate metaphor for describing the way products will soon be created is the "wheel of innovation," which will comprise virtual product development, agile manufacturing, and continuous feedback among producers, products, and customers. Furthermore, the meanings of "worker," "consumer," and "product" will have to change to accurately describe the relationships and activities of tomorrow's participants.

The word "worker" stems from the mass-manufacturing mindset of the Industrial Revolution and suggests a managed culture that dismisses an individual's creative energies. The individual was akin to an interchangeable part, functioning within a disciplined time-and-motion plan concerned primarily with efficiency. In the next decade, technological advances will produce a new body of craftsmen: highly skilled professionals who will possess the education, tools, and expertise to decipher, develop, and deliver specialized products and services directly to customers anywhere in the world. Essentially, their mission will be to elicit from their customers an understanding of what they want, and to then bring the world's best thinking, practices, and resources to bear in order to provide high-quality products at competitive prices. Technology will, in fact, liberate the creative energies of customers and craftsmen and foster billions of potential relationships. What were once merely hands on an assembly line will be transformed into a body of virtually connected, continuously engaged, seamlessly integrated individuals discussing a world of possibilities.

This return to a craftsman culture may reinstate apprenticeship programs even for, say, already highly skilled design engineers. The most advanced craftsmen, with the broadest experience and deepest knowledge, will initially find opportunities for new, highly customized products as they encounter customers in real time. These experts will develop initial sets of requirements, specifications for systems, and details of classical systems engineering that define what the product is. As this information is developed, less experienced craftsmen will use it to tear the virtual product apart, decide what component parts need to be built, and then construct specifications describing their findings.

At the same time, beginning design engineers, or apprentices, will use this design information to actually build the components, put them together, and prepare them for delivery. Because this is a concurrent process, the apprentice—while performing only certain tasks within this process—will no longer be relegated to a downstream position within a sequence of events. As a result, apprentices will be able to learn about the overall product more quickly.

This work arrangement will provide a well-defined culture and a well-defined environment in which new craftsmen will learn their skills, become more proficient, and ultimately perfect their craft. The apprentice engineers will be able to observe their more advanced peers involved in the more creative processes of figuring out how to partition products in terms of how they should work. And, of course, the elite body of expert craftsmen will comprise the most advanced designers and engineers, who will be involved in the even more abstract and creative problem-solving endeavor of understanding individual customers' behaviors and needs— as well as the broader demands of the marketplace. Such a culture will reward its expert craftsmen by allowing them to work intimately, directly with customers, just as the cobbler and the customer used to convene and conspire together.

At the same time, the role of tomorrow's consumer will change dramatically. Indeed, the word "consumer" is too limited to describe the role that individual buyers will play in product development. "Consumer" implies someone who uses something up, engaging in series of repetitive, annihilating interactions with a world of consumable products. Continuing technological advances in such areas as environmental impact, resource optimization, and alternative energies will require individuals to play a more active role in the design, creation, and subsequent re-creation of products they use. "Collaborative customers" is a more appropriate term for the consumers of the future, as it implies the powerful individual voices that technology will convey.

With the power to more effectively transform products according to their volitions and their needs, collaborative customers will enjoy ever-increasing authority, knowing more about how well a particular product functions (or should function) than the producer. Ten years from now, this heightened authority will give consumers unprecedented and un-rivaled power to define such issues as quality, convenience, affordability, and timeliness.

The commonly held conception of products as inflexible material ob-jects will change dramatically. Increasingly, virtual products will exist in a digital state before, during, and after their physical production. These virtual products will allow their performance to be tailored to their users' particular demands and immediate environments. Additionally, they will actively communicate with their creators and with their users. Thus, tomorrow's virtual products will resemble intelligent organisms. Further-more, these products will become full-fledged participants in the wheel of innovation by providing their producers with feedback that can be re-incorporated into the design and manufacture of their same-generation younger siblings produced in subsequent weeks.

Virtual Product Development

Within 10 years, most products will be undergo *virtual product devel-opment,* a process in which a full and exact representation of each product and its associated data will be created, tested, detailed, and manufactured in completely digital form. Employees, suppliers, and part-ners will be tightly integrated through shared data and systems. Custom-ers will actively participate through advanced virtual reality interfaces. All aspects of the product development process—from design to market-ing—will be performed collaboratively and concurrently across depart-ments, alliances, industries, and countries. Geographic constraints will be overcome through a combination of videoconferencing, hardwire networks, and digital wireless communications that will use satellite links to "blast through" enormous amounts of product definition data. In its mature stage, virtual product development will allow true mass customization: product knowledge derived from both the expertise of craftsmen around the world and the real-world experience of billions of collaborative customers and virtual products will be integrated to continuously improve the product.

Let's look at how this process might work at a high level. Generally speaking, the collaborative customer will plant the seed of an idea for a new high-end product. Then, drawing upon its vast knowledge and resources, the producer and its body of craftsmen and other professionals will cultivate the original seed into an even grander idea at a much faster rate than we are seeing today. Once the idea-become-virtual-product has been manufactured, it will continue to intelligently adapt itself in the hands of the customer to meet his evolving needs and preferences. At the same time, the virtual product will serve as an interactive point—a kind of "chat room" in which producers and collaborative customers will engage in a dialogue about the world. In this way, producers will use virtual products as intelligent channels for the ongoing delivery of enhanced services, continuously enriching the quality of customers' lives.

Imagine, for example, golf clubs being produced and functioning in this manner. As you play, the club you selected monitors your swing, the physical characteristics and subtle nuances of the course, and the changing weather conditions, adjusting itself from one stroke to the next in order to optimize your performance. At the same time, the club reports your hooks and slices to its producer and posits explanations as to why they occurred. This real-world data input will not only influence future club designs; it will also enable the producer of clubs to deliver real-time customized services (e.g., enhanced reaction-control programs) to the individual golfer through the virtual product.

Front-End Customer Collaboration

The automobile industry provides an excellent environment in which to explore a detailed scenario of future virtual product development. Consider the person whose car has just died while traversing the Swiss Alps. This person is probably in the market for a new car. But haggling with a salesperson on a steaming asphalt lot full of mass-manufactured automobiles is only a distant memory—one that the collaborative customer can easily dismiss as he reclines in his climate-controlled living room, articulating his preferences in an online statement of intent: "I want to buy, not lease. I prefer this kind of body style, this color, and these features. I drive primarily in these conditions. I have this much money to spend. And I'm looking for this kind of financial arrangement. If you want to do business with me, you must play by these rules. So why don't we roll up our sleeves and get to work?" He will then post this statement of intent on the Internet, opening up a bidding process among carmakers who want his business. Buyers will not have to surf the Net looking for deals. Instead, sellers will have to find buyers. Collaborative customers will not have to use pre-programmed smart agents to research different brands of cars, nor will they have to enlist the services of an infomediary. In this sense, roles will be reversed: the consumer—once a hunter—will become the highly sought-after bounty of producers the world over.

To meet customer demand, producers' craftsmen will employ *intelligent system engines*. More robust than the sales configurators available today, these engines will incorporate many of the customer's initial requests, creating three-dimensional visualizations that represent the sum of those requests. By sharing this visualization, the collaborative customer and the craftsman will begin to explore the customer's articulated needs and unspoken desires. Employing rendering engines that generate interim objects, this collaborative team will define the shape, characteristics, and attributes of the desired product, all of which can be explored in depth.

At each step along this interactive journey, each craftsman's intelligent engines will not only incorporate input from both participants but also draw upon the knowledge of thousands of other expert craftsmen around the world. All the data will be filtered through the intelligent engines, which will generate many iterations of the virtual product before producing a final offering.

The collaborative team will be able to sculpt the object, modifying its shape within the protective boundaries of the intelligent engines. They will drag and drop visible attributes such as color and texture onto the object, review its finish, and explore its expected performance, all the while receiving continuous feedback on weight, recyclability, pricing, payments, and delivery dates.

Using tools that permit dimensional virtual viewing, the collaborative team will also explore the product's interior. Interactively, they will adjust the window placement, instrumentation, control placement and distances, interior lighting, and the physical operation of mechanical devices such as a tilting steering wheel. Employing online libraries of data on luggage capacity, the team will explore storage and packing capabilities until the collaborative customer is pleased with the result. During the entire collaborative scenario, the software tools and communication links used by both participants will be the major limiting factor.

In the near future, this interchange of ideas will be performed with specific "focus groups." Within 5 years, as the technology matures and becomes more widespread, scenarios like the one described above will be played out for high-end custom products and affluent buyers. In 10 years, collaborative customers will not only be able to personalize large, complex purchases (such as houses); they will also be able to virtually experience the final arrangement of nearly all the details before production. Some retailers of high-end swimsuits already allow their customers to design, simulate with visualization systems, and approve personalized suits before they are manufactured. The major gating factors for the speed of implementing such scenarios will be technological performance and acceptance.

Intelligent Reasoning and Decision Making

During the course of the dialogue between the collaborative customer and the craftsman, ideas and concepts will flow at extremely high speed, with each successive idea building upon the previous one. The primary challenge for producers will be to find the intersection between what a customer wants and needs and what is possible from a technical, engineering, and materials perspective. As the field of possibility expands, broader application of intelligent systems will help craftsmen to apply the world's best thinking, practices, and resources to enrich their dialogues with customers and to ensure that products of high quality are delivered at competitive prices. Today, the technology is not fluid, transparent, or fast enough to allow craftsmen to seamlessly integrate customer input, worldwide knowledge, and their own expertise and intuition in real time. As a result, final product designs often reflect only a compromised summary of the knowledge that went into their creation.

In the future, intelligent systems will provide craftsmen with a style of query by which chains of ideas can be connected in a single expression— an important advance over today's relational databases. If craftsmen need to know the outcome of a finite element simulation when looking for some property of a physical system, knowledge-based environments will rapidly perform that complex simulation. Product design environments will ask knowledge bases for the latest and most effective ways to analyze the stated problem. By posing such questions to neural networks and to case-based reasoning programs, craftsmen will set goals for their environments. To achieve those goals, design environments will then connect all the ideas leading from the available information to the means of deriving the requested response, finally performing the necessary calculations. In this special type of query, called a *transitive join,* a knowledge-based system looks for connections between means and ends. Transitive joins combine two concepts: the algebraic notion of transitivity (which is concerned with the relationship among three things) and the notion of being able to join (which describes the unification algorithm of knowledge-based engines). Such queries literally seek solutions to the statement "I have A, and I want C, but I don't know what B is." This application of knowledge-based systems will help craftsmen perform in a matter of minutes processes that now take several months to perform by hand.

In general, when users ask a computer program to solve a problem of this kind, they are asking it to perform an activity called "reasoning." And it is this reasoning activity that most closely emulates the subconscious associations that humans refer to as "intelligence." The set of ideas connected through such reasoning could include the discovery that a minivan's air conditioning system must be changed to manage the heat load of a customer-specified glass configuration. As design environments increasingly handle such low-level details in an intelligent fashion, craftsmen will be more free to explore and imagine the various ways designs can meet and exceed customers' articulated needs and unspoken desires. At the same time, technology will allow individual craftsmen to enrich their own designs with the resonant "voices" of many other experts, ultimately liberating the individual's creative energies in the pursuit of perfection.

Integrated Concept Development

After the initial customer collaboration, producers will enact a completely integrated concept-development effort, which includes concept modeling, engineering design and analysis, customer feedback, and virtual prototyping. A convergence of rule-based management systems, virtual reality interfaces, intelligent systems, and wireless digital-based communications will create the virtual environment in which this integrated effort is orchestrated. Manufacturing processes will also be integrated into this redesign of efforts, with virtual tooling and simulation of fabrication and assembly processes.

Since the 1980s, the time required for collaboration on large, complex development projects for high-end products has decreased from years to days. In the early 1990s, for example, the F/A18-E/F Hornet development program—a joint effort involving three of the world's largest aircraft manufacturers—comprised 350 independent but closely integrated design and work teams. On this project, more than 30,000 plane components were digitally designed and reviewed, not only as individual parts but also in assembly layouts. At that time, the massive databases used for the project had to be updated overnight by batch processing. Today, on development projects for such complex products as motor coaches, similar updates occur within minutes. In less than 10 years, it is likely that real-time collaboration on such large repositories of data will be realized through a combination of high-speed digital-based communications using satellites and localized terabit-per-second fiber data links. The computer internal communications called *system buses* can already exchange data at the rate of 1.6 gigabytes per second. These technologies are being used on several projects, including the terabit-per-second communication network now being completed at the Lawrence Livermore National Laboratories. These technologies will soon become part of producers' telecommunications infrastructures. Linked by high-bandwidth satellite relay networks, these high-performance terrestrial systems will allow global communities of expert craftsmen to participate in real-time concurrent design, engineering, and adaptation of simple and complex products, formulating rapid responses to the changing needs of individual customers around the world.

As we have already witnessed in the semiconductor business, reusable product and process knowledge will be mathematically represented, digitally encoded, and electronically distributed across the virtual extended enterprise. The virtual product and its various iterations and associated process instructions throughout the build-and-break cycle will be continuously managed. Intelligent systems similar to today's information management systems will organize and manage the volumes of data and numerous versions associated with the typical digital model. They will address all the information and applications needed to define the product, including CAD/CAM/CAE files, bills of material, analysis models, video annotations, and cost structures. These systems will then present the data in the product development environment as if it were in a single system. As a result, new and improved product introductions will be acutely managed over a potentially long life cycle, making it easier to keep an ever-changing consortium of partners and suppliers up to date. Today's Internet product catalogs will give way to full knowledge-based support systems that can quickly diagnose and recommend—and probably even repair or upgrade—virtual products. When product information is disseminated in this way, every collaborator will become a part of a digitally based concept-through-support team that includes design engineers, tool operators, purchasing agents, salespeople, service technicians, and customers.

At the same time, tomorrow's man-machine interfaces will allow craftsmen participating in the development of concepts for high-end products to work in virtual design environments that represent information in their respective cultures. Such environments will include intuitive interfaces that offer the essence of virtual reality on the desktop, delivering in-context editing control of the 3D graphical interfaces. This technology will allow craftsmen to simply select objects and manipulate them directly and intuitively.

The aerodynamics engineer of an automobile, for example, will access the work in progress and bring the concept car into his cultural environment. He will then drag the car into a numerical wind tunnel to assess its stability. With access to information about the design of the drive train, this engineer will also be able to make intelligent predictions concerning the car's emissions performance and fuel efficiency without using any physical prototypes. Today, it takes about 10 seconds per frame to visualize the computations required to perform such accurate simulations of wind tunnel fluid dynamics. This is still a bit too slow for the virtual decisions that will be demanded by tomorrow's market. Within 10 years, though, systems will most likely compute at 100 times the current speed, allowing engineers to perform real-time analysis at 30 frames per second (the rate we see on today's televisions).

Meanwhile, the underbody engineer of the automobile will access the work in progress and use a combination of tactile interfaces, neural networks, fuzzy logic, and generative algorithms to integrate such elements as chassis, suspension, drive chain, and steering systems from the libraries of partners or preferred vendors into the available spaces. Again, most of the information in this culture will be represented visually. For example, electrical systems will display wires, circuits, and switches as they actually appear in their physical environment, and hydraulic systems will display tubes, valves, and actuators. As this craftsman uses drag-and-drop interfaces to access libraries of devices, many of the components will be able to actually configure themselves, using automatic routing algorithms to solve spacing and positioning problems. If he is unable to manually adjust the positioning to alleviate the problems, the underbody engineer will be able to collaborate in real time with the body designer to resolve the difficulties. When this step is finished, another function will be used to automatically construct fastening points for everything. This task will use a great deal of intelligent systems technology that is transparent to the engineer. By accessing vast collections of design rules, these intelligent algorithms will solve spatial positioning problems to ensure conformance with company, vendor, industry, and government standards and practices of performance, assembly, accessibility, reliability, and safety. The first generation of this type of technology is being used in the oil industry today by valve manufacturers, whose product designs must adhere to industry standards and practices. Intelligent systems enable these companies to make real-time modifications to product designs based on changes to standards and practices before production. In the future, increased application of such technology throughout manufacturing will allow producers to make broader constraint-driven modifications to their product designs in a matter of minutes, as opposed to the months that are required today.

Technological advances will also give craftsmen greater control over mechanical designs. Researchers in the University of Michigan's Department of Mechanical Engineering and Applied Mechanics have already demonstrated how parts of the mechanical design problem can be solved using an intelligent system that applies a special calculus to assemble machines from a large library of standardized primitive mechanisms. Advancing from the premise that experienced designers create sophisticated mechanisms, in part, by synthesizing abstract representations of simpler building blocks, Sridhar Kota has developed systems that take input from user-supplied specifications and automatically generate alternate conceptual designs. This application of technology will not only guarantee that the mechanism will work and that the materials are strong enough; it will also solve the problem in seconds rather than taking weeks or even months.[2]

As ideas are discussed, simulations performed, and enhancements made, a real-time online diary of all contributions to the development of the concept will be compiled. The knowledge derived from each interactive encounter throughout the process will inform and shape every subsequent interaction. For example, when developing different requirements for vehicles with different uses, craftsmen will be able to study a wide range of variations and discover increasingly better ways to design chassis. The next wave of parametrized methodologies will give us insight into how this will be achieved. Today, one of the most significant problems with parametric modeling arises when a company introduces parametric details too early in the design process. Exacerbating the situation is the fact that many engineering organizations use parametric CAD capabilities to drive requirements and relationships from the bottom up, rather than employing a top-down approach better suited to the engineering of mechanical systems. In the future, CAD systems will combine packaged, discipline-specific content with next-generation process discipline aids to allow higher-quality designs to be created in dramatically less time. Specifically, these systems will allow producers to identify global considerations that may affect several subsystems in a product design and separate them into an associative "control structure." Meanwhile, more local relationships will be integrated into the component parts of the assembly. Such a control structure and an organized work flow will facilitate agreements among various engineering groups regarding the role, scope, and engineering analysis required when changing key design variables.[3]

Broader application of the intelligent systems mentioned earlier will also transform the role of the designer of an automobile's passenger compartment. As he selects a function that uses anthropometric data to determine the shape of the space that will be occupied by the driver and the passengers in the concept car, the designer will position the space for each anticipated occupant. This space will define the constraints on the shape and positioning of the seats, the dashboard and its instruments, the console, steering wheel, the pedals and other controls, the armrests, the windshield, the windows, and the rearview mirror. When the initial design is complete, he will assume the viewpoint of the driver, selecting other functions to reposition and adjusting the placement of the dashboard and console features. This driver's view (in 3D virtual reality) will allow the engineer to more accurately experience the design, selecting specific instruments for each of the displays. The result can be returned to the work-in-progress pool.

At the same time, the vehicle dynamics engineer will verify and tune how the car handles. After accessing the work in progress, he will open the signal dynamics diagram (based on the work of the underbody engineer). This diagram will be connected to an underlying virtual simulation program that can answer questions such as how fast the car will accelerate from 0 to 60 miles per hour on various road surfaces and grades. The vehicle dynamics engineer will also be able to derive other stability data from the simulation in conjunction with empirical models of test tracks. Once the vehicle's performance has been fine tuned, the engineer may choose to download its design to a motion-controlled platform, at which time he can "strap on" the car and take it for a drive on his choice of test tracks.

Motion platforms will be dramatically transformed as the low-cost virtual reality technologies now emerging in theme parks around the world find their way into more design studios and engineering laboratories. Vehicle designers will no longer expend time and materials building physical prototypes to test; instead, they will use advanced simulation. At the same time, visually expressing such things as the signal flow-transform models that underlie vehicle dynamics will become much easier. Intelligent systems will facilitate the interactive exploration, problem solving, and optimization of these complex systems. As a result, the vehicle dynamics engineer will be able to express in visual form everything from a car's geometry and its physics to its simulated behavior, benefiting from visual and tactile presentation of all this information.

Once all the details of the exploration and development process have been satisfactorily addressed, the producer will present the concept car to the collaborative customer for final assessment. In the virtual showrooms of the future, virtual reality systems will enable customers to view full-scale computer-generated models of cars in three dimensions. In such sensory settings, customers will immerse themselves in the vehicle, observe its appointments, interact with and even program onboard information systems, and finally take the car for a simulated spin along almost any stretch of road in the world. Because customers will also be able to view the car's exterior and comment on its styling, producers will be able to verify preferences regarding outer body finish and trim before production.

Photo-realism is particularly critical in an industry such as fashion, where a producer must exactly represent the color and texture to its customers or risk being accused of misrepresenting the product. Today, the quality of real-time visual computing systems with respect to how things actually look in the real world leaves much to be desired. Within 10 years, however, through the combined application of sophisticated rendering algorithms (e.g., ray tracing and radiosity) and advances in hardware, producers will be able to display product designs with photo-realistic quality so customers can experience how the product looks and feels.

As product designs are developed, a host of underlying financial models and the mathematical means of determining the costs of products will be created concurrently in the virtual development environment. Producers' financial and procurement systems will be fully automated and will be linked to the engineering and manufacturing systems across the extended enterprise of partners and suppliers. Once consensus is reached between the producer and the collaborative customer regarding the product's design, intelligent agents representing each of the collaborating entities will finalize their negotiations for parts and services. At this time, the system will immediately begin generating and transmitting electronic purchase orders to the appropriate partners and suppliers.

Agile Manufacturing

As products are being designed by virtual teams of craftsmen (which will include manufacturing engineers), decisions about raw materials, fabrication, tooling, fixturing, manufacturing, and assembly will be made quickly. Drawing on embedded manufacturing knowledge, the manufacturing engineer will use intelligent systems to analyze each iteration, eventually approving a design. These intelligent systems will permit this craftsman to focus on the aspects of the design that have never before been manufactured, singling out these aspects for special attention and leaving the understood, knowledge-embedded portions of the design to the intelligent system. Manufacturing engineers will be able to simulate, redefine, and test the previously unmanufactured design aspects—further developing and refining appropriate processes for various work cells, costing the operations, and inserting that knowledge into the now-defined features for future use. By building up libraries over time, the manufacturing knowledge engine will begin to alert design teams and product line managers of costs and schedules even as they design newer products.

Meanwhile, an agile work cell whose virtual manufacturing process is driven by automation and knowledge engines will create individual parts in much the same way as the original village craftsman did. This cell will be capable of reconfiguring robots, machines, and processes on demand. It will also be able to simulate processes, thereby verifying the combined, coordinated processes required to manufacture complex parts. The cells, operated by suppliers that are in constant contact with OEM producers, will provide manufacturing on demand. Not only will they ensure that a process is valid before raw material is inserted; they will also be able to sense the actual raw material offered and adapt the processes to that material.

Ten years from now, several other technologies will change manufacturing dramatically. Much like the "3D printing" used today to verify design concepts, these technologies will allow for the creation of a network of smaller specialty manufacturers, each capable of producing parts that require special processes to order. These smaller, rapidly configurable supplier networks will develop unique fabrication processes, complex assembly procedures, and subsystem expertise. Networked into the OEM, the specialty manufacturers will use evolving standards like CITIS (Contracted Integrated Technical Information Services) to bid on jobs in real time, much as we see in government procurement today.

With very few exceptions, large, monolithic assembly lines will be transformed into networks of agile cells. These networks of virtually connected manufacturing suppliers will form product-specific virtual teams, producing highly customized goods on demand. The agile cells will be self-contained systems that accept raw materials and convert them into products. Each cell will combine numerical control with real-time simulation, analysis, and sensing. Capable of adjusting to requirements on demand, the cells will consist of manufacturing machines, robots with multiple manipulators, transport mechanisms, virtual positioning systems, and knowledge-based recognition systems. Connected to the Internet, they will allow product knowledge to be developed in the virtual manufacturing systems and transferred on demand.

The build process itself will begin with agile cells producing both individual parts and lower-level subunits. These will be funneled to robot assembly cells, where products will be assembled concurrently (perhaps with stages of assembly separated by considerable distances). Leveraging a logistics network similar to the just-in-time processes used today, these virtual networks will transport their parts and subunits to the correct place for the next step in assembly and finally on to the shipping system for delivery directly to customers.

Any required real-time manual assembly processes will be simulated and animated into multimedia presentations, which will then be linked together to form a virtual assembly process. These presentations will deliver various instructions evolved from the simulation—including interdependency and tolerances—until the final product is completed. For example, the prime contractor for the Hornet program provided the buyers with simulated video verification of the proposed assembly process before beginning production. Similarly, assembly processes for the international space station—especially those required for the final assembly—are being simulated and approved before components are manufactured. The simulations currently provide feedback on clearance, assembly, and mating requirements. They will soon provide accurate feedback by integrating the physical constraints of the actual mechanical system. Such feedback will continue to dramatically reduce the impact of even a single design modification. Today, such modifications require not only considerable resources and software to manage the change but also rapid adjustments to the whole production process, including raw materials, tooling, fixtures, assembly sequences, warranty kitting, and the entire product support network.

Knowledge bases will allow an intelligent process called a *builder* to associate suppliers, foundries, work cells, assembly cells, and transportation systems, implementing the processes specified by a comprehensive assembly visualization. For example the builder, drawing on all the information that has been created at this stage of product development, will go out onto the Internet and begin to locate intelligent agents representing the requisite parts and services, which include work cells, component manufacturers, and transportation providers. At the same time, these agents will actively seek builders in need of the machines they represent. Once a builder has woven together a virtual web of agents that can provide the best products and services at the optimal time and price, it will enter into contracts with the various agents. As these contracts are established, this virtual manufacturing network will begin shipping parts and assembling products.

In many ways, these agile work cells will resemble the virtual factory concept that industry and the Defense Department's Advanced Research Project Agency have been working to develop in recent years. This concept envisions a manufacturing arrangement in which intelligent agents—representing a world of custom-built agile work cells—communicate on the Internet without the need for human intervention. Within 10 years, most high-end products will be created this way. There will be no reason for any single company to own all the materials and machines needed for production. Instead, as customers demand new products, the composition and the arrangement of the virtual factory needed to assemble those products will change accordingly, without the producers' having to refit assembly lines as companies must do today.

As I described earlier, these virtual factories will be capable of rapid prototyping ("3D printing"). Able to produce physical "test parts" directly from digital data, this technology permits physical exploration and evaluation. Using higher-quality plastics and resins than exist today, this technology will create production-grade parts for use in limited-run production. In such scenarios, tooling, molds, and fixtures are bypassed or eliminated. With this technology already expanding into metal manufacturing, the virtual factory is taking its first steps toward producing fully customized products on demand. For more generic products, virtual factories will become more prevalent, with suppliers, foundries, agile work cells, and transportation providers working together to bring products to markets. Ultimately, the molds with which future "cobblers" craft "customized shoes" will be nothing more than sets of constraints in extended virtual design environments. The dismantling of the Fordian Complex is already underway.

Integrating the Virtual Product

Ever since mass manufacturing rendered the intimate dialogue of the village obsolete, customers have continued to freely offer advice, both willingly and unknowingly, about how to improve the performance of products. Those suggestions have, for the most part, fallen on deaf ears. And even when heard, the unsolicited advice has rarely, if ever, been incorporated into a continuous process for improving products.

Today, efforts at virtual product development are just beginning to incorporate feedback loops that allow for continuous communications among producers, products, and customers. But the fact remains that it is almost impossible for the producer to know what the individual customer really wants and needs unless the producer steps into the customer's shoes on a regular basis and sees the world through his eyes. In the future, a combination of intelligent systems embedded in products and advanced wireless communications will enable such continuous feedback loops. Automobile producers, for example, will provide their products with rapid access to product information and expert knowledge. At the same time, drivers and their cars will transmit performance and environmental data back to the producers, who will use that information to make real-time value propositions to drivers and, ultimately, to enhance future product designs.

Much like the learning golf club mentioned above, the more complex products of the future will actually evolve in the hands of customers. As a result, by monitoring the constant interplay of the customer, the product, and myriad factors and forces in the external environment, producers will be able to continuously improve the performance of their products and, thus, enrich their customers' quality of life.

Embedded Intelligent Systems

As automobiles evolve over the next 10 years, they will increasingly become reasoning, knowledge-based organisms that engage customers, producers, the environment, and the world of information in an ongoing dialogue. Intelligent systems embedded in automobiles will give them an information coordination capability, by which they will recombine and reprogram themselves for enhanced performance. Onboard information systems will be smart enough to understand their own structures. As a result, when environmental conditions, customer preferences, or new research findings dictate a change in the performance parameters of an automobile, the internal programs will be able to instantaneously evaluate the impact of the change and then make the change if it is deemed appropriate. Monsanto's genetically engineered cotton seed illustrates the organic nature of this adaptive capability. Genetic information embedded in the seed allows the plant to react differently to temperature, moisture, and pests than an ordinary plant. Implicit in this adaptive process is a constant two-way information exchange between the seed and its surroundings. The next generation of "active control vehicle suspension systems" will function in much the same way. In the past, passive control systems have assigned constant coefficient values to their spring and damper subsystems. As a result, these systems have not been able to adapt themselves to meet changing weather and surface conditions.

In the future, active control systems will employ a variety of intelligent systems to achieve such an adaptive capability. Acting as both sensors and effectors, springs will be assigned adaptive coefficient values. As these springs receive data from the environment, such as a bump in the road or an icy surface, they will do two things simultaneously. A spring will send the physical energy resulting from the bump or slick surface to its own electric generator, which will serve as the energy source by which the spring functions. At the same time, the spring will relay data about the environment to an onboard computer that interprets the data and formulates the appropriate response. This computer will employ neural network technology and fuzzy logic to solve in real time the differential equations presented by the environmental conditions, finally reprogramming the adaptive coefficient of each spring accordingly. Within 10 years, vehicle control systems will actually understand the physical environments in which they function, continuously adapting themselves for optimal performance under variable weather and road conditions.[4]

In the future, neural networks will also be used more widely to enhance a number of safety-related systems, significantly improving a vehicle's ability to distinguish between deployment and nondeployment events in a timely manner. Unlike other decision technologies, neural networks do not make use of predefined threshold or boundary curves. They are inherently tolerant of noise in the input data and capable of producing reasonable responses when presented with novel inputs. Additionally, these networks can simply be retrained when new data become available or when the customer's requirements change; thus, they eliminate the need for a human analyst to modify the existing discrimination algorithm or devise an entirely new algorithm.

For example, neural networks will be "trained" to recognize the need for deployment of an air bag on the basis of an analysis of recent data provided by the vehicle's crash sensor (typically an accelerometer). Once the network is trained, it will be able to determine for itself what features of the crash-sensor data should be used in discrimination. This ability to reason is what makes neural networks more robust than other decision technologies.[5]

Virtual Product Communication

As embedded intelligent systems increasingly record, process, and apply real-time information to enhance product performance, advances in wireless communication technology will radically change the speed, amount, and direction of information that flows into and out of virtual products. For example, continuous communication loops among producers, automobiles, and customers will be realized through a combination of high-speed digital-based communication using satellites and localized terabit fiber data links. As a result, the everyday driving experience will probably evolve into an intelligent telecommute in which drivers and their cars have immediate access to the information they need to optimally perform their respective tasks.

A number of auto manufacturers are already developing intelligent transportation systems to evaluate how various mobile radio frequency communication systems and automotive display systems might be deployed in the future. On the basis of these early efforts, we can imagine that onboard communication systems of the future will integrate radio-frequency communications, display technologies, navigation and route-guidance systems, sensors, and user-input devices. Cars will be transformed into networked adaptive organisms that intelligently assimilate input from drivers, producers, and the environment to continuously improve their performance.

Onboard radio-frequency communication systems of the future will have their coverage area (range) carefully matched to specific applications. For example, information of interest to an entire community would justify broadcast distribution, whereas information relevant to a local area or a single point would need to be transmitted only a short distance. Therefore, communication systems will probably incorporate wide-area and short-range systems, such as digital audio broadcast, vehicle-to-roadside communication subsystems, and global positioning systems.[6]

Vehicle-to-roadside communication subsystems will probably employ multi-use, two-way communication links for short-range applications (approximately 20 to 100 meters). In addition to supporting lane-based and open-road tolling, these local, high-speed, bi-directional digital communication links will provide roadside sign information to alert drivers of road conditions, speed limit changes, services available, and traffic probe data.[7]

When integrated with the overall vehicle-to-roadside communication system, electronic messaging systems will improve the safety and convenience of highway driving by providing real-time dynamic messages in the vehicle for visual and auditory presentation. Because they provide information inside the vehicle, electronic messaging systems will mitigate some of the leading factors in automobile accidents, such as driver inattentiveness and poor visibility. Additionally, electronic messages will be dynamic, with the ability to instantaneously change the content of sign information on the basis of sensor inputs. For example, rather than constantly transmitting the message "watch for ice on bridge," a dynamic sign can monitor ice on the roadway and transmit the message "icy bridge" only when ice is present. Dynamic messages will also provide drivers with convenient information concerning freeway exits for stadiums, concert halls, and other high-traffic areas, as well as for gas, food, and lodging services.[8]

Through some combination of these and perhaps other communication technologies, producers will be able to track in real time how many right turns a particular driver makes, how abruptly she applies her brakes, what speed fluctuations she experiences, and what her car's rate of fuel consumption is. With access to such performance information and to data on weather, traffic, and terrain conditions, the car's producers will be able to inform the driver, in real time, how often she should change her oil or rotate her tires, what type of brakes suit her best, and alternative routes to and from work. Producers will also be able to upgrade the automobile's performance on the basis of its surroundings—for example, by updating its fuel consumption algorithms. Ultimately, all this information will find its way back to the craftsman, who will incorporate it into the following week's designs, thus beginning another spin of the wheel of innovation.

Conclusion

In the midst of all the technology-related change and confusion in today's electronic marketplace, one thing is certain. After all the fiber lines have been laid, the satellites have settled into their orbits, and the digital dust particles have cleared, the roles and relationships of producers and customers will have undergone a startling metamorphosis. If we allow our mind's eye to rise above the fray and wander out beyond the horizon, we will see at once a breathtaking vision of tomorrow's virtual global village and a faint glimmer of yesteryear's golden age before the dawn of mass manufacturing. In that once and future craftsman culture, customers will actively participate in the conception and development of products. Producers will funnel a world of knowledge and resources into malleable molds custom-fitted to individuals' needs. And products will transcend their material manifestations to serve as extended virtual workshops, in which the cobbler and the customer can—once again—sit down together to explore the world of possibility.

Notes

1. Audre Lord, in *Sister Outsider: Essays and Speeches* (Crossing Press, 1984).

2. Sridhar Kota, Associate Professor, University of Michigan, Department of Mechanical Engineering, "Automated Conceptual Design of Mechanisms," SAE Knowledge-based Engineering Symposium, October 1996.

3. Stan E. Kolodziel, "EDS Unigraphics Creates Design Wave," Daratech, Inc., February 1997.

4. Yoshihiro Suda and Taichi Shiiba, University of Tokyo, "A New Hybrid Suspension System with Active Control and Energy Regeneration," *Dynamics of Vehicles on Roads and on Tracks,* Supplement 25, 1996.

5. Stephen J. Kiselewich and Douglas D. Turner, Delco Electronics Corporation, "Neural Networks for SIR Deployment," 1996.

6. Ashok B. Ramaswamy, Randall T. Brunts, and Michael B. Thoeny, Delco Electronics Corporation, "Telepath: An ITS Concept System," 1996.

7. Ibid.

8. Mark Kady, Delco Electronics Corporation, and Peter Shloss, Hughes Aircraft Company, "Electronic Messaging Using Vehicle-to-Roadside Communications," 1996.

2

A Store as Big as the World

Walter Forbes

In the seventeenth century, the Quakers discovered a revolutionary principle of marketing and retailing. If they eliminated the concept of bargaining and fixed a single immutable and non-negotiable price for each of their products, they could save an enormous amount of time and expense—and offer their products, in the end, more cheaply than any of their competitors who continued to bargain on each sale.

Changes in the retailing landscape since then have been as much about size and scale as about the fundamental nature of the way goods are priced or sold. The megastore and the mall are, after all, little more than brightly lit, marble-lined versions of the bazaar of Istanbul. It is often said that the Internet is the first new medium to be introduced since television. Perhaps more significantly, the revolution in retailing with the arrival of the cyber marketplace is as profound in its own way as was the pricing mechanism of the seventeenth century.

It is as close to a perfect market as has yet been created. The evolution of the market since man first swapped one rock for another, down through the Quakers, on to today's mega-malls, and now into cyberspace, has been the functional equivalent of moving half the distance to the far wall, then half the distance again, and so on. We have approached the perfect market, but we are not yet there. The cyber market brings us within touching distance.

What economists call a "perfect market" establishes a perfect balance between supply and demand, between satisfaction and gratification, and between want and need. The price to be paid satisfies all three of the principal parties to every transaction: producer, seller, and buyer. As the perfect market is approached, the nature of each of these parties will change very slightly, perhaps morphing one into another so that we are left with an essential and seamless process of information transferal—moving from conception of product and conception of need at both ends of the continuum toward a central point of satisfaction which is the marketplace itself.

This is the new world we are entering—a world where a marketplace exists only in space and time, where bricks-and-mortar retailers are an anachronism from the twentieth century, and where parking lots and suburban malls can begin to return to their rightful places as parkland and green space.

The marketplace of the twenty-first century—an interactive one, or a "cyber market," or even a "perfect marketplace"—is about time and space, and this is its fundamental difference. From the manufacturer to the final consumer, the cyber market has defined a new concept. For the first time, the market is bigger than the marketplace. Indeed, in many respects there remains no such thing as place. There are a thousand, a million, and eventually a billion points of entry and exit, production, and consumption. Above all, it is a market of multiple (indeed infinite) points of contact.

The only way to capitalize on such points of contact is for the manufacturer and the retailer to be at once everywhere and nowhere—to know and to understand deeply, second by second, what the customer wants and what the manufacturer can produce to satisfy these desires. Above all, it means the end of the bricks-and-mortar retailer for most retail transactions.

The evolution of the interactive marketplace is being driven by specific socioeconomic trends: people are spending more time at work; more and more families are relying on two incomes, which even then seem insufficient; the population is aging; and the fear of crime is growing. These trends are complemented by equally influential consumer trends: people are demanding larger amounts of comparative information before they select and purchase a product; retail stores are failing to maintain service levels; manufacturers and retailers continue to increase the number of products and features available, while high turnover and tightening profit margins force salespeople to be thinly spread, uninformed generalists. These phenomena coincide with decreases in the prices of computer networking and databases and with an overall decline in the cost of all forms of communication, with the increasing costs that accompany bricks-and-mortar enterprises, and with the increasing costs of personnel (including the overhead of health care, taxes, and administration).

These changes are occurring against the backdrop of the continued worldwide entry of personal computing into consumers' homes and a commensurate growth in interactive services. People are going to be spending more time getting their own information and obtaining goods and services directly. They will increasingly expect to interact *and* to transact.

The enterprises that provide the content of this interactive marketplace will be winners no matter what hardware, platforms, and sources of delivery they marshal. At least they will win to the extent that they can provide information, an ability to transact, savings, and a dynamic environment. Along the way, interactive content becomes more valuable than passive content. Microsoft's interactive encyclopedia EnCarta® is more valuable than the traditional encyclopedia, electronic bulletin boards are more informative than magazines, an interactive electronic "street atlas" in your car or truck fleet is more efficient than a paper map, and digital listings of apartments for rent and used cars for sale are more useful than classified ads in newspapers.

The interactive marketplace is a highly personalized one. Every consumer's experience is unique. This brings with it the advantages to business of one-on-one marketing. Businesses in this marketplace can anticipate the consumer's requirements, and can in fact evolve their offerings in tandem with the growth and the changing needs of the consumer's family. The consumer, in turn, inhabits an environment of extraordinary flexibility, able to wander free, to be guided by experts, or to explore the marketplace with people having similar interests.

A range of complementary, maturing technologies support the construction of this "perfect marketplace": networks supporting increased bandwidth to the consumer, ever-faster processors and methods to combine multiple processors to act in concert, advanced messaging, security and encryption, streaming media, Internet telephony, neural networks, profiling systems, and smart agents. But the viability of the interactive market has less to do with technology than with content, with little commitment to fixed assets, with short product or service life cycles, and with the essential ability of buyer and seller to interact directly and intimately. How might this market look?

Back to the Future

In order to describe my vision of the future of shopping, let me first posit what technological advancements will be ubiquitous or at least generally accepted by, say, the year 2008.

In 2003, a breakthrough in compression algorithms allowed a descendant of the twentieth century's cable modem to surpass the residential transmission rate of 100 megabytes per second, allowing generous growth in bandwidth for channeled phone lines, traditional cable television channels, and Internet connectivity. Homes no longer need to be separately wired for phones, cable, ISDN, etc., since this channeled cable bandwidth is sufficient and convenient to deliver and transmit all sorts of broadcast and point-to-point communications. As a result of this advancement, the once-clear product delineation between televisions and computers, challenged in the late 1990s by such products as WebTV and Compaq's cable-ready personal computers, has been left to the historians. The telephone has become a collector's item, since the new computers accommodate streaming audio-video and full-duplex audio as seamlessly as older ones handled word processing.

As dependence on computers burgeoned at the end of the twentieth century for not only business functions but also for day-to-day home and entertainment uses, the demand on premium hotels and vacation centers to expand their "business centers" was met with the installation of networked computers in each guest room. Airlines and train lines have not yet begun supplying computers in economy class, but at least they provide network ports for passengers desiring to connect to the Internet while in transit.

New cars come with an onboard computer as standard equipment, and used cars are easily outfitted. The function once served by GPS-based mapping displays is now served by software loaded onto the onboard computer, whose display replaced the dedicated GPS display of the 1990s. Advances in wireless packet-based communication allow the onboard computer to connect, as needed, to the Internet, to provide the driver with geocentric maps of service providers, restaurants, nightclubs, historical points of interest, and the like.

With the advancement and acceptance of debit cards, cash is seldom used. The many ATM facilities once maintained by banks have been replaced with public, networked computer terminals for the convenience of citizens and visitors. As more and more tourists looked to the Web for information on towns, cities, historical sites, landmarks, and entertainment centers, visits to public information centers decreased. Visitor information, local weather forecasts, and any other information that visitors might seek on the Internet are now provided by computers housed in converted ATM facilities. Since the Internet also supports full-duplex telephony and video, public phones have been made obsolete by these public computer terminals.

In short, computers are everywhere by 2008, and they are relied upon to serve humanity for a whole new order of essential home, entertainment, communication, and business functions. A large-screen computer in the living room is used to order groceries in one window, to watch an old movie in another, to converse with Grandma and her aging sister Bridget in a video conference call in a third, and to get an update on the household's finances in a fourth. A smaller-screen computer in the car is used to track the progress of a trip in one window, to order take-out Portuguese food in a second, to turn down the car's computer-controlled stereo system in the third, and to join in the video conference call with Grandma and Great Aunt Bridget in the fourth.

Let us take a drive down whatever "Miracle Mile" of retailing might exist in the vicinity of any American city in the year 2008. The sprawling malls of asphalt and concrete are now only secondarily centers for shopping. Theme restaurants and specialty shops still exist, depending in part on the draw of passing customers on their way to the cinemas and virtual reality gaming arenas now anchoring the malls, where once stood the mega-stores of the preceding century. Some of the land once paved to provide parking for the malls has been reclaimed for green space. Some of the largest parking garages have been converted into training facilities for Olympic skateboarders and mountain rollerbladers; smaller ones stand empty or have been razed.

This transformation was not initiated by a deep recession, but by a lack of time and will to shop in the traditional way of the twentieth century. And it happened fast.

Retailers were the first to spot the trends, although, like all benign rulers facing revolution from below, they had little idea of what to do to fend off the upending of their mall-based prosperity. For more than a decade, trends had been going against these traditional retailers. Most American women (the largest demographic segment in the history of shopping) were working full or part time. And everyone seemed drastically to be paring back the time they spent shopping, and going to fewer shops when they did venture out. Their tolerance for the imperfections of the shops they were visiting less frequently also began to shrink. Even a 30,000-square-foot "hypermarket" was ever less an attraction—as were the selections, the hours, the locations, and the amount of useful product information attainable from the salespersons, who were not only fewer in number but shorter on patience and helpfulness.

Even the outlet malls that once attracted throngs with lowered prices were striving desperately to attract the last remaining shoppers still prepared to drive to market. They slashed prices even deeper on brand-name merchandise, and they offered discounts on the charge cards they issued as an added incentive, but to no avail.

Some retailers recognized early on that they had to reexamine the economic fundamentals to survive. The cost of most items they sold was piled heavily onto the product only after it left the factory and began moving through distribution and sales: perhaps a 100 percent markup to the wholesaler, another 100 percent to the retailer. A 50-percent-off sale at Saks may still have left a dress or a suit at twice the price it cost leaving the factory, which in turn may have been twice the price of the labor and the fabric that went into it. Any retailer that didn't drastically control costs and cut markups perished. Bradlees and Caldor, with respective expense ratios of 29.4 percent and 24.2, went into Chapter 11 bankruptcy. K-Mart managed to cut its expenses to 22.2 percent of sales but could not cut them further.

Way back in the 1990s there were 18.6 square feet of retail space for every man, woman, and child in the United States—twice the amount of two decades earlier. And whereas every square foot generated an average of $175 in sales in 1975, 20 years later it generated $166. At the same time, expenses were skyrocketing. Even the superstores were not looking so super in comparison with cyber retailers, who populated a market no less competitive yet far more immediate and omnipresent than any physical shopping district. A cyber retailer could slash its expenses to barely 14 percent of revenues, while operating costs relative to sales were rising at almost every downtown or suburban retailer. At the same time that costs and prices were plunging in the interactive marketplace, a cyber retailer could be leaping over the traditional providers of goods and services to build a global presence for hundreds of millions of additional buyers. With no inventory, no display space, and no old-fashioned stores to service, sales per square foot had become irrelevant for the cyber retailers of 2008. And the new generation of shoppers in cyberspace found no full parking lots, no jostling crowds, and no "sold out of size 14." Parking lots had been replaced with bandwidth, jostling crowds with server consumption and transaction speed, lack of inventory with just-in-time manufacturing and next-day drop shipping.

On the shop floor in the late twentieth century, there were perhaps 30 models of portable stereos on display—ten brands, with three or four speaker configurations. Buying such a stereo in 2008, you simply suggest to your personal agent that you want the speakers to be separable. In a flash, all those models with stationary speakers disappear from the "shelves." Say you want a twelve-disk CD changer. Gone in the blink of an eye are all the one- or six-disk models. You want a built-in graphic equalizer. Suddenly, there in front of you—from 3800 models available on your doorstep tomorrow morning—are five, displayed with brands and prices. The entire process has taken 5 minutes of your time. Before you could even have gotten the attention of a harried clerk with five other pushy customers waiting to elbow you out of the way, you have found the portable stereo system that suits you best, and your family will be listening to it at tomorrow evening's barbecue.

Not only will your purchase be delivered promptly to your doorstep; it will be there at a price 20 percent below the best price on the shelf of a national discount store. Why? No rent and no salesclerk to pay, no heating bills or parking lot attendants, and no inventory to float. No inventory, yet total availability. Instead of a salesperson, the cyber retailer becomes an information and mediating agent. The manufacturer becomes an assembler. This is the shape of the new "mall" of cyberspace. Who is populating it, and what are they buying? What do they expect? What will it take to sell to these buyers?

Retailers in the twentieth century used to order various goods in a mix of styles and colors from a range of manufacturers, perhaps once for each season or for the projected duration of each fad. The manufacturer's reliability extended only to producing a fixed model with specified color and style, being able to deliver it in bulk to a wholesaler or a retailer, and being able to promote and advertise it so that the retailer would find a ready demand for it when it appeared on the shelves.

The twentieth-century retailer was responsible only to display goods in an attractive and accessible manner, with hopes that customers would arrive. In 2008, however, things are very different. The retailer is a rich source of both positive and negative feedback on products. Whereas in the twentieth century the form of feedback was limited to initial and subsequent bulk purchases of products, now a whole new granularity of data is supplied by the retailer to the manufacturer. Each time a particular product is eliminated from consideration by a shopper, owing to lack of features or uncompetitive pricing, that valuable piece of information is supplied back to the manufacturer. Near misses were never capturable in the twentieth century retailer's world, because no insights into a shopper's thoughts regarding a product were available except as implied by a final sale. What is more, the twentieth-century sale was often too strongly believed to imply complete satisfaction with a product's features—discounting the likelihood that the product selected was an acceptably imperfect fit with the shopper's criteria, and thereby missing an opportunity for product improvement.

In 2008, manufacturing is much more than just-in-time production to meet bulk retail orders, as the order is for an individual consumer. The retailer and the manufacturer share the responsibility to fulfill the order of every customer who visits the cyber market. The manufacturer plays as important a role as the retailer as development and production steadily penetrate the process of selling—a logical consequence of the telescoping of the factors of time and distance.

In 2008 it is up to manufacturers of jeans to determine the best sources of denim fabric, navy thread, and brass rivets. Cyber manufacturing gives them the capacity to "assemble" each pair of jeans, as each customer is able, should he or she so desire, to select a style of rivets, type of patch, and a precise kind of fabric. Each pair of jeans can be made specific to the body that will wear it. And each retailer knows which manufacturer will fill an order most efficiently, achieving the best integration of quality and speed. With a Dutch cargo plane manned by a British crew waiting at Jakarta Airport (all this having been assembled by a freight forwarder at Kennedy Airport in New York), a retailer can be confident that a paint-fitting pair of jeans from Jakarta will be sliding into position in Darien before one manufactured in Duluth and trucked to a staging area at Grand Rapids has fought its way through "two-day" mail at Lansing.

Cyber retailers' effectiveness and profitability depends far more on the ever-renewed data on products and on the flow of knowledge than on any piling up inventory on the shelves with which the cyber market seeks to dispense. Cyber retailers are highly and increasingly sophisticated go-betweens—a role that can be extraordinarily profitable in any society, and steadily more so in the information age. Knowledge has always been power, and now we have a greater ability to know than in all history. If necessary, that knowledge can be used in real time between buyer and seller.

If store shelves are not cyber retailers' key objectives, what is their contribution? First, they must maintain the highways, and certainly the road maps, though the customers furnish shelves and parking lots. It took quite a while to build a critical mass of each of these components that allowed the cyber retailing to become any more than the video game of a handful of computer nerds.

At the same time, the pricing of the services that would allow the computer to become as integral a part of shoppers' lives as the automobile was also shifting in favor of the cyber retailer. Once online services were priced at a flat rate, the meter was no longer running on Internet connectivity. Free shopping software was easily downloaded, and online access to the cyber mall was embedded directly into scores of computer programs. And once on line, the sophisticated software of the cyber retailer could not just quickly guide shoppers to their intended destinations, but could lead them to others they had not even thought to visit, strolling them through a virtual shopping mall.

Security, too, improved in tandem with the development of online merchandising and invoicing. As online banking and bill paying proliferated from the original ATMs, customers became habituated to online orders and payment, the next essential steps toward an amiable extension of the routine shopping experience. As debit cards gained in popularity, the consumers able to make electronic purchases extended from credit card holders to all those with active checking accounts.

All this familiarity made the computer as unthreatening as an automobile or a television: shopping could be as simple as opening the refrigerator door. Instead of spending 20 minutes jockeying through irritated traffic, the cyber shopper could sit at a computer and, with a few clicks, float inside the cyber mall to try on "the latest Paris fashions" in forms that have had no other bodies inside them.

The Electronic Executive Assistant

The first "smart agents" arrived on the scene in the 1990s, in tandem with profiling systems. Each of these technologies attempted to produce a highly tuned match of content to the individual, but they attempted to apply the tuning at opposite ends of the formula. The explosive volume and dynamic nature of information available on line led many neophyte online denizens to feel completely overwhelmed and lost. Agents attempted to tune the process by requesting and searching for content as the proxy of the individual, on the basis of in-depth information about the individual entered by the individual. In accord with the old adage that less is more, less peripheral information and more relevant information was displayed to the end user, thereby improving the individual's experience on the Internet. In an academic sense, search engines could be considered "agents" for end users, insofar as end users utilized them to locate topical information. The search engines of the late 1990s, however, were necessarily weak agents, hindered by their lack of context and by their literal handling of search criteria. One would certainly not expect a vintage-1998 search engine to locate the "best dog collar for

Elmer," since the search engine would have no information about Elmer (in particular, his neck size and his owner's constraints in defining "best"). One would, instead, search for "purchase+dog+collar" and do the rest of the qualitative searching by hand.

While agents attempted to tune an individual's request, profiling systems attempted to dynamically tune a service's content to be delivered in response to that request. Profiling systems were intended to target content, typically in the form of advertisements and product descriptions, from a service to an individual, on the basis of available demographic information, purchasing history, and any personal vital statistics offered up by the individual. Since the prize for success was a marketing edge in the electronic "New World," every pebble was turned in search of the perfect profiling system. The models produced and the methodologies attempted were exhaustive, including models based on direct questioning, inference engines, psychographics, and neural network technologies.

By the beginning of the new century, companies employing neural-network-based technologies enjoyed sweet victories. Neural networks were utilized by the large search engine companies to mine the universe of Web pages for key words and categorization. The profiling systems based on this same technology proved to be superior at matching content to individuals through a three-step process. A company's corpus of product and advertising content was processed to produce vertices in an N-dimensional space representing their respective positions in the mathematical equivalent of the company's content universe. As new products became available in a company's line, those products were similarly processed. Next, the pages traversed by individuals were similarly processed, and were combined to determine an individual's coordinates in the company's content universe. This processing was able to occur in real time, thanks to the ever-increasing computing power of multi-processor servers. Finally, two flavors of questions could be asked of the profiling system: What content is in the proximity of an individual? What individuals are in the proximity of a product? The former question was used to tune content returned by servers to individuals, significantly raising the click-through rates for advertisements, increasing product sales, and doubling the length of sessions, and thereby feeding more data into the profiling system. The latter question allowed email promotions of sales items to be targeted to the narrowest possible set of highly potential customers, avoiding negative customer sentiments.

Toward the end of the twentieth century, many companies with small amounts of content were inclined to join profiling co-ops. Profiling on their own had produced only marginal improvements in targeting content, since the average individual did not spend enough time (or, more correctly, did not request enough pages) on a company's site to produce a meaningful profile, regardless of the technology on which the profiling system was based. Advertising revenues for search engines and large destinations skyrocketed, while small companies scrambled to keep enough bargain-basement banners active to fill their empty spaces. By 2008, profiling co-ops were nothing more than historical oddities—failures owing to lack of in-depth, proprietary data such as the constituent companies were willing or able to supply.

Although profiling systems matured around 2004, much continued to happen in the development of a superior agent through 2008, with no sign of slowing. Online content increased exponentially over the last decade, while individuals' disposition toward copious amounts of semi-useful data became acutely rebellious. The agents of the 1990s were limited in their intimacy with the details and behaviors of individuals. Their descendants of the 2000s have the advantage that computers are integrated into an order of magnitude more daily events and processes in the lives of their respective masters.

As an electronic executive assistant and confidante, the 2008 cyber agent has access to an individual's financial records, exhaustive purchasing history, qualitative preferences, and vital statistics. Cyber agents assist in a wide gamut of processes, saving the individual time and avoiding errors easily detected by a computer. Email and phone messages are filtered by the cyber agent as adeptly as by the most seasoned executive assistant. Television and radio commercials are likewise filtered, and progress reports on the day's assignments are delivered in the time slots they would have occupied.

Access to personal information and preferences is supplied out by the cyber agent according to assigned levels of trust, and cyber agents can communicate with one another as needed. My cyber agent, for example, will ask my wife's cyber agent for her preference in necklace length while assisting me in purchasing a birthday present. If my wife has given me sufficient permission to receive that level of information, my cyber agent will ensure that she is pleased with the length (if with no other detail of the gift). In the absence of that datum, my cyber agent will use information from my previous purchases to fill in the information, and will initiate the product-selection process by indicating to relevant electronic stores that *it* is in the market for a necklace. Notice that the cyber agent shops in my stead, and that it supplies information to electronic stores on a "need to know" basis and in strict accordance with the levels of trust I have established. Membership-based cyber services in the year 2008 have almost an unfair advantage over transaction-based cyber retailers, since they are typically trusted at a more intimate level than their traditional shopping counterparts. They are joined, after all, with the expectation that they will act in partnership with cyber agents to bring the member incomparable value. The cyber service of 2008 is the cyber agent's cyber agent.

Retailers a Breed Apart

This direct point-of-contact with the shopper is where the cyber retailers' responsibility begins—but that responsibility is very different from the responsibility of the slightly bored human salespersons. The new sales "personnel" are parallel to the products themselves. These cyber clerks fulfill a dream of the "human use of human beings"—maximum transactional fit without endless petty fiddling. Before the Quakers began fixed pricing, sellers and buyers bargained by item. Merchants had to know their never-very-uniform products intimately if they were to guide their shoppers and maintain the kind of one-on-one give-and-take that would result in a match of price, goods, and, not least, time consumed. By the 1990s, the flesh-and-blood salesclerk was all too frequently little more than an unskilled, uninformed order-taker without the artistic involvement that makes for manners, enterprise, and creation.

Further, since the development of profiling and cyber agents, cyber retailers know the maximum applicable information about each individual customer, while the customer's cyber-agent coordinates and negotiates with the impalpable staff of the great house of cyberspace. Much as the local tailor or the high-priced couturier knew his customers' every dimension, color preference, and body type as a result of previous interaction, the cyber clerk can use the customer's profile and updated information from the customer's cyber agent to create the functional equivalent of a changing room. Dresses or suits appear instantly on a generated body type that fits the shopper perfectly, modeling it from every angle. Colors and materials change at the click of a mouse button. Let the same shopper enter the market for a car instead of the latest dress suit, and the "small talk" with the cyber tailor about looking great in earth tones will cause the display models to favor brown and tan interiors, while the stereo sound system will play the same digital recording ordered last week from the cyber record shop.

Moreover, the economies of all these customizations—above all, that of scale—surpass anything ever available to the scattered, harassed, ill-coordinated armies of the old retailing.

Meanwhile, during the twentieth century's last decade, the supermarket gave way to the megastore. Home Depot moved from a standard 103,000-square-foot format to 135,000 square feet, while Office Depot increased the size of its superstores to 45,000 square feet from 30,000. Wal-Mart added 50,000 square feet of grocery space to its existing discount stores, finding that its surveys showed half the food shoppers buying other merchandise. Discount merchandise sales increased by 25–30 percent. The shoppers could wander from deli meats to designer jeans—if their feet held out. And Circuit City set up CarMax auto superstores to sell used cars with a unique concept: 500 to 1000 cars on each lot, each at a fixed price. No stress, no haggling. All these steps were taken to meet the trends that were working against these powerful merchants.

But what about giving those same automobile customers access to not 1000 listings but 100,000, and the freedom to match maximum preference of style, and even accessories, with odometer reading—all this accompanied by a history underwritten by a money-back guarantee? And what if the prices were 30 percent below anything sitting on asphalt lots, no matter how large and innovative?

Instead, shoppers in the superstore not only of 2008, but well before then, can wander from deli to designers without leaving their armchairs, choosing among foods and recipes, clothes and cruises, life insurance, clubs to join, real estate to buy or rent.

Ultimate Economies of Scale

These are the ultimate economies of scale combined with diversity of interest and best use of time. Eventually, even the superstore or the megamall must collide with certain all-too-numerous limits on their capacities: absolute constraints of size or of hours. Nine AM to 11 PM is fine if your shoppers don't have to be at work at 8 AM and be back to give the children supper and put them to bed at 10 PM at the latest. Simple geographic accessibility must hit its barriers—even thousands of 250- to 400-square-foot Sunglass Huts can keep only so much proximity to so many customers. Not even McDonald's can build a store on every street corner.

Moreover, even the largest superstore can carry only so much merchandise, offering a finite spectrum of selections. Inevitably one model of television, one kind of cream cheese, one brand of salsa, one color or size or shape will be—to some accusing eyes and palates—glaringly absent from the shelf. A building cannot be a world. Nearly ten years ago, Tandy experimented with outlets large enough to qualify as theme parks. Its Incredible Universe stores were the largest ever created—with 185,000 square feet, each stocking more than 85,000 models of electronic products and home appliances, each generating $55 million to $65 million in sales in their first year—and still they have not so much as broken even: indeed, by the mid 1990s their sales were falling.

Overall, bricks-and-mortar retailers saw same-store sales increasing by only 2 to 3 percent from year to year by the mid 1990s, while the cyber retailer was posting same-store gains in terms of multiples.

There are several contributing factors. First, chains like Incredible Universe never created a compelling reason for customers to shop in them. Finding the right product at a good price was no reason to undergo the total assault on body and mind perpetrated by such upscale environmental sinks. There are physical limits on how far a shopper can walk without exhaustion. "Shop 'til you drop" is not a twenty-first-century concept. "Strolling" from deli to designer under one mega-roof could entail a walk longer than the previous generation's trip to the "corner" store five blocks away. Cities fall down when the farms are set too far distant; as do malls when they expect too much of their customers.

For now the cyber retailers are lifting the visit to market from grinding wheels and weary ankles to concentrate upon making it entirely what it centrally is: an *informational* transaction. The perfect marketplace consists of as many points of sale as there are customers, each point directly accessible, every conceivable product available in every conceivable size, style, and color able to compress to the minimum the delays imposed by distance and complexity. Virtual assessment being obstinately compelled to act upon real objects. Some lapse is inescapable, but layer after layer of unnecessary reality is going down like the Berlin Wall. This is not magic. No product will simply materialize on the doorstep. In spite of efforts to proliferate publicly available networked terminals, not every customer will have access to the hardware or software necessary to enter the cyber market, but enormous progress is being made.

Inevitably, such progress generates a proliferation of systems and points of entry, an intensification of competition, whereas in a perfect market there would be no competition. For every product would be available to every customer at every point of entry—a rather static perfection, illustrating Schumpeter's dictum that a perfect system wouldn't work. Particularly in a transitional phase as bricks-and-mortar retailing gives way to cyber retailing, there will be felt a need to build awareness of the new systems, to clarify the still rather surreal duel between the electron and the countertop.

The ratio of knowledge-as-capital to inventory, human resources, and bricks is lower, much more static, and less fine-structured. Wal-Mart and Home Depot don't need to profile their customers for the fundamental reason that their customers' computer interactions—at the checkout counter—represent the weary end of the relationship, not its fruitful beginning. But the cyber retailer's very store is built out of knowledge and staffed by knowledge, and it can expand through knowledge alone.

As soon as the customers "stroll" in, their histories, their patterns of taste, and their temperaments leap to electric life. We are very likely to know the sizes they wear, the colors they prefer, the books they read, the types of car they drive, their jobs, hobbies, and sports. The sophisticated hardware we have developed builds an unlimited number of instant bridges to their realms of preference. They may have come in for a new portable television for the boys' room, but having bought that they may have time to look at a new videodisc player, and then to be gently moved to the video and music store for discount CDs or videos. Let them be seeking a home gardening video and we can show them, out the window, the gardening supply store across the parking lot. Sovereign in their living room, they can be glancing through seed catalogs or kicking the virtual tires of a new tractor-mower. We can monitor how long and carefully they consider each item as well as register the final choice. The next visit will be even more rewarding—for our customers, each of whose visits serves to focus and crystallize our sense of their present tastes and requirements, and for us, who are being enabled to expand the horizons of what we have to offer them.

Still, there remains the central question of how to get them through our doors of perception in the first place. Advertising, marketing, and promotion will continue to be as important on several fronts of cyber retailing as in historic merchandising. At the outset comes explanatory marketing. The nature and value of cyber retailing must be conveyed to individuals sensibly reluctant to entrust their money, credit, and personal secrets to a faceless avatar on the other side of a computer screen or at the other end of a telephone. For a decade, home shopping by television or telephone has been laying the foundations for such confidence, while familiarity with and confidence in the computer as a tool rather than an adversary is crucially establishing a sense of the friendliness and dependability of the newly shaping cyber world.

Some central techniques of past marketing retain their power—for instance, alliances, referrals, and simple word of mouth. A father calling a Holiday Inn 800 number for a week's hotel reservations for his family in Orlando may be asked if he'd like one free night for a four-day stay, then be switched directly to the phone room of Traveler's Advantage where he will also be told about the online version. At his local bait and tackle shop, the fisherman hears about the North American Fishing Club. A cable television advertisement for discounts with the Dining on Us Club is followed up by direct mail with a pitch for membership in MasterCook.

Links with software providers and educational services prove of even greater value in guiding would-be members to new and uncharted vistas of cyber shopping. A CD-ROM encyclopedia can hook callers into a remote database of up-to-the-minute academic research on a chosen subject, then immediately spot interests of the student or scholar and point out the appropriate boutique within the cyber mall. An inquiry about plant physiology can lead to the cyber garden shop where, out the virtual window, the shopper can spot the cyber golf shop across the way or the cyber bookstore, which offers every title currently in print at wholesale prices. Sierra's 3D Land Designer CD-ROM for garden builders displays an icon connecting directly to the same cyber garden shop. Video games need connectivity capability, so a child entering The Realm can be alerted to a real fantasy land with the toys and games that can enhance his experience—just click the online icon. Embedding shopping alternatives and online connectivity into every form of software on the market is the most powerful key to the widespread use and acceptance of cyber shopping. Playing golf with the CD-ROM golf game can suggest a vacation in Pebble Beach and a quick online trip to the travel service, and every such foray can lead to another online shopping transaction.

Such instant synergy is one of the many substantial advantages that online shopping has over telephone purchasing (the transitional phase to true cyber retailing.) It embodies the difference between mere richness of contact and functionally infinite connectivity. The shopper can swoop from one opportunity to another—complete homework and buy a shelf-full of books from the same desktop, fold a whole "in" tray of paper business into seconds or minutes of direct electronic communication, and so on. And there is the incredible lightness of being one's own intermediary—dispensing with the need for bringing in other people who have to be informed from scratch about one's needs and habits, and who may be understandably distracted. Instead, why not have, literally at hand, real experts who are immersed in a particular customer's lifestyle and budget? The cyber retailer can also minimize the cost of relying exclusively on telephone sales personnel, who may be considerably less adept than a computer at drawing customers into the larger cyber marketplace. The screen can help bring the customer into expanding vistas of glorious possibility, unconstrained by having to put halting phrases through an earpiece. As conventional direct-mail retailers discovered (and rediscovered), a catalog and a color photograph by a high-level professional may be far more persuasive than a tired voice on the telephone. Imagine being able to follow a moving image, pan across a range of alternatives, change color, size, and style in a flash, place one's real body in a suit or dress, and then spin it before a virtual mirror.

Experience confirms that online shoppers buy five to six times the volume of telephone shoppers, are more likely to go on to visit and join alternative shopping and membership sites—and all this at far lower cost to the merchant.

Once we have passed the entry phase of cyber retailing, in which customers are persuaded of the concept's value, convenience, and utility, we enter the second phase: differentiation. Initially, the few cyber retailers that there were seized the advantage to build vast databases of individual consumers' tastes and styles. At the supply end—that of manufacturers, designers, and transporters—they built alliances in order to position themselves as the vital "go-betweens." But of course the pioneers' very success attracted competitors.

The first new arrivals in cyber marketing already possessed extensive databases—telephone companies, overnight mail carriers, even the Postal Service. So cyber retailing's second phase of advertising and marketing entailed brand differentiation, less an issue of price advantage than of the nature and responsiveness of the system itself—manifested in its software and hardware, its database of information about individuals, its consistent ability to create and deliver swiftly, exactly, specifically. In the world of cyber retailing, at least in its early years, one strike and you're out. Just one wrong size or color, one three-day delivery delay, makes a convenience a nuisance. Reality, if not the devil, is in the details.

Likewise, profit is in the details. Detail is married to the capacity to persuade developers, designers, and manufacturers that *their* ultimate success lies in powerful harmony with a go-between who can serve as the producer's eyes and ears—every day gathering millions of voices and distilling the ever-shifting wants and needs of customers, synthesizing and spotting trends before the breaker crests so that the manufacturer can ride the mounting wave rather than flail frantically behind it.

At the same time, cyber retailers must demonstrate that they deserve consumers' confidence. The go-between must be trusted with a body of data that however much it may be composed of empirical dots of information accumulates to a gallery of rather naked portraits. The cyber marketer is moving toward the trusted role of members of the professions: only the professional level of discretion can or should retain working confidence. Where such powerful bodies of data are shared, they must be shared only in strictest anonymity, aggregated as blocks of statistical data, not segregated by individual preferences.

Already, cyber retailers have the capacity to batch-match individuals' buying habits in exquisite detail. Patterns previously unnoticed leap into clarity when databases flash the last 50 people who bought a particular type of large-screen television and at the interval of a week, a month, a year bought a similar type of VCR. Offer them that VCR immediately. Why not, for instance, suggest that the manufacturer package them as a unit and offer them as an ensemble?

In virtually every creative offering there is the prospect of instant feedback. The buyer of the latest John Grisham courtroom thriller, automatically notified of the next Grisham blockbuster, can have the new book arrive on its publication date—no long line at the stores, no signs that it has been sold out. And readers who like this sort of book can have every comparable book run past them without having to sift the book reviews. Moreover, publishers confident of a committed number of advance sales can order their initial print-runs, and even offer signed copies at a premium to the online shopper. In turn, the producer of a would-be Hollywood blockbuster can test multiple endings on line using a carefully weighed national cross-section of moviegoers, the texture of whose whole pattern of taste and interest lies before the entrepreneurs. This also generates word-of-mouth publicity before the film even opens, bypassing jaded reviewers by sweeping the drama in its absolute first-moment freshness directly to its target audience.

Such links between producer and customer will transform the entire commercial landscape. The creative environment changes as consumers who drive the market and vote with their money are able to provide the positive feedback to pull what they desire into existence.

Effectively, the cyber retailer becomes the ultimately objective go-between: he seeks to maximize choice and minimize price for the consumer and to maximize the creativity and reach of the manufacturer. In the past several decades, the Quaker doctrine of single price for a single unit—eminently fitted (morally and economically) to the minute interfaces of two or three shopkeepers, two or three suppliers, and consumers all within walking distance—has been disintegrating under the communication revolution. If there was no one necessary place, there need be no radically determinable price.

Cutthroat discount retailers therefore sprang up like useful mushrooms. Suddenly, no one, especially in North America, believed in a single, fixed price any longer. It was always possible to find that one discounter who would knock another $20 off the VCR or $200 off the new car. If you pressed AT&T hard enough on its One-Rate Plan of 15 cents a minute, you could find the One-Rate Plus Plan of 10 cents a minute with a $4.95 a month fee. Press the button again and they'd waive the fee for the first 6 months or throw in 100 minutes free. Indeed, the bricks-and-mortar retailers became so desperate to offer the best price that they welcomed (or at least frantically endorsed) "comparison shopping," spied on competition, and offered to match any competitor's price. Then, when customers dared to challenge them and wrote down prices, the bricks-and-mortar retailers even had them arrested, as Best Buy stores did in Reston, Virginia.

With the arrival of cyber retailing—if a place both everywhere and nowhere "arrives"—the Quakers drastically return. There is one price per good, no markup, no room to shave prices. Competition is swept onto new grounds.

Incentives will become increasingly important as price differentials evaporate, and will indeed evolve into altogether new products. Eventually, incentives themselves may become new products. A century ago, Wrigley's began making chewing gum to package as an incentive with the baking powder that was its core product. Ultimately, the chewing gum became so popular that they eliminated the baking powder and sold the chewing gum. But it took long market experience to dictate this reverse. In those days, such trends took years to become apparent. In the cyber mall, they can be spotted in a heartbeat.

Ushering in Cyber Economics

An entire new economic system will accompany the arrival of true cyber retailing. The traditional structure of margins, overheads, and markups dissolve before the power to price goods precisely and provide them at a cost that dispenses with the inputs and outgoes of bricks and mortar. Memberships will be king. The cyber retailer will charge only an annual entry fee to his mall—as a go-between, he will be selling knowledge, contacts, and ability to deliver. This is his business, rather than his adding to the prices of what he sells his customer. Economies of scale will be intensely compressed. Once the hardware and the software have been installed, the incremental inflow of new knowledge or the recruitment of new members will be all profit. For the consumer, all that is necessary is to show up—which can be done on a couch.

Profit and loss will be rethought. Capital expenses will be amortized over the entire membership base. Operating expenses will primarily be the cost of acquiring new members. Profit will lie in the constant attraction of new members by new services. Effectively, profit will derive from the true strength of the go-between—the power to amass relevant knowledge at an unprecedented order of magnitude and still to engage it in a timely and creative fashion.

The real key to profitability is the capacity to renew and extend membership. Acquisition costs make the shopper's first year a loss leader, though even these costs are beginning to drop as word of mouth induces a broadening stream to "walk in" to the electronic mall. Profits begin with second-year renewals. Hence, the endless need to provide further incentives to renew and to generate word-of-mouth. This upward spiral of innovation, novelty, and expansiveness complements the concept of "membership" and helps distinguish the cyber retailer in the electronic marketplace.

In short, with price competition flattened by the new efficiencies, competition will have to define itself in terms of convenience, access, speed, efficiency of delivery, and creativity for specific customers, opening up carriage-trade flexibility to anyone in the system. The next giant leap past Quaker pricing will be the establishment of a simple universal price for each product.

Theoretically, the membership-based cyber retailer is in a delicate position. His bricks-and-mortar predecessors and competitors wanted to maximize shoppers' visits. The store most likely to succeed would be packed with the greatest range of saleables, since, advertising not withstanding, this was the only way to jog the customer's elbow at point of sale. But the cyber retailer's position is quite other. He may actually want to *minimize* visits past the first one that elicits the membership fee, since subsequent visits and subsequent purchases add no revenue and indeed are a load on the "network." But that view is likely to be short-sighted. In fact, ongoing visits to his electronic world reinforce habit, which may be hoped to generate interest and brand loyalty that can be crucial to the producer-partner upstream.

From the consumer, the cyber retailer wants renewals and, scarcely less, referrals. For the producer, the cyber retailer wants to provide a constituency large enough to win the exclusive arrangements, bulk pricing, incentive promotions, and just-in-time delivery essential to retain the consumer. Growing the market will ultimately grow the marketplace—and vice-versa. This returns us to the ultimate nature of the cyber market, whose ultimate vista is that it exists only as an infinity of connectivity and imagination for maker, supplier, and buyer.

This parallels the difference between the effective powers of print, radio, and television. Print created sound and images in the reader's mind, relying heavily on his imagination. Radio removed one dimension, yet most imagery—sights, smells, even the subtle texture of sound—still had to be filled in. Television contracted imagination's province yet more narrowly. The resonant if imprecise castles of the mind were shoved aside by those of Mr. Disney's minions.

The cybermarket re-empowers its visitors' imaginations. Suddenly, where the modest store shelf was the limit of material variety, now possibilities proliferate like the desert after rain. Instead of 100,000 volumes fighting for place higher and higher off the floor at a Borders megastore, 2 million volumes crouch like greyhounds on line. Now the idea of anything from a style of blue jeans to a "Starship Enterprise"-class video camera is available on line.

At the systems level, a number of the doctrines governing existing global retailing will also have to be rethought. Indeed, many of the restraints on commerce that have underlain generations of international trade disputes will dissolve before planet-wide facilitation. Controls on the number of dealerships General Motors can establish in Tokyo or of film kiosks that Kodak may set up in Osaka will become meaningless when consumers can buy far more efficiently by typing on a keyboard anywhere to access most anything. No foreigners allowed as members of the Paris Bourse or the Tokyo Stock Exchange? But there will be excellent de facto boards of governors. The securities admittedly will be traded on line a dozen time zones away, or mutual funds can be purchased from the cyber broker with a momentary pause to download the offering prospectus.

Ultimately, production and distribution locations will place themselves according to their adaptability to the new online universe whose key is proximity to the consumer. The neighborhood restaurant could deliver meals ordered on line, just as the supermarket can deliver an order, routed by a computer searching its database for the nearest source for the cyber shopper's order. McDonald's and Burger King once made their reputations by taking their menus as near as then possible to the customer, at thousands of street-corner locations. The cyber restaurant will take the menu to the customer in his or her own home. The cyber street has 10,000 corners, equally close.

Manufacturing will find proximity to transport routes and locations equally if not more important than to raw materials. Prime center-city retailing locations for upscale boutiques at premium rents will give way to distribution centers closer to the consumer at home, not the consumer as pilgrim. Already, banks that coveted street-level locations to show the flag all over town are beginning to discover how easily cyber banking can replace "Roman temple" banking. Branch locations are being decommissioned by the thousands each year as online systems pull in hundreds of thousands of customers and hundreds of millions of transactions.

As online banking unfolds, confident in its security and confidentiality, the general acceptance of cyber payment will match psychology with technology. And operational benefits follow the attitudinal ones. One of the early problems facing television shopping networks was the reluctance of many consumers to divulge their credit card numbers on the telephone. Checks not only bounced frequently, but delays in simply getting them through the mail and then clearing them entwined an infuriating paper chain around the order and the delivery. Electronic commerce technology had given the cyber retailer instant verification that the customer can cover an invoice. The purchase is on its way before the buyer has logged off. Since charge and debit cards are the consumer's entree into the world of electronic shopping, banking alliances form a critical component in identifying potential new members.

No part of life is unsusceptible to the online experience. All that is necessary now is for this momentum to reach escape velocity. With computers installed in almost half of all creditworthy American homes, the potential exists for critical mass well before 2008. Other areas of the world, at the moment, seem a decade behind—but computer adaptivity can strike like lightening.

Linking the World

Europe has at least as many creditworthy homes as the United States, and much of Europe, East Asia, and Southeast Asia will have been deeply penetrated by computers and modem links within the first two or three years of the new century. Although half the people alive in the world today have never made a phone call, this will change fast.

Despite ideological or material barriers, word cannot be kept from most remote corners of the world that the computer does not simply process words or play video games but is also the gateway to the world economy. Indeed, in accordance with the law that when backward societies at last get going they do not have to recapitulate the old paths to the present, New Guinea may be ordering from the Mexican clothing market before anyone in Port Moresby, its capital, bothers to begin building a shopping mall.

Moreover, the arrival of vast numbers of cyber shoppers on every continent will compound for truly global and fundamental efficiencies of scale and production. Ford's attempt in the early 1980s to launch a "world car"—one designed and manufactured identically for sale on every continent—had mixed success. But the steadily freer circulation of people and ideas across national, even continental, boundaries means that ultimately world-standard tastes will begin to develop. So great a change is still hard to anticipate, but it surely will embrace a synthesis of the highest standards of different cultures—say, Italian car design with

Japanese manufacturing quality. And with these cross-border fusions and initiations of taste and possibility will come global economies of scale, global combinations for production, and global methods of distribution.

Already, many American teenagers are being dressed from head to toe by Chinese who have never (yet) tasted a Big Mac. There must of course be casualties as more efficient sources of production displace less efficient ones, and some spheres of activity, like Quaker pricing, will come full circle centuries later. In Marco Polo's day, merchants returned to Turkey from China with silkworm larvae concealed in their garments to build a silk industry that predominated in Western markets, out-competing the Chinese until Chinese economies of scale, given lower wage rates and improving quality and reliability, coupled with the development of global transportation and distribution networks, burst over the Turkish industry like a tidal wave. Now, Turkish producers are reduced to buying raw silk from China to imprint with their own designs; and the handwriting even for this is on the wall. Italian designers have caught on and, given their superior sense of international taste and quality, and a comparable access to Chinese raw silk, promise to strip the Turks of their final competitive advantage. It is unlikely that this armada of global shifts bearing down on us will doom national styles to the cosmopolitan blandness of, say, international airports. Rather, they will provide greater flexibility and choice, as well as lower costs to consumers and cyber merchants alike.

As cyber retailing expands overseas, economies of scale will kick in even more vigorously. Where once government and industry trade missions examined price differentials between the United States and Japan, now the cyber marketplace will be examining these differentials and deciding in the blink of an electronic eye the source for the best product at the cheapest price with the most appropriate delivery system. Arbitraging products and prices between countries and across continents will be an important function of the cyber retailers' systems.

Consumer pressures will also flatten the myriad regulations and multiple standards that have been speed bumps for global marketing. When a consumer in Moscow can see on line that he is paying a premium for a television set configured for the Russian SECAM signal over a single standard common to Europe and Asia, pressure will mount for a single global standard.

Equally, the arrival of broad currency blocs will facilitate common global pricing and further accelerate the expansion of cyber retailing. The European monetary unit, for instance, will create a second major currency zone as a counterweight to the dollar zone, allowing two price quotations to cover much of the consumer-driven world. While multinational companies have had to deal for years with the impact of multiple currency fluctuations on their earnings, now an increasingly broad network of producers, distributors, and merchants will have to take on similar burdens. Currency swaps and interest-rate swaps as hedges against sharp swings in banking and currency markets hold the promise of becoming as ubiquitous as the corporate checking account. Cross-border tax problems, also once the purview of multinational giants, will also become the concern of an increasingly broad cross-section of players in the new global cyber marketplace. Again, with the proliferation of mass pressure for resolving these problems could and should come the standardization of tax levels and procedures.

The New World

Above all, cyber retailing provides a new world of possibilities for imagination and creativity, opening up new markets for new products that have still not been conceived. The compounding effect keeps working. Where once a startup enterprise could take years to grow from a garage workshop to a factory floor, online advertising, sales, distribution, even financing time frames can now be compressed to months, even weeks. Indeed, the cyber retailers, the "go-betweens," as the first to spot new trends and new fads, can themselves become venture investors—building upon their unique knowledge base, they can help move an early-stage enterprise into a new product with a new assembly line in a remote corner of the world. Knowledge builds upon knowledge. The retailer as manufacturer or even talent scout has been explored in the past: Wal-Mart, for instance, has long provided encouragement and seed capital for small domestic manufacturers. The global cyber retailer has an even broader playing field, the ability to identify and develop opportunities more quickly, and access to global resources of physical and intellectual capital.

3

The Ascent of Content

Edward D. Horowitz

Fifty years ago, at Bell Laboratories, two seminal events were unfolding almost simultaneously. While one group of engineers was discovering the transistor, another group was hard at work defining the fundamentals of digital transmission. Today, we stand at the threshold of a new electronic age that will reap the benefits of these twin efforts in ways unimaginable even a few years ago.

The marriage of the transistor and digital transmission is about to be consummated with the emergence of the electronic marketplace, which in its current embryonic form we know as the Internet or the World Wide Web. More than 35 million US homes are projected to be on line by 2000. The Internet is rapidly on its way to rivaling the ubiquity shared only by telephones and televisions.

Many things have to happen, however, before the Internet reaches the enviable 99 percent penetration level of homes of the telephone and television. For one, the costs of its basic components—bandwidth and memory—must continue to collapse. For another, the Internet content providers must meet the challenge of developing innovative and engrossing interactive content that is user friendly enough to appeal to the 65 million US households that are projected not to be on the Internet by the end of this century. To achieve this, those in industry segments beyond entertainment will have to recast themselves in a new and unfamiliar role as content providers in an interactive age. This chapter examines how and why content will play such a dominant role in the emerging interactive digital era.

The Economics of Change

The economy has evolved from addressing basic needs to providing a wide range of products and services. Electric toothbrushes and cosmetic surgery are examples of non-essential products that have emerged to satisfy narrower market demands. Sustained economic growth will depend on even more targeted marketing in order to stimulate demand for increasingly customized consumer products and services. A highly developed economy that can target the individual will require a wide range of sophisticated and interactive marketing tools matched with comparable transactional capabilities. These tools will cater to the numerous simultaneous demands for an infinite range of goods and services. Only an electronically based market environment is capable of providing these tools, and it will in the process revolutionize global commerce. The Internet appears to have that potential.

John Kenneth Galbraith observed in *Economics in Perspective* that "economic ideas are always and intimately a product of their own time and place; they cannot be seen apart from the world they interpret" and that "the world changes—is, indeed, in a constant process of transformation—so economic ideas, if they are to retain relevance, must also change."

Electronic commerce will force many changes on the world's economic structure. Traditional economic theories and practices will have to be revised in order to stay relevant in this entirely new commerce paradigm.

The number of steps involved in the production and distribution of goods and services will almost certainly decrease. The digital era will herald the demise of traditional intermediaries. Stockbrokers, real estate agents, and other market makers will find their roles severely altered if not altogether eliminated by the proliferation of online marketing tools. Entertainment conglomerates, whose traditional roles are largely limited to the packaging and marketing rather than the creation of content, will find their middleman role at considerable risk as their "value-addedness" is challenged. Until now, the commercial value of content has largely been realized through replication, distribution, and promotion—skills which the creator himself often does not possess.

Conducting transactions and generally managing business processes over a global electronic-based network in a secure and reliable manner will be crucial. Achieving the ability to do this, however, will be no easy matter. Today's Internet is certainly not up to the task of supplanting many business transactions which require a high level of security. Such a usurpation will require many new protocols and many new commerce-specific computer applications programs to be developed and implemented. Only then will the Internet be viewed by the business community and the general public as able to handle their most confidential content securely. Meeting and overcoming this challenge will drive electronic commerce and will define the very essence of the electronic marketplace.

Content

Content is the packaged commercial matter, born of creativity, that courses through the delivery pipelines. It is art with commercial intent; more precisely, it is the creative endeavor fused with economic intent. By 2008, content should have transcended its means of delivery and emerged to dominate the electronic marketplace. Content in electronic form traverses today's broadcast TV, cable TV, satellite, and telephone delivery systems. By 2008 it should have transcended its means of delivery and have emerged to dominate the electronic marketplace. It will become an essential part of all electronic commerce transactions. Content, made readily accessible as entertainment, news, sports, financial, and numerous other services on the Internet, creatively packaged and merchandised, will deliver the necessary mass of users to the electronic marketplace. Educational content will stimulate learning when presented in a manner that plays to the natural interactive strengths of the Internet. The most compelling content in all these various forms will frequently overwhelm its user and evoke a response in ways never before envisioned.

Is the Super Bowl "content" when played in an empty stadium? Not unless some enterprising individual "commercializes" it in some other way. However, one should not define content too narrowly. It is as much the roar of the crowd (the rudiments of interactivity) as it is the event itself unfolding on the field of play. In the broadcasting era, content has been like the sound of one hand clapping, or an overfriendly car salesman engrossed in his sales pitch. It has suffered from a lack of engagement with its audience. "Interactivity" at its most Byzantine (and least confrontational) was Neilsen ratings and Arbitron boxes. The broadcast content providers both suffered and benefited from their decidedly noninteractive perch. During the "golden age" of television, people would watch test patterns—such was the novelty of this remarkable new technology. Content was little more than something to fill the screen in order to prolong or heighten what, at heart, was an overriding fascination with the medium itself. To quote the oft-quoted McLuhanism, the medium was indeed the message. The Jack Benny Show and others of its ilk were animated scribblings that careened across the screen because something had to careen across the screen.

The Russian comic Yakov Smirnoff once joked about the dearth of programming choice in the Soviet Union, where, he said, there were two TV channels: channel 1 and channel 2. Channel 1 carried the boring state-sanctioned fare. On channel 2, a burly individual would instruct viewers to turn back to channel 1. Although Soviet television was clearly oligarchy at work, it does bring to mind television in the United States in the 1960s and the 1970s. Three channels, programmed by CBS, NBC, and ABC, shared the national television audience. The blandness of television programming in those days is widely acknowledged. But it was this very blandness that attracted the mass audience to television by offending no one with its programming crowded around the arithmetic mean. Much to the chagrin of their "elitist" critics, the television networks aimed at the heart of the bell curve, making mediocrity in the "vast wasteland" their mainstay. Though social critics will forever chastise early broadcast television for pandering to the lowest common denominator, it is a mathematical fact that the lowest common denominator yields the largest share. Creative and thought-provoking content, which by its very nature appeals to smaller more discerning audiences, was denied access to the airwaves in television's early days. Television in the United States was first and foremost an advertising medium driven by commercial considerations. The television services in other countries were funded by central governments. Indeed, quasi-governmental agencies ran the television services in most countries, the Soviet Union being a prime example. The channel constraints of early television were, from the standpoint of content, the age of the free ride. The audience was truly captive to—as well as captivated by—the sheer magic of television. As long as something emanated from the screen, early viewers were fascinated with the strange new glowing box that was fast becoming the centerpiece of family life.

In the mid 1970s, communications satellites that could "see" all of the United States, including Hawaii and Alaska, began to change the economics of content distribution and challenge the networks' dominance. The monopoly Bell System, which furnished the television networks with terrestrial-based program-distribution facilities, was staving off the potential competition from MCI as Western Union and RCA moved into the domestic communications satellite business. It was RCA that provided the cable TV programmers with their initial satellite capacity, enabling the cable TV industry to quickly dwarf the combined program-distribution capabilities of the three networks.

We were witnessing the first crack in the armor of distance as a major controlling factor in content distribution. Satellites gave new content owners a low-cost means of distributing their programming, bypassing the TV networks and their local TV stations and going directly to local cable TV. New "networks," such as Home Box Office and Ted Turner's "superstation" WTBS (an erstwhile bankrupt UHF station in Atlanta), began to capture sizable pieces of the viewing audience.

The videocassette recorder, introduced in the 1970s, created another alternative to broadcast television. The distribution dam that had controlled television's content flow for more than 20 years had been breached on two fronts in the space of a few short years. The three networks suddenly found themselves in a period of viewership attrition, which continues to the present day. In the mid 1970s they shared more than 90 percent of the viewing audience. By 1997 their cumulative share had dropped to 30 percent, and all indications are that it will continue to drop as more and more distribution channels become available to other content providers.

The Death of Distance

In the world of telecommunications, the 1990s will be remembered as a decade dominated by "the death of distance": the phenomenon of collapsing international telephone calling rates as nationally owned telephone companies were increasingly subjected to privatization and the markets they serve were opened to competition. This downward price trend is likely to continue through the balance of the 1990s, with international calling rates between the United States and other industrial countries projected to drop to 10 or even 5 cents per minute by 2000—a decline of about 95 percent in less than 5 years. The market dynamic is a familiar one: with the introduction of price competition, technology innovation is encouraged, yielding lower-cost capacity. Meanwhile, all participants benefit as the expanded capacity stimulates increased demand and has a market-enlarging effect led by lower unit costs.

The practical effects of these developments are even more far-reaching and dramatic. The price/cost differential between international and domestic US long-distance telephone service is narrowing fast and will soon become negligible. Indeed, the terms "long distance" and "local" may soon become relics of a bygone regulatory era. The relative distance or proximity of one's called party is rapidly losing market relevance. Market forces, working together with technological advancement, are erasing distance as a cost determinant in the telephone business. Clear evidence of this is emerging as, increasingly, the Internet is used for long-distance voice and fax calls. The long-distance telephone companies will be compelled to seek new markets in order to obtain relief from the effects of commoditization.

Will the Death of Bandwidth Be Next?

A large number of low-cost broadband digital transmission services are in the planning stage and will become available to consumers over the next decade. For example, the Federal Communication Commission plans to award each of about 1650 TV stations in the United States a second channel over which programs can be broadcast in digital form. By 2008, each of these stations should be broadcasting a digital television service. Although the FCC originally intended that these channels be used for the broadcasting of high-definition television (HDTV), it now appears that the HDTV programming will be broadcast for only a portion of the day. At other times, the channel will be used to broadcast multiple standard-definition programs and a variety of data services. With each channel capable of transmitting almost 20 megabytes of data per second, it will be possible for a single TV station to broadcast as many as six TV programs simultaneously (and, during the night, to deliver a newspaper electronically in about a second). Despite its lack of interactive capabilities, digital television's channel capacity should allow broadcasters to remain a potent force in the content-delivery business well into the next century.

In addition, most local cable TV companies will have capacities of more than 500 channels by 2008. This will allow them to expand their pay-per-view service and to carry many channels that they are not able to carry today. At the end of 1996 there were more than 150 national cable TV programmers and only 53 channels on the average cable system. The decline in viewership of broadcast network TV over the past 15 years can be attributed directly to the growing viewership of basic cable service. This can reasonably lead one to the conclusion that the typical viewer simply wants more choice in programming. If that is so, then, as cable adds more basic TV services, and as it increases channel capacity, we will witness a complementary decline in network television viewing.

Local telephone companies will be offering high-speed data links to the home over a variety of wired (copper, coaxial, and fiber) and wireless-based connections well before the end of 2008. These systems will be able to offer a "virtual cable TV" service of essentially infinite capacity, limited only by the number of TV programs collected at the "head end," and also ushering in the video-on-demand service that the telephone companies have long promised.

By 2008, a number of operational advanced-technology satellites will be capable of providing fast two-way data services directly to the home. These satellites, in conjunction with direct-to-home television satellites, will constitute considerable competition for the multimedia delivery aspirations of the local cable and telephone companies.

A new terrestrial wireless technology, Local Multipoint Distribution Service (LMDS), will be operational in many areas of the United States by 2008. LMDS will be able to offer a "wireless cable" service with 200+ channels and two-way broadband data services directly to the home.

In summary, digital broadcasting, cable TV, local telephone, satellite, and LMDS-based services will collectively create a multi-lane broadband highway for delivering all kinds of content to the home. Bandwidth-delivery wars, reminiscent of the long-distance telephone battles of the 1980s and the 1990s, will cause the cost of content delivery (bandwidth) to slide inexorably down a commodity curve. This commoditization will relegate the delivery systems to a relatively minor role as arbiters of content. Unfettered by the constraints of distance and bandwidth, content providers will lose their delivery-based self- consciousness. The world's knowledge, as practically defined by the electronic marketplace of the day, will be readily accessible by means of a desktop computer or a TV set. It will be the prime source of news, information, entertainment, and advertising content, far exceeding the capabilities of television.

Another major technological development that will effectively increase the availability of bandwidth and decreases its cost is digital signal compression, which allows a television picture to be transported in about approximately one-fiftieth of the bandwidth that it would otherwise require. Today's direct-to-home television satellites employ digital compression. Broadcast TV, cable TV, and all the other multimedia delivery systems of the future will also use it to increase their capacity.

The broadcasters' motto of the 1960s and early 1970s might have been "This is what we think most of you will watch." Today's motto might be "We think there is something here that you want to watch." Early in the next century, with the deployment of digital multi-channel two-way transmission systems, the question may well be "What would you like to interact with this evening?"

Low-cost, high-capacity data storage devices will also proliferate during the next 10 years. Most notably, the digital versatile disk (DVD) player should see wide use. The DVD will supplant the CD-ROM, becoming a standard feature of personal computers before the end of this century. With a digital storage capacity of approximately 17 gigabytes, a single DVD has almost 30 times the storage capacity of a CD-ROM and can store a full-length movie. Personal computers will also have considerably more storage capacity than they do today—the capacity of a hard disk may exceed 20 gigabytes by 2008.

The new high-capacity storage systems, particularly when used with the new digital delivery systems mentioned previously, will open up many new opportunities for the creators of content. Multimedia content, transported over the Internet without the current bandwidth constraints, will find widespread use in homes, schools, and businesses by 2008. Microsoft and Intel, proponents of international standards for Internet-based multimedia services, will give content a new meaning in numerous business, entertainment, and educational applications. New Internet protocols will facilitate the prioritization and delivery of high-quality multimedia content to television sets that will be compatible with personal computers and with the Internet. Video conferencing, video telephone, video mail, and a profusion of other telecommunications services will be in widespread use in businesses, homes, libraries, and schools by 2008.

The ability to call up content on virtually any subject in text, visual, and oral forms will be like having the contents of the Library of Congress on your bookshelves. The year 2008 will find us with the bottlenecks in the content-delivery pipeline largely eliminated and a world of information at our fingertips. We will have access to a massive amount of intelligence at the click of a mouse. But will we be more informed, or will the digital age take us to the crest of Sisyphus's hill only to fall back in the face of an information onslaught?

In a tale of determination and diligence (and future success), Bill Gates has described setting out to read the *World Book* as a child. Having reach the P volume after 5 years, he abandoned the effort when he discovered the "greater sophistication and detail" of the *Encyclopaedia Britannica*. He dropped that too when he found a new and even more fascinating passion: computers. Owning an encyclopedia is a far cry from reading it. In fact, having all of the world's content at one's fingertips can be overwhelming rather than empowering. At the end of the day, access is not power; information is.

Recent market studies project that one-third of the homes and businesses in the United States will be using the Internet for online services by 2000. However, the vast majority of homes, and many businesses, will not be on line. How then to achieve universal adoption?

To become a viable electronic marketplace, the Internet will have to converge on universal coverage. To achieve this, there will be a need for user friendliness and ease of access. It will need to be multi-generational, addressing various socio-economic and aptitude levels. It will have to be adaptable, capable of supporting the needs of the "turbo user," who might otherwise be turned off by excessive diagnostics but at the same time be supportive of the less knowledgeable user who will require extensive graphical user interfaces and diagnostic windows. Bandwidth on demand will also be a necessary service in order to accommodate the heterogeneous user loads resulting from low-intensity applications such as email all the way to complex multimedia content that will require very high bandwidths.

In short, the Internet will have to be everything to everybody. This kind of feature-breadth capability will be essential in order to attract the regular television viewer who purchases an Internet-compatible digital TV set and who, one evening, explores the online experience for the first time. If a second visit is to be ensured, then the maiden voyage must be smooth and painless. Luring this large audience of consumers onto the electronic marketplace will surely be the greatest challenge for the architects of Internet-based commerce. The broadcasters' digital television initiative will help immensely with programs and advertisements linked to the Internet's transactional services. The world's greatest advertising medium will be the key to the average consumer's transition from strictly passive TV viewing to active participation.

The TV-PC and the PC-TV are two new kinds of consumer products that will be introduced in the market before the end of the 1990s. The TV-PC is essentially a digital TV that can access the Internet. The PC-TV, on the other hand, is a PC capable of receiving digital broadcast TV. The TV-PC will generally have a large screen capable of displaying HDTV pictures and be manufactured by the traditional TV set manufacturers. The PC-TV will generally have a smaller screen, will not be capable of displaying HDTV pictures, and will be manufactured by the PC manufacturers. These products will enable the Internet and electronic commerce to penetrate many homes that are beyond their reach today. They will also be the prime motivating force driving interoperability between the Internet and digital broadcasting technical standards. TVs and PCs will have to be compatible with the Internet TCP/IP protocol and with the digital television broadcast standard in order to be commercially viable in the age of electronic commerce. Bill Gates's prediction of a PC in every home maybe turn out to be prophetic—provided, of course, the PC is also a TV.

Safeguarding Content

Content comes in many electronic forms, including the written word, data, video, audio, and voice. It is transported on magnetic tape, transmitted over regular telephone lines, and broadcast by wireless means. To have copyright merit it must embody original work in tangible media such as those just mentioned. To have commercial value, it must be informative and/or entertaining and distinguishable from other content. Unfortunately, many of the tenets of copyright law break down in the age of electronic commerce. Without proper safeguards, it will be relatively easy to pirate the creative works of others. The unbounded nature of the electronic marketplace will further exacerbate matters without international agreements on these matters.

Many national and international bodies are beginning to address the commercial implications of electronic content. The Working Group on Intellectual Property Rights of the Information Infrastructure Task Force has suggested changing the law to better protect the rights of content owners. It is specifically addressing the uniqueness of digitally based delivery systems such as the Internet. The World Intellectual Property Organization—a UN body—is attempting to revise and update the Berne convention on copyright to address the many new issues emerging as we enter the digital age. The European Commission recently issued a draft directive that would extend copyright protection to databases.

Protection of content owners' rights is essential if the electronic marketplace is to fulfill its promise. The laws of intellectual property bestow on the owner monopoly rights to exploit the work for a limited time. They alone control the decision whether to sell or give away their content. One can never presume the content owner's consent. Content is never available for free without the owner's explicit authorization. Many business executives do not believe that the protection of content on the Internet today is adequate. Their primary concern is not with the pirating of movies or music. They want protection for their content, which might, for example, be a description of the proprietary services they offer their customers. Lacking assurances that the Internet is secure, businesses will be reluctant to use it for their critical business transactions. They will instead use an Intranet, which by design has limited access and a controlled audience. Consumers' rights will also have to be addressed. For example, interactivity implies joint authorship of many bodies of content. Consumers participating in a survey conducted as part of a market research study might contribute substantial value to the research. In such an instance, the consumer deserves some degree of ownership in the research report's content.

Instituting effective measures to protect content ownership will be a key factor in making Internet-based commerce a viable business proposition. To contain piracy in the digital age (particularly on the Internet), anti-copying technologies are essential to protect the illegal dissemination of content. Synergistic solutions combining enforceable laws and technology constraints will have to be developed. Unfortunately, piracy is nothing new in the electronic content distribution business. It is a worldwide problem affecting all sectors of the electronic media industry. For example, in this age of software-driven telecom systems, fraudulent use of telephone service is relatively easy for a moderately talented hacker. This costs the telephone industry hundreds of millions of dollars a year. The illegal copying of recorded material is a multi-million-dollar black market business and represents a major global problem. The Motion Picture Association of America maintains offices in many countries and spends millions of dollars to thwart the efforts of those who sell unauthorized videocassette copies of American movies on the black market. The International Federation of the Phonographic Industry, which tracks the pirating of compact discs and audio cassettes, estimates that one in five copies of recorded music is an illegal copy. The Business Software Alliance, which monitors the sale of computers and software, estimates one out of every four software package sales is illegal. Bill Gates could not have sustained the development costs associated with Microsoft's computer system software had the potential revenue losses not been retarded to some degree by copyright law. The satellite TV distribution industry experienced and overcame similar serious problems a decade ago. Many individuals purchased backyard satellite dishes and intercepted movies being distributed by HBO, Showtime, and other programmers who were using satellites to distribute their content to cable TV headends. Ultimately, encryption used to stop this piracy. Once encrypted, the movies were accessible legitimately only if the owner of a home dish subscribed to the service and installed a de-encryption box. This was the birth of direct-to-home television service via satellite.

A corollary to minimizing piracy is the need to have relatively simple methods of payment for the legal use of content. Convoluted or obtrusive payment schemes will simply drive business away from legal channels. Excessive charges will likewise act as an accelerant to illicit content distribution. People will only use their perception of exorbitant pricing as a rationale to engage in content theft. Whoever develops a universally accepted payment method will indeed inherit the keys to the city. Recent research indicates that consumers make 82 billion transactions each year, of which 35 billion are cash transactions, 33 billion are check transactions, and 12 billion are credit card transactions. Businesses also write about 30 billion checks a year. The ability to transfer funds securely will open up a huge business for electronic commerce on the Internet. Personal banking will require "firewalls" and site-visit identity checks. New protocols and software will make bank transactions more secure. These measures will increase consumers' confidence in electronic banking, especially in banking from the home. They will also stimulate the development of many new financial services. Today, for example, tax returns can be submitted to the Internal Revenue Service electronically. In the near future, the preparation of tax returns will be handled electronically by banks, which will monitor their customers' incomes and expenditures and compute the applicable taxes automatically. This service will be one in a menu of comprehensive financial management services. Others will include stock portfolio management, monitoring utilities consumption, telephone service purchases, vacation and business travel planning, frequent flyer mile records, and auto maintenance checkups.

These services will be customized primarily by banks to meet their clients' individual needs. The number of US households using online banking services could reach 18 million by 2002. Financial services for businesses on the Internet will grow at an even faster pace to include reports and analysis of sales performance, preparation of tax returns, financial reports, and company annual audits. In the electronic market-place, distance-managed health care will demand a similar level of security not currently available on the Internet. Keeping personal health information confidential will be essential.

MasterCard and Visa have been supporting the development of *secure electronic transaction,* a procedure for conducting electronic business transactions in a secure manner. There are many security-focused software packages under development. Some will let consumers visit Internet sites anonymously. Others will allow an Internet site to establish the identities of site visitors before completing business transactions with them.

The reluctance of the marketplace to embrace the Internet as a commerce medium in the recent past was due to a number of factors. Businesses and consumers had little confidence in the security of the Internet. The ability to transfer funds in a secure manner was and remains one of the biggest challenges facing the Internet. Providing a secure means of conducting business electronically is a vitally important challenge for the Internet. Universally appealing solutions are elusive. Government-mandated encryption of electronically transmitted information is a subject of considerable debate. Balancing the needs of national security with the rights of privacy is by no means easy.

When looked at in proper perspective, issues of security are not unique to the Internet. Business and consumer confidence in email, the telephone, and even surface mail is generally not much higher. Despite the concerns about security, Internet-based sales should quadruple to almost 25 percent of all sales in the next 5 years. Also, business-to-business electronic commerce should reach $66 billion by 2000, with 40 percent annual growth. Overall, the Internet economy could reach $200 billion by 2000, up from $15 billion in 1996.

Managing Content

The success of many companies in electronic commerce will very much depend on their acuity at managing sometimes far-flung databases. Establishing and maintaining a comprehensive multi-dimensional customer database will be among the most important tools for Internet success. The companies that excel will have considerable expertise in serving their existing customers and marketing to new customers through a well-structured database. Companies that place a high degree of importance on maintaining and regularly updating their databases will be among the most successful ones. All divisions in a company, especially the customer billing and service groups, will need access to these databases. Proficiency in database management will give a company a distinct competitive edge in the electronic marketplace.

These databases will include a detailed profile of every customer relevant to the goods and services provided by the company. Only this attention to detail will ensure that the services offered meet the customers' needs. Interpreting these databases accurately will also help attract new customers through targeted advertising of products and services. New-product promotions will also be more effective if customer databases are used to identify customers who match a prescribed profile. Special offers, such as vacation and travel packages, will have a much higher "take ratio" if the customer databases are properly exploited. "Half of the money I spent on advertising and promotion was ineffective; the only trouble is, I don't know which half" is an adage that will have less validity in the electronic marketplace.

Of course, a marketer's dream may become a libertarian's nightmare. Unprecedented amounts of personal data streaming through a public network present a very real privacy issue. Keeping business data secure and confidential will be crucial. It is not as though databases haven't been repositories of sensitive information in the past. What has changed is the ease and velocity with which this information can be transmitted around the world.

Databases are increasingly being stored on very large database servers (VLDBSs). These servers need to be highly scalable in order to process queries and transactions (data inserts, updates, and deletions) from multiple clients on a simultaneous basis. Scalability of VLDBSs is getting a lot of attention in the computer industry. Transparent or seamless linking of distributed database servers with users will be another key need of the electronic marketplace. Structured query language, a high-level computer language used in conjunction with relational database management systems, will see widespread use in linking VLDBSs and enabling them to be accessed over multi-user networks.

The need to access and manage data is not just a preoccupation of the business community. Consumers too will have a strong desire to assert control over the torrents of data threatening to engulf them. "Push technologies," for example, deliver information where a prior interest has been registered by the user. There are two basic approaches in providing such a service to the consumer. The first is branding, in which the consumer tells the service provider what he wants to see by name. The other involves offering the consumer an Internet search engine, which then conducts the search on the basis of some previously established choices. Despite some misgivings about these kinds of services, they could prove valuable, for example, to those who want to prevent pornography and "junk email" from entering their homes via the Internet.

The Content-Management Engine

As the PC and the Internet converge with the TV set and its traditional programming services, their respective search tools will merge. It has been Netscape versus Microsoft in a browser battle, with Microsoft also talking to the Justice Department. The new alliance among IBM, Novell, Oracle, Sun Microsystems, and Netscape, reportedly committed to developing a new Internet-based open platform that would challenge Microsoft's dominance, is indicative of the high stakes in this contest. Microsoft and some other companies have made no secret of their interest in gaining a foothold in the market for set-top boxes The victor will command unprecedented access to the eyes and, of course, the checkbooks of electronic commerce's users.

Digital television broadcasting, scheduled for a 1998 rollout, will have its own search engine equivalent, commonly referred to as the Electronic Program Guide (EPG). Just as it is in the current digital DBS satellite TV service, the EPG will be a key component in terrestrial broadcast TV and cable TV services. The EPG common to DBS services helps the viewer sift through a sometimes overwhelming 170 channels as well as facilitating pay-per-view ordering. In the DBS model, the regular telephone line provides the upstream channel from the viewer's home to the DBS program control center. EPG functionality—residing in a new set-top box—will become more crucial as the local cable channel universe expands to more than 500 channels. Similarly, as local TV broadcasters "go digital" with collective offerings of 35 to 40 channels in major markets, the new digital TV sets will have embedded EPG capability. Unlike the Internet search engines, the EPG has, to date, received scant attention outside the TV industry's engineering committees.

As a programmable and interactive tool, the EPG will not simply arrange and order existing content; it will contribute content to the viewing experience. It will have "pages" containing programming information and other relevant data, in all likelihood interspersed with the banner ads common to today's Internet browsers. The EPG embedded in the set-top box will be programmed by the local cable company, while the EPG embedded in the TV set will be programmed by the individual providers of TV programs (primarily the broadcasters).

Might there be a clash of EPGs as the cable TV audience (70 percent of all homes) is presented with one service by the cable company and another by the broadcasters? Interestingly, the recent Supreme Court ruling that prohibited local cable companies from preempting local broadcast signals with their own programming choices addressed only the current analog TV service. The Court was silent on cable's preemptive prerogatives with regard to the impending digital TV broadcast services. At the industry's request, the FCC plans to answer this question in the not-too-distant future. This cable carriage debate is one example of the tremendous power that stands to be accrued by whatever entity acquires programming control over the EPG.

Ultimately, the convergence of the EPG and the Internet browsing engine will give way to a fully integrated tool that will allow the viewer to jump, seamlessly and interactively, from one platform to the other. Amid the clutter of a seemingly endless array of content choices, the growth of electronic commerce will depend on a navigational agent. For the purposes of this discourse, I will call this agent a *content-management engine* (CME). The CME, as an evolutionary outgrowth of its predecessors, the Internet search engine and the EPG, will break down many of the semantic walls that currently differentiate "TV" from "the Internet." The ubiquity that the Internet seeks will be greatly aided by this confluence of functionality. The mass audience of television viewers (PC neophytes, if you will) will simply find themselves on the Internet. Moreover, this will be accomplished in Trojan Horse fashion: the members of this Internet-reticent audience will not be forced to confront their aversion to computers. In perhaps one of the great ironies of the digital age, Internet ubiquity will be accomplished, not through the PC, but through television.

The CME will perform numerous functions in the electronic marketplace of the future. For example, suppose you have just returned from a busy day at the office sometime in 2008. You flop down in your favorite easy chair and turn on your TV—or is it your large-screen PC? No matter.

On pops your CME multimedia-driven menu asking you if you want to see your video mail and other messages before watching regular TV? OK, you respond.

On flashes a brief list of messages on your customized electronic bulletin board. Tomorrow is Mother's Day. "Do you want to send flowers?" asks your friendly florist. She already knows you have not done so, as your financial records have just been scanned and you have not made any such purchases in the past week or so. You answer Yes, and she responds by holding up a bunch of fresh roses and offering to have them delivered tomorrow morning for only $49.95. You click OK and then move on. Another message is from your financial counselor at the local bank. You need to file your tax return by tomorrow, and according to a review of your tax file records which he has prepared and keeps updated you owe $250 to the IRS. With your approval, he says, he will send in your return tomorrow and electronically transfer $250 of your hard-earned money from your electronic bank account. You give less-than-enthusiastic approval.

Having dealt with all the urgent messages of the day, you now move on to the next item.

On pops your local video provider. He tells you the movie you ordered is now in his video server. It is available at $3.95 now, but if you wait and download it to your PC after midnight it will cost you only $2.99.

Next is a personalized summary of news, sports, and stock market items of interest to you. Reviewing your stock portfolio, you may be prompted to make some adjustments. The sports results come next, beginning with your favorite team. You might request a more detailed report to see who played, who scored, the team's standing, and so on.

You now move on to watching "regular" TV. Your favorite quiz show is about to start, and you won a couple of free round-trip tickets to Florida the last time you "participated."

This is just a brief summary of the kinds of functions that could be embedded in the CME.

Microsoft has already made known to the cable industry its eagerness to develop a set-top box that will incorporate a high-speed modem for access to the Internet. Netscape's subsidiary Navio is developing software to link a TV to the Internet. The TV set manufacturers Sony, Mitsubishi, and Philips have similar plans, as does the video game manufacturer Sega.

Who will be the gatekeeper of this CME device? A distributive model could evolve wherein each content provider (cable company, phone company, bank, etc.) would maintain its own relevant subject matter. This might be the more egalitarian approach. But there will almost certainly be conflicts as the various content interests, recognizing the importance of a presence on this central device, jockey for prominence.

Home Computing

Another issue that will have to be addressed as we approach the full-scale adoption of an electronic-commerce-based society is the future of home computing. In order to benefit fully from all the services available to us in the electronic marketplace, will we want to access an increasing volume of complex operating and applications software packages. This will require the installation on our home PC of a large-capacity server that can be remotely updated by our local cable company or our local bank.

If the prospect of having all this computing equipment in your home is not appealing, you may prefer a network computer (NC)—a much simpler machine that will connect you to one or more massive computers at the local bank. The network computer, in time, might prove more attractive to the regular TV viewer, whose direct use of the Internet will in all likelihood be quite limited in scope. The typical TV viewer will almost certainly balk at the idea of purchasing a home PC with expensive and complicated peripherals and excessive "intelligence overhead." The network computer is more like a conventional appliance. To the extent that "desktop" software is needed, it can be downloaded from the central server, perhaps on a metered basis. The NC's advantages suggest that it, rather than the PC, may be the instrument that makes the Internet ubiquitous. We may choose instead to let the network rather than the desktop do the work. In any event, later generations will almost certainly look back bemusedly on the "Heathkit" computer era of the 1990s. With vast stores of content available for our entertainment and home business affairs, who will have time for RS-232 cables with bad pins, or for intermittent COM ports? By 2008 we will be captivated by the content and no longer captive to the technology.

Many large companies with thousands of PCs, servers, and routers are contemplating this very issue today. The NC concept has garnered a lot of attention and is not likely to go away soon. It is a new approach to the world of business and home computing whose time may have come. Many believe it to be a much less expensive solution than constantly upgrading the PC.

As expanded bandwidth allows more system intelligence to migrate upstream and off our desks, the PC-versus-NC debate promises to become more heated. The computer market will probably fragment into a range of options, from the PC through various PC-NC hybrids to the NC. Microsoft is already moving to develop a middle-of-the-road solution with its MS-CE software package. Product variation is probably the best way to accommodate the needs of a range of consumers, from the novice to the "turbo user." While the latter will be looking for almost instantaneous responses and for some degree of difficulty or challenge, the former will want something simple and easy to use, like a television or a telephone.

The year 2008 will see the media-delivery issues largely vanquished; content will have "come of age" as the reason why we grappled with all the gadgetry in the first place. By this time, our dependency on the electronic marketplace will have been affirmed. No longer a technological plaything, it will be an integral and indispensable part of our lives.

The primary concern for content owners and for consumers as we move to an electronic marketplace will be restricted access to content. However, the restriction will not be due, as in the past, to the unavailability of channels or the high cost of bandwidth. Instead, it will result from distribution covenants arising from exclusive carriage-right agreements crafted and imposed by business conglomerates. Avoiding this may entail regulations excluding companies that own content and content-packaging interests from owning the means of distribution and vice versa. Perhaps this is how we can be best assured that content will flow freely and will thus become the dominant ingredient of an electronic-marketplace-based economy.

Conclusion

If the journey to the digital age has taught us anything, surely it is that the barriers to ready access to content posed by distance and bandwidth were surmountable and perhaps less formidable than we once thought. Far more intractable are the barriers related to broad-based consumer acceptance of these newly liberated means of communication. Without a doubt, powerful marketing challenges lie ahead if the public's general reluctance to adopt exotic new technologies is to be overcome. However, this battle stands to be won on generational grounds. Today's children, weaned on computers, will undoubtedly harbor fewer of their parents' apprehensions with regard to paperless transactions and the "legitimacy" of non-tactile media. In this respect at least, the simple passage of time favors the successful emergence of an electronic marketplace.

I have only touched on what may be the most stubborn variable of all and on the peculiar challenge it presents to the commercial content providers of the twenty-first century. This variable is our time. Barring any physiological alterations to the makeup of our brains, time promises to be as scarce as ever. Indeed, the relative value of our time will undoubtedly increase as a torrent of media choices compete for our attention. This battle for "the favor of our gaze" will usher in smarter, more sophisticated information intermediaries. Though there are many security and privacy issues to consider, these mediation tools will, of necessity, be more intrusive than their forebears. The sheer mass of available information will demand that we reveal ourselves more fully in order to extract relevant information in a timely and meaningful fashion.

This mediation function is exemplified by the CME, which will straddle the two main repositories of tomorrow's content (digital TV and the Internet), serving as a gatekeeper and ordering the larger world in radically new ways. Among other things, this central content-storage device will, in a sense, protect the consumer from information overload and content burnout. Its role will be as much reductionist as inclusionary. However, it will need to have a bifurcated personality, allowing the high-end user to browse as he or she sees fit while offering the low-end user bite-size nuggets of useful or titillating information.

Finally, human communications and content sharing will emerge from a sort of delivery-imposed hibernation. We will learn in a hurry that much has not been shared between us for want of a more effective medium. For years, bandwidth, cost, and distance conspired to allow only the most commercially compelling communications to criss-cross the world. The real ascendancy of content lies with ordinary people sharing their humanity with other equally ordinary people. This is the content that stands to enrich the world in ways unprecedented and heretofore unimagined.

II

Reaching through the Screen for Better
Services and Goods

4

The Digital Utility: Premonitions of the Future of the Last Great Monopoly

William D. Bandt

A dream that is not understood remains a mere occurrence. Understood, it becomes a living experience.

—Carl Jung

"I was standing in a tollbooth," the young executive told the sage, "leaning forward to collect the toll as a large black limousine drew closer. As it neared, it sped up and passed through the tollgate with complete disregard. As I turned and watched it go, I saw that it had no driver and that it was occupied by seven mannequins. As the limo accelerated away, I found myself disoriented by what had just happened. In the distance, I heard the din of small engines and was surprised to see seven small cars approaching. I stepped back and watched all seven of them race past my station. They seemed to be chasing the limo like a pack of predators. Seconds later I heard a loud crash, saw a ball of fire, and realized that the seven small cars had crashed into the limo, and all the vehicles were engulfed in flames. Almost immediately, the seven small cars emerged from the inferno and sped even faster into the distance. I really don't know what to make of this story, but I am troubled by it because it resembles a dream I have had many times before."

The sage asked: "Are you a spectator in this dream, or are you a participant?"

"I am the tollbooth attendant," replied the young man (an executive at a very substantial electric utility company). "I find myself caught up in the excitement of the speeding cars and the thrill of the crash, but have no idea what to conclude."

"Did the small cars have drivers or passengers?"

"Each had a driver but no passengers. I also noticed that each of the cars was different, having very little resemblance to the others."

"This dream," said the sage, "reminds me of one which Pharaoh called upon Joseph to interpret. The limousine occupied by the seven mannequins symbolizes seven good years of affluence and plenty for your industry. In those good times your earnings will be solid, your growth will be sound, your shareholders will be happy, and you and your colleagues will prosper handsomely. The seven small cars symbolize seven years of famine. Their conquest of the limousine symbolizes the impending decline of your industry under pressure of stark scarcity. As Joseph advised Pharaoh, I will tell you that the seven years of your current affluence must soon come to an end and will be followed by a period of disarray, conflict, and unsteadiness, which will make you reevaluate what you are and where you are headed as your industry transforms under the onslaught of deregulation, technology, and changes in the very markets you monopolize today."

"You may be right," said the executive. "My industry is beginning to undergo change, and we all know that more is headed our way. Everyone is worried. Some of my peers prefer the old order; others are impatiently arguing for even faster change. My opinion is that things are proceeding a little more quickly than they should, and I would like to see the rate of change decelerated so it can advance at a more cautious pace."

"Don't count on it," admonished the sage. "The forces already in motion are powerful, and the outcome is as inevitable as gravity. I would like to give you a treatise I have written and suggest that you read and think through it. Afterward, we should get together again."

"Thank you for your thoughts," said the executive humbly. "I'm not really thrilled with your interpretations. Nonetheless, I want to read the treatise. I also want to add one thing about my dream that I forgot to mention. I alluded to the fact that it kept coming back. It first came in 1992, more than five years ago."

"That," said the sage, "means you are already five years into your era of plenty, and you have only two to go before the famine."

"That's more than a coincidence," said the executive. "In many ways, the Energy Policy Act of 1992 unchained us. Many expect that before the millennium the industry will experience upheaval throughout the country."

"We should talk again, and soon," advised the sage.

The next morning, while driving to work, the young executive thought through the dream, its symbolism, and what it might mean for his company and for the entire utility industry. However, his thoughts of the future quickly subsided as he pulled into his parking space and took his private elevator to his palatial office. His secretary brought him coffee and a scone. As she handed him his newspaper, he told her to cancel his morning appointments so he could read the treatise, which was titled "The Disintegrated Utility."

The Disintegrated Utility

Historically, the operating model of the public utility has been one of a regulated, integrated monopoly. In this model, utility shareholders have owned and operated the power plants, the transmission lines, and the local distribution network that supplies electricity to individual businesses and residences. This integrated operating model has been based on a regulated construct whereby the state regulatory commission grants monopoly powers to the utility to operate within a local franchise. In return for this market power, the utility must comply with the oversight of the regulatory commission, including submitting the financial rates of return it authorizes. Though the role of the Federal Energy Regulatory Commission has been important over the years, state regulators have wielded most of the authority over the specific operations of utilities under their jurisdiction.

But several powerful forces are attacking this historically sacred model and will ultimately alter it if they don't overthrow it. First, there are the changes brought about by deregulation. Most of America's great cartels, including those in banking, airlines, and telecommunications, have already been undone. Though no single model has been employed in these deregulations, the overarching principle has been the reduction or elimination of regulation and the concurrent end of monopoly powers. The ultimate result has been to create or enhance competition in previously monopolized markets. Today, federal regulators are encouraging the states to move toward competition and customer choice. (Some states are taking more aggressive action than others.)

As America's electric utilities—its last great monopolies—are deregulated, several recurring themes emerge. The first is the inherent goodness of deregulation and its benefit to the consumer. Second, deregulation is thought to lead to a better allocation of resources by employing price as the mechanism for allocating resources in a market offering open access for all customers. Finally, competition, while painful for some utilities, will ultimately be beneficial to American society and the American economy because of the substantial benefits consumers will gain if given the right to choose their energy supplier.

Besides the regulatory changes, significant technological trends are reshaping the energy industry and society at large. Chief among these is the increasing impact of microprocessors in virtually all aspects of peoples' lives.

Even in 1995, approximately 20 million microprocessors were installed as central processing units in computers, and more than a billion were installed as "embedded intelligence" in cellular phones, pagers, wristwatches, microwave ovens, and air conditioners, their primary object being system operation rather than computation. As embedded microprocessors get cheaper, they will become even more pervasive.

Another fundamental shift in technology is the migration toward networks. As devices are combined into a network, the network's power grows exponentially with the number of devices. We have embarked on the age of pervasive computing—a development that is extremely important for the utility industry because the devices that are the hosts of embedded intelligence are most often connected to a source of electric power, which is largely the domain of the electric utility. As intelligent devices become pervasive, utilities have both an opportunity and a mandate to take advantage of the networks of smart devices. The opportunity this chain of events gives electric utilities to create value is both enormous and nonlinear.

A third force driving the changes in the utility model is the trend toward convergence. Advances in computer power and bandwidth, when combined with the digitization of media, form irreversible forces that are transforming many industries, energy utilities included. Utilities must understand these changes, integrate them into their operations, and capitalize on their inevitability in order to create value for both their shareholders and their customers. In fact, connecting utilities and their customers to the emerging communications infrastructure will have the same profound effect on the economy that the interconnection of power grid infrastructures had in fomenting the growth of electrification in America and the huge industry that this nourished.

As the vertical structure of the electric utility industry disintegrates, what becomes of the components of what were previously operated as vertically integrated utilities? Today, utilities typically own and operate an integrated set of power plants, transmission systems, and local distribution businesses (power grids). In the future, the previously integrated utility will be deconstructed into a complex of businesses which will sell their services as non-integrated participants in the energy value chain. The competitive supplier of choice to the customers of a disintegrated electric utility will pay for the generation, transmission, and transport through the grid of the power that the utility markets to its customers. This will relegate the regulated utility of the future to the role of an asset manager, realizing the regulated return on the assets utilized in delivering the power to the ultimate customer.

Disintegrated utilities will become mere shadows of their former integrated selves. If they aspire to grow and to create superior value for their shareholders, one of their greatest obstacles will be getting out of their own way. The role they stand to inherit as the managers of the denominator in the return-on-assets equation derives from a financial regime in which earnings-generating assets could be created by buying new office furniture. Rather than merely acting as toll takers on their regulated assets, the utilities must be create value in the energy-supply "food chain." Each of the three major disintegrated components of what used to be an integrated utility will be assigned a separate business function within a loose corporate structure, enjoying no cross-subsidies. At best, they will be separate businesses, doing business at arm's length while still belonging to the same shareholders. At worst, they will end up as separately owned and operated businesses, competing for their shares of the energy-supply food chain and facing the possibility of ending up as road kill on the digital highway of commerce as energy rapidly becomes commoditized and its distribution channels become digitized.

The successful utility of the twenty-first century must be inextricably tied to the information highway, confronting the ever-increasing digitization of an ever-expanding component of people's personal and business lives. This goes far beyond investing in the physical carriage of bandwidth, which appeals instinctively to denominator managers. It means finding nonlinear approaches to value creation for customers in digitally defined transaction space—a necessary condition for prosperity if not for survival as these powerful forces descend on a very traditional industry.

About a month later, as the inquiring young executive prepared for his next meeting with the sage, he rehearsed how to open the discussion. His mind had been filled with thoughts of the first meeting and with the treatise the sage had given him. "Well, here goes," he said to himself as he knocked on the sage's door.

"Come in," said the sage as he ushered the visitor into his suite. "I'm glad you came back. I assume from the length of your absence that you had a lot to think about."

"Indeed I have," said the visitor. "Our conversation and your interpretation of my dream have been troubling me. And I have had another dream: I had been invited to play golf with several of my friends who help run other utilities. We had all agreed to meet at the course on a Saturday, but instead of a golf foursome I was greeted by a rock band. The musicians were all middle-aged men, dressed in faded jeans and in tie-dyed shirts printed with the band's name: The Sadducees. Screened on the back of each shirt was the expression "We're just GRATEFUL we're not DEAD." To my amazement I recognized the faces of all the musicians. They were the CEOs I had agreed to meet for golf! Instead of golf clubs, each of them was carrying a guitar with no strings."

"Before we begin talking about the dream," said the sage, "I would like to discuss your business, since we didn't get to do much of that during your first visit. To start with, can you tell me what business you are in?"

"I produce, distribute, and market energy to my customers."

"Produce, yes. Transport, of course. Market? I hope so! As you read in my treatise, the disintegration of your industry will force each of these functions to be separately commercialized, and your firm may or may not end up being in all, or even any, of those businesses. What is important for the sake of our discussion, as well as for the interpretation of your dream, is that marketing is something that you have not done very well. In fact, it stretches my imagination to understand how marketing was more than an afterthought to you, the monopolist from whom customers had no choice but to buy their energy. Nonetheless, I think it will make for an interesting dialog to look at how the changes in the world around us are affecting the utility business.

"As competition comes to your industry, it will be valuable to think through the ways in which the *un*-monopolized playing field will be leveled. As your industry deregulates, and you face the twilight of monopoly, the changes that occur will be profound, particularly with respect to the way you confront the marketplace.

"Now let's spend a moment talking about the dream. The musicians have aptly characterized themselves as Sadducees.[1] They are extremely wise about the markets they serve today, but they lack the wisdom that will be required as markets move rapidly toward a competitive state. Their attire symbolizes their infatuation with their past. Their lack of guitar strings symbolizes the colossal failure of imagination in the electric utilities they have run so well. Sadly, these monopolies have been the breeding grounds for non-innovation, although they have been meticulous in their attention to financial detail and to the care of their customers. Thinking forward to the electronic marketplace in which they will find themselves doing business in the not-too-distant future, I suspect they really *will* be grateful if they're not dead. In sum, this dream foreshadows their resistance to the changes that are about to occur in their very basis for doing business.

"In order to gain a better perspective on this industry in which you find yourself, let's look at some changes in a larger context.

"Looking back over the last 300 years, we can see that the roots of the United States are in an agrarian society and culture. As mass production came to the United States within the last 100 years, we entered a golden age in which very strong and successful participants emerged as they were able to conquer the economies of mass production and to create products that would satisfy their customers' needs. The auto industry is a case in point.

"After the golden age of mass production, the information age was born. Fifty years ago, the computer was virtually unheard of. Forty years ago, IBM's early mainframes found limited deployment in scientific and business applications. Thirty years ago, elementary computers enjoyed substantial success in multiple sectors. Twenty years ago, IBM dominated the world market for computer mainframe hardware. In the early 1980s, the Macintosh was introduced; it was soon followed by the IBM PC.

"By the late 1980s, IBM's mainframes held a worldwide market share of only a single-digit percentage of the world's installed computer base. They had been largely supplanted by the seemingly unstoppable trend toward desktop computing, which was the genie let out of the bottle by the introduction of the Macintosh and the PC. Now, those widely distributed computers are being connected on networks at an explosive pace. They are being connected so quickly that Scott McNeely, CEO of Sun Microsystems, has stated that 'the network *is* the computer.' By that he means that there is more computing power installed in the networks that connect computers than there is in the computers connected to those networks.

"As we retrace this rapid 50-year journey through computer history," said the sage, "it is valuable to ask what parallel progress has occurred in your industry."

"Not all that much," sighed the young executive. "When I look at that 50-year time line, which is longer than my own life, I am chilled by the fact that my industry has hardly begun to avail itself of these new powers. That's not to say that we aren't successful in using computers in operating our enterprises. But I fear we have fallen far short of the available opportunities to implement computing and network technology in our product development, marketing, and customer service programs."

"Precisely!" exclaimed the sage. "Bill Joy, the Vice President of Research at Sun Microsystems, tells me that we are at a point of change in the history of the United States that is equivalent to the 1980s' move to microprocessors, which led to the wide distribution of processing power and its ultimate connection on networks. As so much of industry rushes headlong into the world of network-centric computing, you had better make sure that you and your Sadducee brethren pay close attention to these developments and to emerging technological trends, lest you face extinction. You have truly reached a strategic inflection point.

"Are you old enough to remember the admonition 'Do not fold, spindle or mutilate?'"

"No," said the young executive, "I can't say I've ever heard that."

"Another affirmation that you're a member of the digital generation. Old paradigms die slow deaths. Although that phrase was around for a long time, the only place to find a punch card today is in a museum of computing history. It is both interesting and instructive to think 10 years into the future, and to contemplate which of the things that are so real to us today will have been put to rest.

"Let's take this paradigm notion a little further. Since so much of what we have been talking about involves technology, do you think you could make a list of the top ten players in technology today?"

"Let's see. I'd have to include Microsoft, Sun, Netscape, Novell, Cisco, IBM, AT&T, Hewlett-Packard, Compaq, and Intel."

"Very well," the sage nodded. "Do you realize that 10 years ago more than half of those companies were mere startups? It would be interesting to think ahead to the marketplace 10 years hence and to try to guess which of those companies will still be on your top-ten list. My point is that the creators and purveyors of technology we have been discussing are rushing into the future at warp speed. Actually, they're *inventing* the future at warp speed."

"My own industry could hardly be accused of that," quipped the young executive. "At best, we are mere extras in the movie."

"Right on, to use another archaism," responded the sage. "As the world changes around you, and you anticipate the loss of your monopoly power, you can no longer afford to be insular. Now I'd like you to make up a list of today's top ten energy companies. If we were to look forward 10 years, I wonder what that list would look like. I can assure you that the players will change. I don't mean that the existing players will simply change positions on the list. Those who know the new rules of the markets being created by the new technologies are those who will compete and prevail in the new digital marketplace. With the full implementation of deregulation, the incumbent monopolists who have become so accustomed to protection in their franchised markets will have no rules and no regulators to protect them. They will only be able to call upon their own wits and ingenuity.

"I have another treatise that I'd like you to study. It should give you some points to ponder regarding the way the new technologies will force changes in the marketplace and will demand some completely new thinking from the utility of the future."

The New Rubric of the Digital Utility

The emerging technology infrastructure, which connects people, places, and things as never before with digital communication links, will change economic activity as significantly as the creation of a national electric network did at the beginning of the twentieth century. Just as the installation and connection of the universal electrical power grid in the United States and other developed countries made electricity universally available and facilitated advances in industry and lifestyles that could not have been achieved in any other way, the new communication infrastructure will make information and communication available to all, thereby forcing a reconsideration of the way parties at both ends of the communication pipe do business with each other. As the number of points connected grows, and as communication bandwidth increases between these points, people, businesses, and institutions will pump huge quantities of multimedia text, sound, image, and video back and forth, utterly reworking the fundamental structures of how people, institutions, and businesses relate.

In order to compete in this newly connected economy, a very clear strategic architecture will be essential to establish links between today and tomorrow—an architecture that identifies what must be done right now to grasp the future. The impact of this new world of unimagined connections will be as profound as the invention of the printing press, the discovery of penicillin, the creation of the transistor, and the development of the microprocessor. In the electronic marketplace of the twenty-first century, utility companies will have to develop and deploy distinctive competences in doing business on a broadband high-capacity communications highway connecting virtually all major points in the economy. Consumers as well as businesses can and must get connected to this infrastructure as the necessary condition for buying and selling in the next century. And so, the utility industry will go through profound and dramatic change, either suffering or benefiting from the growth of this new digital umbilical cord. The jolt of this change should come as no surprise to the utility industry, which has benefited from, and ably exploited, the development and connection of the national electrical grid infrastructure.

In order to get their unfair share of the forthcoming digital harvest, utility companies will have to become experts at developing new competencies that have to date only been dreamed about, or anticipated with trepidation. Much of this will be about marketing through the new information infrastructure, which will prove to be both the greatest opportunity and the greatest threat to the utility of the future. It was recently noted in Fortune magazine that "in industry after industry, power is moving downstream toward the customer, the person with the dollar bill in his hand." Deregulation will make this transition possible, but the new electronic marketplace will implement and accelerate it.

The challenge for the digital utility of the future will be the successful separation of the product-delivery channel for energy (the wires) from the customer-care and marketing channel (the medium). Marketing in the digital age will be substantially influenced, if not dominated, by the proliferation of new multimedia connections. This will allow, if not require, the development of a virtual multimedia customer-care and customer-interface platform—a trend being accelerated by the convergence of information enabled by digital multimedia technology, but also by the industry convergence evidenced by cross-investment between software and cable TV companies and between telecommunications and entertainment companies. It is said that an increasing proportion of consumers' dollars will ultimately end up in the hands of the company that controls the sales channel. Eventually, less and less compensation for value will end up back at the factory (or, in the case of utilities, as compensation for the energy commodity).

Rising from the ashes of the traditional utility will be the digital utility, a new enterprise motivated to exploit all that the new technologies creating the electronic marketplace have to offer. Of paramount importance will be the new virtual channel to the customer, the advent of intelligent agents, and the rise of a new breed of intermediaries which will occupy a growing position between the supplier and the ultimate consumer of products and services. The coming shakeout in the utility industry will be profound. Today the local telephone, gas, electric, and water utilities all claim to have 100 percent market shares. In fact they do, but not much longer. The battle for the control of the single customer, who is today provided with segregated utility services by each individual monopoly utility, will ultimately meld into a channel-dominated digital relationship with a supplier of aggregated utility services. That is not to say that each utility as it exists today will have the luxury of creating its own separate marketing relationship with its existing customers through the new information infrastructure. Such economics no longer work. In fact, there will be a wave of consolidation of breathtaking financial magnitude, creating a new breed of meta-utilities which will become the purveyors of multiple services to the same customers in a relationship dominated by the new digital infrastructure.

The ultimate winners in this battle will be those who are able to develop the best and most pervasive digital customer-care platform. The traditional business model is "buy low and sell high." The new approach in the digital marketplace will add value and create wealth by developing and exploiting new channels and new forms of connection and relationships with the customer, giving rise to a new breed of intermediaries in the race to create new value-added relationships. They will collapse the distribution and sales chain that today separates suppliers from buyers. In addition, new markets will be created, or existing markets will be grown, by providing customers with direct digital access to the sales chain. Finally, the digitization of media and communications will allow customers and suppliers to exploit heretofore unavailable data, using new technologies that blazed into existence with the advent of the electronic marketplace. As the existing industry structure disintegrates, this rebirth *of fundamental structures will put the integrated local utility company at great risk.*

It has been estimated that the cost of software, marketing, distribution, and fulfillment on the Internet is between 1 percent and 3 percent of the cost of performing the same functions through retail stores. Not only does this call into question the economic viability of the current vertically integrated utility structure; it also forces a reconsideration of the very basis of the marketing and supply of the energy in a deregulated marketplace, which will inevitably give rise to a new breed of digitally enabled intermediaries who are nimble and innovative in bringing together buyers and sellers, thereby creating new digital sales channels which will be independent of the existing industry structure.

The electronic marketplace, further energized by the forces of deregulation and the quest for survival, will force the energy industry to transform itself from an industry of integrated utilities into one of energy intermediaries that bring buyers and sellers together to consummate energy transactions. Opportunities for profit in this new marketplace will devolve from the factory, or its products, toward the providers of the tools and content of commerce in this new medium. It is there that the value will be created for the customers, not in the wires, the pipes, or the bandwidths. Sources of competitive advantage for the digital utility will be found in proprietary databases based on a universe of point-of-sale data concerning energy transactions, and in the ability to evolve control networks into data networks that allow energy-consuming devices to be connected and to be made active, intelligent members of the communication networks on which they reside.

The new energy intermediary will realize that the contrarian economics of the electronic marketplace will probably require that the winning long-term play will be to give away, or inexpensively bundle, the tools required to create commerce opportunities, standards, and distribution possibilities in the market space to which sellers and buyers come together. Notable examples from other industries that portend the future of the utility industry include Netscape and Adobe. Microsoft made DOS the standard operating system because it was bundled and distributed through nearly all the IBM-compatible personal computers sold directly and through retail channels, so that it was essentially "free" (but not a

*choice) to the customer purchasing a new computer. The ability to dis-
cover and exploit the free-goods "quirk" of the new economics of the
electronic marketplace will prove to be a pacing issue as traditional
utilities and electronic intermediaries struggle for shares in the new
marketplace.*

*What will make the electronic marketplace a dramatically altered
infrastructure for business transactions will be its ability to expand the
scale and the scope of conventional economic activity for both buyers
and sellers, inviting innovators to reinvent the value chain by exploiting
the flow of market information. Monthly visits by the meter reader will
be supplanted by live, real-time, market-shaping data flows, which new
energy-information intermediaries (essentially specializing in the development and control of information about the energy market) will exploit
to occupy an increasingly large position in the value chain between sellers
and buyers and to serve as agents for their clients, helping them to
navigate vast oceans of information to make the right energy choices
(whether digitally available or not). The value proposition they will offer
is the analysis and contextualization of customer data (e.g., lifestyle
preferences, usage patterns, and constraints) to make raw customer data
decisionable and actionable by the seller of energy and energy services.*

*In this electronic marketplace, utilities will have to become information
intermediaries in order to avoid being replaced by knowledge brokers.
The pure act of energy delivery will occupy only a fraction of the value
chain. The new connectivity of the energy marketplace will provide a
powerful means for connecting supply and demand. There are many
completely new sources of information about commerce, and there are
new communication techniques to enhance the abilities of energy producers and consumers to conduct electronically enabled energy commerce. The goal for a new digital utility will be to achieve strategic
advantage through the conduct of proprietary commerce, on dedicated
channels, utilizing tools that exploit competitively unique sources of data
which are enabled by the new digital medium.*

*Electronic commerce in energy will lead to the development of com-
pletely new sources of added value. One of these will be the reduction
in the cost of searching for the best deal. When energy customers ultimately do have the right to choose, how will they discover the best deal*

and make the best choices? Tremendous opportunities for adding value exist for those who can enable these functions. Second, the creation of new electronic commerce channels will for the first time enable collaboration between sellers and buyers, thereby evolving the industry beyond the current relationship, which exists around episodic transactions, into more symbiotic relationships based on the mutual development and utilization of forecasts, quantity and price commitments, usage timing, and mitigation (formerly thought of as demand-side management) to the extent that it is mutually and symbiotically beneficial. This new digitally enabled relationship developing in the energy marketplace will cause the digital utility to look hard and long at its distribution costs as new channels are developed and maintained.

Ultimately, utilities, as they become energy information intermediaries, may adopt the same philosophy toward customer service as retail banks, which clearly prefer digital transactions to human involvement. As in the banking model, it will cost more to conduct a transaction at the utility's walk-in customer service office than to pay a bill or make an inquiry electronically. It has been estimated that from 50 to 80 percent of the costs of consumer products in the retail marketplace can be attributed to distribution. Not only will new technologies lead to the development of new channels; they will also be able to eliminate many of the unnecessary costs currently incurred in distributing energy and in managing product and service channels by simply making the distribution chain digital. This will allow the energy intermediary to unbundle pricing and other aspects of a proposed transaction for transparency, and then rebundle them for the customers' operational convenience, allowing the micro-segmentation of the market down to the individual customer.

When the channel is digital and the marketplace is electronic, this will be feasible for the first time. In the new digital energy marketplace, where comparison shopping for the best deal will be just a click of a mouse away, the tasks of brand equity development and brand management will be daunting. "Online brand equity" may become an oxymoron. In the electronic marketplace, attracting and holding customers will require the development of a completely new view of customer loyalty and customer retention. The digital attributes of comparison shopping will make the customer's choice set essentially infinite and will place nearly all of the power to control the transaction in the customer's hands. In the past, the role of intermediaries in modern society evolved to that of "gatekeepers" who obtained, filtered, packaged, and delivered information, facilitating the choices for their clients. This was as true in the case of political parties as in the retailing of consumer products, where retail stores determine which products will be available to their customers. The growth of the electronic marketplace will not only completely disrupt these activities of traditional intermediaries and the value that they bring to (and extract from) transactions; it will also create entirely new intermediary functions. The new energy intermediaries will integrate the data they have collected and filtered into decision-making systems that will deliver packaged solutions to their clients.

So far, the closing in of ruthless forces of deregulation of an industry unaccustomed to competition, coupled with advances in communication technology and the digitization of media, has elicited more questions than answers about the future of the utility industry. Nonetheless, several aspects of the future of the industry are coming into view. First, to survive, much less thrive, utilities will have to become digital, exploiting rather than studying or even resisting the opportunities of the new electronic marketplace. Second, the digital utility will have at its disposal the tools to reinvent the value chain, in order to become an energy intermediary. This will allow it to develop new means of value creation in the marketplace by exploiting digitally enabled information to provide unique solutions to customers while excising costs from the distribution chain. In fact, the new energy intermediary may well control, if not own, the value chain itself. The new tools for collecting, analyzing, and exploiting customer information will shift the balance of power from the utility to the customer. The electronic marketplace will enable real-time price and service comparisons, thereby stripping today's utilities of any remaining vestiges of the market power they enjoyed in the past. This new and somewhat radical notion of "decision division" (coined by Alvin Toffler) calls into question not only the direction but also the magnitude of the value proposition in the electronic energy marketplace. Many, if not most, of today's utilities will not remain in their present forms in tomorrow's electronic marketplace. The challenge ahead for this huge industry will be not merely to renew or even re-engineer itself in order to get ready for the future, but to reinvent itself fundamentally in order to compete in the electronic marketplace.

Several weeks later, as the executive arrived in the sage's office for his third appointment, he was particularly nervous.

"What's wrong, young man?" asked the sage. "You seem troubled."

"I am," was the reply. "I put a lot of thought into the conversation we had the last time, and into the second treatise you gave me. I'm disturbed by some of the possibilities you raised. I've been working hard to change the culture of my utility company to get ready for competition. That effort has been like turning a battleship 90 degrees while it is going at flank speed. Maybe I've been wasting my time."

"No, no, no!" responded the sage. "I would never say you are wasting your time. I would only ask if you are doing enough and are doing it fast enough."

"It really goes deeper than that," lamented the young executive. "You see, I've had another dream, and it has left me even more puzzled. Let me share it with you. One evening, after I got home and finished dinner, I was sitting down at my PC to check my email. As I logged on, I discovered that my computer's modem was actually plugged into the electric wall outlet just above the one into which the PC's power cord was plugged. For a moment, I feared the PC would blow up. It didn't, and as soon as I got onto the Internet I was pitched an ad. This ad was for a free E-card good for 20 kilowatt-hours of electricity and 1000 cubic feet of natural gas for every five pay-per-view cable TV movies I prepaid through the First Virtual Energy Company. In order for this offer to be good, I had to make my purchase while I was logged onto the session, and it had to be purchased through the Internet's E-channel. Not being able to pass up this deal, out of either curiosity or economics, I clicked on the ORDER NOW button and turned on my TV to watch a mystery."

The sage responded: "I am glad you came to me with this dream while it was still fresh in your mind. You'll like what you hear as the explanation of this dream unfolds. I'll let you interpret this one yourself. I'm going to ask you to exercise your ingenuity for a few minutes. Close your eyes and think about the poorest Third World country you can imagine. No power, no phones, hardly civilized. What would you do to help that country develop?"

"Well," said the young executive, "I'd get the people of the country connected with one wire if I could."

"Which one?" asked the sage.

"Mine, of course!" responded the young executive. "But how?"

"That's not the point. If you could, what would you do?"

"Well, I would build a single infrastructure, and I would be the single service provider. The communication and energy industries would never have the chance to converge, because it would start out as one. Why install phone lines if you could make phone calls over the power line? That's the way I'd do it if I knew how to."

"Nice job," responded the sage. "You've broken the code. What you had dreamed and the way you have answered my questions are completely consistent. You may well not be aware of it because you have been too busy being a utility, but the technology to do most everything that occurred in your dream is now available. It is not commercial yet, but it is available in the laboratories and operating in limited market tests. I've seen electric meters read over the power line, logged myself onto the Internet, made a long-distance phone call of perfect digital clarity, and conducted a video conference in which the cameras in an office building were connected only over the active power line."

"You must be kidding," responded the young executive, visibly agitated. "If that's true, my industry will never be the same. I'm in the driver's seat when it comes to the convergence of the communications and energy industries, and I'm in a position to dominate the commerce that occurs if I can do it over my power lines. With the deregulation of telecommunications, I become the alternative access provider whether I decide to be the phone company or make a deal with competitive telephone service providers to use my lines. You're right, I feel great! But is this for real?"

"Not only is it for real," the sage responded, "it is deployed in several places today. Not only can you bet on it; you will soon be able to take it to the bank."

"Speaking of the bank," said the young executive, "I don't think that even one of the thousands of people who work for me has a clue as to what you are talking about or how to make money from it."

"I guess you'll have to fix that if you are serious about the future," said the sage. "But there is more to the story than we have uncovered so far. Lou Gerstner of IBM has also told me that the computing industry is moving rapidly toward the era of network-centric computing. By that he means that computers which stand alone and process independently are becoming rare. The evolution of client-server technology, and the rapid increases in the availability of bandwidth and the decrease in its price, have caused the computing industry to look for growth in network-oriented high-bandwidth applications. Remember what I said in my last treatise about stepping up the value chain? The promising opportunity for you as a utility executive is to look at how you can apply this new technology to your business.

"The key lies in the idea of embedded intelligence. As I told you before, not too long ago more than a billion microprocessors were installed in devices sold for applications other than basic computing. Only 20 million microprocessors were installed in computers; the rest were installed in devices. The microprocessors make those devices smart. You are standing at the cusp of a revolution in the energy industry that is enabled by this creation of smart energy applications.

"In this technology lies the opportunity for your industry, and even your own company, to differentiate itself and create a value proposition that will be unique and sustainable. I understand that you are suffering from a great deal of competitive anxiety, but you should take some heart in smart energy; it will open up new opportunities that you have never imagined. We have talked before about the new communications infrastructure which will enable widespread electronic commerce because of its ubiquitous connectivity. This will be one of the primary components in your becoming a digital utility. Think of the developing communications infrastructure not as a single network but as a network of networks. Think of it as a great hybrid that will provide nearly universal connections and interoperability. One of the major components in that hybrid is your power line. I'm referring to your power line as it connects premises to external points, as well as the power line that operates within the premises. The power line within the premises (residential or commercial) provides a readily available topology for the installation of a private local-area network (call it a P-LAN). This P-LAN becomes the domain of the electricity supplier, which has the opportunity to turn it into an active communication network for the purpose of external connectivity.

"Now stir in some embedded intelligence, which already exists in almost all the electricity-consuming devices that contain microprocessors, and you have the makings of an extraordinary value proposition for your electric customers. Today you measure, or meter, the consumption of electricity at a customer's premises, typically monthly. You do that through a very dumb meter that simply counts the amount of electricity that passes through it. Utilizing embedded intelligence in the devices that have become smart through the microprocessors they contain, if you connect those devices to the P-LAN you will be able to measure the use of electricity in real time down to the device level. You can forget about planning for submetering. What I'm talking about is device metering."

"Then as long as the devices are smart and connected to my power line premises network, I will be able to sell a customer electricity at one rate for his air conditioner and another rate for his clothes dryer."

"You've got it! That gives you the potential to engage in the ultimate in microscopic marketing, segmenting your marketplace not just into individual customers but down to the individual device. And when the technology is fully developed and commercially available to do it all over your power line, you may choose to become an ener(gy)-tainment company, since you will already own the physical carriage into all the premises in which you do business. In fact, as an ener-tainment company you will be in the position of providing energy and energy services as well as content. The content provided over the power line (a communication channel you already own) may be ener-tainment, entertainment, or electronic commerce.

"The part of your dream about getting free gas and electricity with pay-per-view movies is really about ultimately bundling and jointly marketing those services in order to realize and maximize the margin obtained by the package provided to your customer. In fact, your dream was more than a dream, it was an uncanny premonition based on what

I know is nearing commercial availability with respect to communications over your power lines.

"It gets better. In my treatise I talked about evolving the customer relationship from episodic energy transactions to a mutually symbiotic relationship. Here's how that will occur. When your customers' devices are smart (utilizing embedded intelligence) and are connected to the network of the power line, each device's energy demand and usage can be separately measured, managed, and controlled. When that occurs, the symbiotic relationship becomes one in which the aggregated individual demands of virtually all of the smart energy-consuming devices that are connected to the network can, in real time, be aggregated to create a demand curve for the power plants that serve them with the requisite end-to-end connectivity. The story is now complete, because the symbiosis occurs as the output of the power plants literally follows the load created by consumers' consumption choices as connected, smart energy-consuming devices interact with the source where the power is generated in response to real-time pricing signals."

"I surely do feel better now than when I walked into your office," said the executive. "I hope you'll understand that I need time to digest these thoughts, which are new to me. I can't believe you found all of this in my dream."

"You give me too much credit," said the sage. "After all, it was your dream. I believe we have covered enough ground for today. I hope you'll come back one more time, however, because there is a lot more to be discussed than we have covered so far. Though you'll find much of it encouraging, you'll also find in our next conversation several factors which will be very disquieting to you."

The young executive stormed into his next audience and seized control. "Until this morning, I really wasn't sure why I was getting together with you again. I thought I had the answers I was seeking after our last meeting. Then last night I had a disturbing dream. I can't make any sense of it. For the first time, I had a dream in which I was a bystander, not a participant.

"The setting of this dream occurred a number of years in the future. My daughter, who is now a toddler, appeared as a pre-teen. The other child, apparently my son, is about 3 years younger, and is someone I have never seen. The children are fighting over who gets to use the mouse to click on an icon that will tell Alphie, our Personal Digital Agent, what amount of energy to go out and buy for the next week. It seems that the icons on the screen require someone to select what temperature the house is to be, when the refrigerator is to defrost, when the dishwasher is to run, and when the micro-generator in the basement will come on in response to price signals (received through the online electronic market-place) that the market price of energy is high. This is beyond my imagination today. The concluding screen says 'Thank you for your business. We appreciate the opportunity to serve you at any time in any place.' The message is from the American Interactive Energy Exchange.

"I had a little trouble swallowing the power line discussion, but I liked what I heard. The dream upset me because I'm not sure who everybody in it is and because I'm not sure what I'm going to be doing for a living if it comes true."

"I believe I can help," responded the sage reassuringly. "Your dream is an ideal foundation for me to give you my last treatise. Rather than take it with you, sit quietly in my office and read it while I go about some other matters. We need to discuss it immediately."

Micromarketing in the Digital Age

The art of marketing will become the science of marketing in the digital age. Rather than begin with a discussion of how it will impact the energy industry, let us look at the more immediate consequences for other industries.

The first casualty in the traditional value chain will be the supplier who relies upon a fully vertically integrated organization that spans from production to customer delivery and service. Look at the travel industry. Travel agents are being replaced by electronic tickets and online ticket purchasing. The airlines have been quick to learn that, with the availability of enabling technologies, they have identified a new form of value added. Most notable here is the electronic presentation of American Airlines, which was introduced as American's "Newest Terminal." Travel arrangements can be made, flight schedules can be checked, and tickets can be purchased directly from the airline, thereby obviating travel agents' commissions and giving the customer a new and direct intimacy with the actual producer of the service. All the airlines that are now on line, and many of the hotel groups, often distribute free software that allows direct access to their online services. Not accidentally, this software is proprietary to them and works only when used with their system, thereby providing a very subtle element of competitive advantage and customer retention. Said another way, it is unlikely that every customer will acquire and master the use of every airline's software in order to be able to shop all the airlines simultaneously.

The travel agents have also been supplanted by a new breed of electronic travel agents who, instead of providing personal service, provide (at a low cost) fare-optimization capabilities that allow a customer to craft a trip according to his own personal needs and not according to the preferences of the travel agent, much less the commission structures offered the travel agents by airlines to induce them to feature their services.

It is more of a stretch to imagine electronic trading and transactions coming to the stockyard business. Nonetheless, it is a documented fact that the Calgary stockyard conducts two-thirds of its annual transactions on line. A variation has now come to the marketing of new automobiles and to the business of selling used auto parts. There is no reason to believe that the utility industry will be excluded or immune.

Let us think through this circumvention of traditional marketing channels. Imagine a virtual music store, Bandwidth Buster Music, that offers every current CD for sale, always at a 25 percent discount from the list price. If you order from Bandwidth Buster, you can get your music in either of two ways. If you are willing to pay a service and handling charge, they will send you a CD or a cassette. If you want it for the lowest possible price, all you have to do is click on the order button, download your music, and go from there. (Of course, the distribution and licensing rights of the music companies are carefully preserved in these transactions.) Before the digital era this could not have occurred. However, now that channels are becoming digital, markets can become virtual, and the multiple layers of distribution and their consequential economics can be circumvented and even eliminated. The elimination of these multiple layers in retail channels is the essence of the disintermediation (more nearly digital intermediation), which eliminates the functions of the "middleman." Digital networks replace the costly but relatively unproductive steps in the chain of marketing and distribution that intervene in the direct relationship between the original creator of a product's value and the ultimate consumer of the product. In a moment I will discuss how this provides a heretofore unavailable opportunity for the creation of a direct digital relationship between the supplier and the ultimate consumer, not only circumventing the middleman but also allowing the customer to be a buyer on his own terms, according to his own personal preferences, and permitting the supplier to create a direct microchannel to that customer so that his needs can be assessed and specifically met.

What does this mean for the energy industry of the future? The disintermediation that is now manifest in the energy industry will evolve into a structure in which ener(gy)-mediaries will take over the role of physical merchants. These will be nothing more than mercenaries who look to bridge the relationship between utilities and their ultimate customers. Will those digital intermediaries be the agents of utilities in reaching the end customer, or will they be third parties with whom the utility competes?

The utility industry that exists today will be unrecognizable in a decade, because digital markets will be separate from physical markets. As the tidal wave of technology pummels the old-paradigm utilities, a utility's ability to understand and capitalize on the emerging electronic marketplace will determine its success or its demise. The digitization of markets and marketing channels and the coming pervasive connectivity will move the locus of the value chain from the physical layer to the network. The new technology will require all parties to rethink their positions on the value chain between the original producer and the ultimate consumer. The physical exchange will become virtual as transactions and communications become digital and networked. In this way, the value chain really will become a virtual value network.

The rise and ultimate fall of physical intermediaries and their evolution into digital intermediaries will occur when their services, first personal and then electronic, get replaced with hypertext entries on the communications network. A necessary condition for this to occur will be the universal connection of customers. This will enable, and ultimately force, *the digitization of markets. With the digitization of markets arrives the unique opportunity for the development of a new micromarketing model that will bring sellers and buyers together in a one-on-one relationship. The increasing utilization of microprocessors in energy-consuming devices and the connection of those smart devices to the network (whether it is the power line or some other network) will enable an energy customer to buy precisely the amount of energy he wants, when he wants it, at the quality level he wants, from any supplier he selects. And there will be many suppliers to choose among. One might say that this will create a perfectly efficient market for energy. There will be no obstacles and no friction in the marketing, because sellers and buyers will be able to interact with perfect information and to make the optimum deal between themselves. Today's utility counts in its "customer universe" the number of meters and the amount of energy that passes through them. The digital energy market of the future will allow the mass customization of virtually every market, with a single customer occupying a market segment size of one. The new digital utility will become a micro-merchant in order to capitalize on this segmentation.*

In this transformation, technology will be the bridge, and maybe even the crowbar, that forces the proactive change in the paradigm. Digital markets will be very different from physical markets. Comparison shopping will have no boundaries in digital markets, and the notion of differentiation will take on a very new meaning due to the collapse of differences in time, place, and information access when the playing field has been leveled. Companies with truly different products, with differentiated features in their offerings through the electronic marketplace, or with unique pricing methodologies will rise to the top quickly, but will face an inevitable future struggle to stay there. The perfect efficiency of digital markets will force the expression "We will not be undersold" to take on a draconian new dimension. Differentiation in the electronic marketplace will be extraordinarily difficult to achieve, but when accomplished it will provide a valuable source of competitive advantage and customer retention.

The electronic marketplace will exhibit a voracious appetite for new products and services, exacerbated by micro-segmentation and by a new one-on-one relationship between suppliers and purchasers. The new science of product creation in the digital marketplace will be of para-mount importance in achieving aspects of sustainable differentiation. Compaq, now the world's largest manufacturer of personal computers, enjoys between 80 and 90 percent of its current revenues from products it did not have on the market 2 years ago. The new electronic marketplace will be very unforgiving of lack of innovation, and very hungry for a seeming endless stream of new products and services to satisfy the indi-vidualistic requirements of the new micro-segmented electronic market.

The pace of the molecularization of the marketplace will be governed by technological progress in several areas. These include the migration of communication over networks from analog to digital, advances in database and data-mining technology that allow digital networks to become neural or learning networks, and further development of com-puting away from hierarchical computing structures, evolving into peer based interactions (similar to the Internet model). Finally, continued increases in available bandwidth will permit these peer-based, Web-fashioned networks to communicate seamlessly with full multimedia capability. As these technologies continue their rapid advance, the disso-lution of the big, crude market into innumerable fine-tuned micromarkets will continue as information barriers and communication discontinuities are removed. This will put a great deal of buying power in the hands of the consumer—the reciprocal of the way that the traditional utility model has vested a great deal of power in the hands of the seller. Each buyer, or his electronic representative, will have a form of monopsony buying power in the marketplace. As the intelligent devices that consume energy on the premises of the customer become smart, this will allow the marriage of the customer's personal preferences with the ability to indi-vidually manage the consumption of each of the devices on his premises' network, thereby forming an individual personalized demand curve that can be adjusted dynamically. The buying representatives of each individ-ual customer can be designated as agents that will surgically and imper-sonally construct that demand curve for that customer.

Where is the utility in this model? Marketing to the masses as practiced in the past will evolve to molecular micro-marketing as the marketers seek to identify specific customers, or groups of customers, or indeed single customers, at given times of day, as likely candidates. Because of the data available in the digital networks, their marketing programs can be tailored to individual preferences or to aggregated preferences of groups of individuals, thereby permitting efficient price discovery and negotiation by parties on both sides of the transaction. With the availability of networking technology in the electronic marketplace, buyers will be able to network themselves into clusters allowing the aggregation of their demands, thereby substantially increasing their buying power and subsequently improving their negotiating position in dealing with suppliers—almost the diametric opposite of today's model. In fact, this future model of the electronic marketplace turns the tables on the monopolist, delighting with its populist tendencies regulators who are ambassadors for competition rather than trustees for oligopoly. Notably, all of this will be empowered by the advent and maturation of networking in the electronic marketplace.

And how will this be implemented? By the use of intelligent agents. These agents should be regarded as virtual personal assistants that effectively automate word of mouth in the process of price discovery and in the negotiations between buyers and seller. An agent is an adaptive, autonomous, network-centric learning software algorithm able to navigate heterogeneous computing environments while maintaining the ability to learn and respond independently. An intelligent agent should not be compared to a spellchecker. Rather, it should be thought of as an equational complex that goes beyond the checking of spelling to contextualize the word whose spelling is being checked in order to determine whether the proper spelling of the word within context is (e.g.) "their" or "there." On this contextual analysis, the correct spelling is either verified or corrected on the fly as the text is being typed.

An agent should be thought of more as a verb than as a noun. It must be able to search, learn, and execute instructions involving transactions, whether in word processing or in transactions in the electronic energy marketplace. In the energy marketplace, intelligent agents could aptly be called "e-bots," meaning electronic software robots which are more finders than browsers. As e-bots shop for the best energy deals on behalf of their clients, they will become bargain-hunting electronic nomads visiting virtual storefronts. As they learn where the best deals are and what terms are available to consummate those deals, this learning can be combined into neural network systems of purchasing on behalf of the micro-segmented individual customers, or on behalf of the aggregation of these customers into buying clusters on the network. Essentially, this will be the combination of human and silicon-based intelligence. The evolution and ultimate maximization of the latter will be directly dependent upon advances in networking technology and on the pervasive connection of buyers and sellers to the digital network. In the era of networked intelligence, it is likely that agents will have their own agents. This will allow the market to clear even more rapidly and potentially in real time. In fact, it will be mediator agents that seek to make a match between the agents of buyers and the agents of sellers in order to fulfill in the most efficient manner the transaction opportunities in the market, based upon the information and expressed preferences of the individual intelligent agents of the parties on both sides of the transaction.

Thus, the advances in networking technology and the proliferation of electronic agents, as well as the agents of those agents, pretty much have to reposition the techno-industrial infrastructure substantially. As this new era of the electronic marketplace dawns, traditional market structures that have relied on institutional rules for their current success will be under great pressure to change or die. This will be particularly true in industries that have grown up with substantial artificial protection, such as government-authorized and government-regulated monopolies. The noncompetitive economic structures developed over decades by these industries will no longer function. The traditional and often anachronistic economic paradigms that have served them in the past will rapidly become dysfunctional as their current forms of marketing and transacting will come to be replaced by hypertext entries on the network of networks.

The young executive finished reading, lurched up, shook his head in consternation, and asked the sage: "When all this occurs, what will the digital utility really be?"

The sage responded calmly: "Not much like the old. It will not be vertically integrated. What the new digital utility will do is manage, control, and even dominate the symbiotic relationship between the customer and itself through the electronic umbilical cord of online commerce. It must do this while struggling to compete against parties whose current competencies are in communication and networking technology and who will be able to buy their energy from any number of suppliers while struggling to carve out a sustainable, profitable position in the electronic marketplace."

"Will I be the dog or the bone?" the young executive demanded.

"Both," responded the sage. "The ultimate outcome will be what you make it. I think we have discussed enough for today. In fact, I have given you much to think about as you go your way and continue to run your company. If you feel the need to get together again, I will of course be available. However, I think the future will really be up to you as you chart your course in dangerous waters."

The executive said goodbye and went to his new company car. As he settled into the plush leather seat, the cockpit automatically configured to his personal ergonomics. As he spoke the word "Home" into his digital car phone, voice-recognition technology speed-dialed his wife so he could notify her that he would arrive shortly. As he sped into the fading day, he settled back comfortably and spoke the word "End" to terminate his call, comforted in the belief that technology was his friend and servant rather than a disruptive adversary.

"The sage was a bit carried away with himself," thought the young man. "A little too nonlinear, dipping too deep into the deep end. Couldn't happen that way. No chance." Then he trembled at the prospect that the sage might be exactly right, and he realized how much more interesting life would be if that were so.

Notes

1. Saducees: a priestly, aristocratic Jewish sect, formed in the second century B.C., that adhered strictly to religious traditions and accepted only written Mosaic law as doctrine.

5

PASHAs: Advanced Intelligent Agents in the Service of Electronic Commerce

Denos Gazis

Electronic commerce had a slow start on the Internet, but it is gaining momentum as we approach the end of the millennium. Much work will be needed before electronic commerce will compete with the ordinary variety; however, a lot of work is already underway, and international competition is likely to accelerate progress. Europe, in particular, did not want to be left out of yet another computer revolution, and so it enthusiastically endorsed electronic commerce as the way of the future.

The European Union's admirably broad definition of electronic commerce includes purchasing over the Internet, email, fax, electronic data interchange, and electronic payments. By that definition, parts of electronic commerce are certainly well established. Making the whole of electronic commerce a dominant part of our lives no matter where we are in the world will require the development of technological tools that will correct some of the shortcomings of today's Internet.

In this essay I shall discuss the development of a tool intended to make the Internet friendlier and thus to make a wide range of applications, including electronic commerce, ever more widely accepted. I shall demonstrate the use of the tool by discussing a few applications that are likely to affect the lives of everyone—Eurocrat, Silicon Valley entrepreneur, or Malaysian manufacturer.

When we talk about anything involving the use of computers, including electronic commerce, we should keep in mind the different attitudes of different people (especially people of different ages) toward computers. It is probably fair to say that those who today control the greatest percentage of purchasing power are not likely to easily accept computers as intermediaries in their purchasing activities, although I am hopeful that some of them may be convinced to join the activity if the medium can be made substantially friendlier. The picture, however, is going to change in the coming years, as purchasing power shifts more and more into the hands of the generations for whom interaction with computers has been a way of life from childhood.

The above remarks pertain mostly to purchasing activities of consumers. Purchasing by businesses may be different, insofar as it depends more on business needs than on personal preferences. Even the current shortcomings of the Internet do not appear to diminish the eagerness of businesses to pursue electronic commerce, which, by everyone's estimates, is going to provide substantial savings to businesses in the years to come.

For both consumers and businesses, the future of electronic commerce will depend on its ability to deliver to buyers what they need, preferably better than the old-fashioned marketplace does. I shall concentrate on buying over the Internet, because this is the most likely evolution of electronic commerce; however, virtually everything I say here applies to transactions over any other communication network. The network must supply the information needed for initiating a purchase, and it must carry out the necessary financial exchanges.

It is in supplying information and customized service that we run into trouble when we use the Internet. The sheer volume of information that the Internet offers has been a problem for many. With the current technology, finding things over the Internet is a process that appeals only to people endowed with a certain degree of submissiveness. First, there is the difficulty, even for computer-literate people, of coping with the vagaries of the "user-friendly" computing equipment that accesses the Internet, and with those of the associated "user-friendly" software. A person who masters the act of extracting information from the Internet then faces another problem: the Internet is just too efficient in disseminating information, thus producing information overload in most cases. It is easy to get swamped by the volume of information obtained over the Internet, which today resembles a superb dictionary published in nonalphabetical order for people with time to kill.

A number of search engines are currently available. These are capable of searching a large number of home pages of people who have something to offer and finding a list of pages that contain references to key words supplied by the user. Such searches typically produce a list of hundreds of thousands of home pages, usually ranked according to the frequency of appearance of the key words. Sorting out this volume of information, much of it often repetitious and/or irrelevant, is a formidable task that discourages all but the most dedicated Internet users. But help is on the way.

Enter Intelligent Agents

The use of intelligent agents has been increasing, particularly in constructing improved search engines for the Internet. This has been a natural reaction to the early frustrations of Internet users from volumes of largely irrelevant information produced by early versions of search engines based only on keyword searches. Today, some modern search engines are capable of analyzing the text of search results obtained by keyword search in order to ensure relevance to the needs of the user. They do this by utilizing various degrees of natural language processing to ensure contextual relevance. Another technique contributing to relevance is the "profiling" of users, consisting of contextual delimiters supplied by the user.

While the use of such agents has made substantial inroads toward improving Internet searches, it is fair to say that the agents used thus far are relatively limited in scope and capability. For one thing, the early agents have addressed largely only one application: the linguistic processing of text. There is a lot more that agents can do toward improving the quality of life by assisting humans in carrying out a variety of applications.

PASHAs to the Rescue

I have named the tool I have in mind a PASHA, which stands for *personal application-specific hyper-intelligent agent*. This acronym delineates some essential differences from early intelligent agents.

A PASHA is *personal* in that it is designed to accept personal wishes of a specific user and to act according to these wishes. It will be able not only to engage in a search for useful information according to the user's wishes but also to take actions pre-authorized by the user. The personalization of a PASHA subsumes the profiling of a user, although it is best limited to a specific application.

A PASHA is *application specific*. It is foolhardy, and virtually impossible, to design an IA that will do everything for everybody. Fortunately, that is also unnecessary. It is sufficient to design a PASHA that can carry out a specific task well and (perhaps) solicit the help of another PASHA specialized in another area. Moreover, a PASHA will not be constructed by a computer specialist alone; it will require the collaboration of a specialist experienced in a specific application. This is an important distinction between PASHAs and the early intelligent agents.

The awkward term *hyper-intelligent* (chosen in part to properly complete the acronym) conveys a special message. A PASHA will not be limited to the kind of intelligence possessed by its early progenitors. It will be endowed with an advanced capability for natural language processing, and with speech recognition capability where that is needed. The idea is to produce something that communicates with humans in the way they prefer to communicate, not as an ordinary "user-friendly" system communicates today.

The information processed by a PASHA need not be confined to information obtained over the Internet. PASHAs can be used as intelligent assistants in carrying out everyday tasks around the home or the office, based on information available on site. But it is in improving the use of the Internet—by relieving humans of the inordinately high loads of processing Internet information, doing their job around the clock, and delivering their service exactly when it is needed—that PASHAs can have the greatest impact.

A PASHA will have a natural language processing capability and user interfaces substantially superior to those of any agents developed to date. First of all, by limiting the use of a PASHA to a narrow domain of a specific application, we can improve the efficiency of linguistic processing, which is inversely proportional to the breadth of context. Combining less-than-perfect recognition of speech transmitted over noisy channels (e.g., telephone lines) with natural language processing will enable users to communicate with PASHAs by voice, in ordinary English, albeit over the limited context of a specific application. A PASHA will also generate relevant text, following the completion of a search and other necessary tasks, in order to inform its user and/or to carry out transactions within a range pre-authorized by the user.

The increasing capability of linguistic processing and speech recognition with narrowing of the contextual range can enable performance that would at first sight look unattainable. In the early 1990s, researchers at IBM's Research Laboratory were eager to advance speaker-independent recognition of continuous speech. They achieved immediate success by simply limiting the text to that published in the *Wall Street Journal*. This was sufficient to make the distribution of utterances in the linguistic space more easily distinguishable than they are when speech is permitted to roam into unconstrained territory. PASHAs will not be required to understand Shakespeare (unless, of course, they are designed for a Shakespearean application, which may provide its own contextual constraints).

One of the key advances incorporated in a PASHA will be the ability to go beyond information retrieval to "computational enhancement" of information leading to a recommendation and/or an action. This enhancement will involve processing of information obtained in any way, including by means of the Internet, in order to extract information to be used by algorithms specific to an application, leading to a decision. For example, a PASHA assisting the management of a portfolio may obtain information concerning stock market activities as well as news concerning specific companies, then derive inputs necessary for the use of portfolio management algorithms appropriate for the needs of its master.

Thus, the computational enhancement of information will generally involve three steps:

input preparation The raw information will be processed in order to obtain the necessary input parameters in the form required by the available computational algorithms. This step may require linguistic processing in order to extract appropriate data from a text and then convert the data to the required input format. In other cases, the information may be obtained in some numerical form but may have to be converted into a different input format. Eventually, the PASHA will also be able to extract information from images (e.g., a color-coded diagram).

computational enhancement of information The agent will carry out computations based on algorithms appropriate to the specific application in order to obtain an improved characterization of a system in terms of appropriate state variables. At this stage the agent may evaluate the outcomes of "what if" type questions and compile results suitable for decision making.

decision making At the discretion of the user, the agent may be allowed to make a decision based on the preceding computational results, and it may initiate appropriate action through interaction with other agents or by entering an order for a transaction.

A PASHA is intended to combine the capabilities one expects of intelligent agents, such as linguistic processing of text, with capabilities one would associate with a management system running a particular application. Such an integration of capability can be viewed either as enhancing the ability of an intelligent agent to manage a system or as enhancing the ability of a management system to search for information and communicate with humans. Either way, the combination follows the successful history of combining software capabilities to achieve synergistic advantages. For example, operating systems have been expanding their horizons to include graphics processing and, eventually, an Internet browsing capability. In the case of PASHAs, combining information processing with system-management capability would generate the nearest thing to a superb human assistant, or even an army of assistants, that computer technology can offer. Object-oriented programming can make the construction of PASHAs modular, permitting modules common to more than one application domain to be reused.

The use of a PASHA or of any other comparable aid for electronic commerce over the Internet will change dramatically both the nature of the process and the degree of participation. Businesses are likely to derive the earliest and biggest benefits from the use of PASHAs as they provide personalized service to operating units and even to individual employees.

Now let me discuss a few possible applications of PASHAs. This discussion is certainly not intended to be exhaustive. It includes applications that can be implemented relatively soon, either because the requisite technology and algorithms are available or because they can be expected to be developed shortly. These applications are also chosen because they are likely to be attractive to a large number of users, thus maximizing the potential for return on investment.

Management of Credit Cards and Other Financial Transactions

Users of credit cards are often invited to subscribe to a service, or otherwise commit to periodic payments, by means of regular periodic charges to the card. However, many users have been frustrated by the inflexibility of the current practices in accommodating desired changes to those charges. For example, charges to a credit card often continue after cancellation of a service, requiring lengthy communications in order to stop and reverse charges.

A PASHA can be authorized, with the agreement of the card-issuing bank, to clear all or some of the charges to a credit card before they are made. A user would only have to communicate with the PASHA, in natural language if he desired, in order to instruct a bank to withhold payment. The same PASHA could be asked by the user to stop payment of all charges to a misplaced or stolen card. The communication with the PASHA might require a keyboard, but advanced releases may use speech recognition to make possible voice communication, even over the telephone. The relatively constrained context domain would make such communication eminently possible.

The PASHA could reside in the user's computer and could, over the Internet, negotiate appropriate arrangements with the financial institution's intelligent agents. Alternatively, the PASHA could reside in the financial institution's computer and receive messages from the user over the Internet or by telephone. The latter option appears to be advantageous in terms of cost, security, and reliability.

A related service performed by a PASHA might be an improved replacement for the automated telephone services offered by most institutions that deal with large numbers of customers requiring a relatively limited range of services. Currently, these automated telephone services tend to be rather time-consuming, sometimes onerous, and often frustrating. With the assistance of a PASHA, a user could enter a request in natural language. The request would be translated into the appropriate sequence of number inputs, which would activate the proper response of the automated telephone service.

Trading in Equities

Trading in equities offers a huge opportunity for the use of advanced PASHAs to optimize transaction choices and timing. Trading of common stock and/or stock options requires close monitoring of the price movement of stock prices and option premiums, even if the trader limits the choices of transactions to a specific list of equities. For optimum performance, the investor would like to have information on any stock market activities that might offer opportunities of pursuing his financial objectives.

A PASHA could be instructed to follow market activities and news releases concerning individual companies and market trends, and to assist a user in mapping out and revising an investment strategy in response to these inputs. The PASHA could be trained to follow accepted portfolio management theories and practices and/or individual preferences of the user. It could advise the user on investment opportunities. It could even generate transactions according to pre-specified instructions from the user concerning individual equities.

Managing the Distribution of Electricity

The management of the distribution of electricity has been undergoing a drastic change since the deregulation of electric utility companies, which has uncoupled the production and distribution of electricity. Deregulation is changing the business of electric utilities from one of just selling energy to one that includes various elements of service, and the service content is likely to continue increasing in the coming years. It will affect the distribution of energy to all customers, from households to large commercial sites.

Let us first look at the simple challenge of serving households. Electricity is currently sold to consumers by very simple, and perhaps outdated, methods. Consumers are charged a fixed rate per kilowatt-hour or, at best, a dual rate that charges less during off-peak hours.

Emerging competition among energy companies, stimulated by the ongoing deregulation of energy monopolies, may force these companies to rethink their pricing strategies. One possibility may be to allow virtually every appliance to negotiate the best time of operation, and a correspondingly reduced price of energy. This can be accomplished by mobilizing a PASHA to activate some or all the appliances of a household in a way that optimizes timing and reduces cost to the user. The PASHA would be programmed to follow the user's commands and either carry out the task of an appliance immediately or negotiate with the electric company an optimum time and price of operation. The PASHA would reside in a computer, either the user's or the utility company's. The

PASHA would negotiate energy use for a number of appliances and activate them through remote switches. Full implementation of PASHA capabilities, including advanced user interfaces, would facilitate making desired changes, regardless of the location of the host computer.

Large customers have considerably more complex needs than households and are served differently. Their needs involve containing the cost of energy, guaranteeing satisfactory performance of equipment that uses electricity, and satisfying environmental requirements.

The cost of electricity to a large commercial customer is often determined not only by total consumption but also by the level of peak demand. Thus, it is advantageous to a customer to suppress the peak demand, in addition to containing overall consumption.

Monitoring of performance involves, first of all, guaranteeing that a piece of equipment always operates within an allowable range—for example, that a freezer stays within a certain range of temperatures. In addition, monitoring of appropriate sensors aims at detecting incipient failures of equipment and calling for preventive maintenance. A wide variety of built-in self-test and built-in self-diagnostic systems are often available to make this enhancement of preventive maintenance possible.

Finally, environmental quality control involves monitoring and controlling air quality, such as ambient CO_2 level, in order to initiate possible corrective actions, such as increased ventilation.

It is easy to see that the above requirements are intertwined, since minimizing energy consumption and/or suppressing peak consumption is influenced by distributing energy to the entire range of equipment in order to satisfy performance and environmental requirements. This leads to a complex task requiring the following the following capabilities of a management system:

prediction The system must be capable of anticipating fairly accurately the demand for energy of the entire site and its various pieces of equipment.

scheduling The system must schedule the consumption of energy in order to achieve consumption objectives, such as suppressing peak demand and minimizing overall consumption.

monitoring The system must monitor the performance of all equipment to guarantee satisfactory performance and environmental quality and to detect incipient failures.

real-time adjustment The system must be able to adjust the operation of equipment, in real time, to achieve desired levels of performance in response to unanticipated fluctuations in demand, weather, and other conditions.

As the complexity of a system providing the above services increases, a customer is faced with the problem of finding operators capable of running the system. Let us see how a PASHA can meet all these challenges.

A PASHA residing in a computer will be linked to sensors and to every piece of equipment at the site, and also to the Internet. The PASHA's database will contain data on past activities at the site, historical records of past energy consumption, and other relevant information: past and expected weather conditions, projections of future events that may influence the activities at the site, and so on. The database will also contain profiles of individual units of equipment consisting of normal readings and indications of readings warning of possible incipient failures.

The PASHA will receive sensor data from the site containing information concerning activities at the site, operational characteristics of the various pieces of equipment, and environmental quality measurements. It will also receive, over the Internet or through direct communication with relevant information providers, current and projected weather conditions and news of any events likely to influence the performance of the equipment at the site (e.g., events that might produce unusually large crowds).

On the basis of the above data, the PASHA will define, in real time, a projected allowable range of operational characteristics of all pieces of equipment (e.g., lighting requirements, ventilation requirements, and cooling requirements) and the associated levels of energy consumption.

The computational enhancement will be based on algorithms to be developed by modeling the physical behavior of all pieces of equipment, and the site as a whole, as a function of operating the equipment within the allowable ranges. The objective of the algorithms will be to optimize an objective function, such as minimizing total energy consumption and/or suppressing peak demand, subject to constraints on delivery of the services provided by specific equipment units. For example, a freezer may be lowered to the lowest permissible value during a period of otherwise low energy demand at the site in order to reduce its energy consumption during periods of high activity and energy consumption through lighting, air conditioning, and the like. It is this component of application-specific computational enhancement of information that distinguishes a PASHA as an advanced intelligent agent incorporating the knowledge of an expert on the management of energy consumption at the site.

The computational-enhancement component will also include considerations of environmental quality control and monitoring of the status of the various equipment units for the purpose of initiating preventive maintenance. Both these considerations influence the constraints on the operational ranges of the equipment, and they will be appropriately incorporated in the optimization algorithm.

For obvious reasons of cost containment, equipment operators are unlikely to possess deep technical knowledge of all aspects of the functionality of the equipment and the computerized energy-management system. However, advanced user interfaces may be used by the PASHA to permit exchange of information with equipment operators in natural language and/or speech. It will be able to receive queries from the operators, to respond to such queries, and to advise the operators on recommended actions beyond those that may be programmed as being within the purview of the PASHA itself.

The use of PASHAs for energy management appears to be a natural evolutionary step after the deregulation of electric utilities. Since it can provide value to the customers of electric utilities, providing PASHA service as part of a service contract to customers will give a company a competitive advantage.

Improving Transportation Systems

If electronic commerce flourishes according to everyone's best expectations, how are all the wonderful things that will be purchased over sophisticated communication links going to reach the buyer? To be sure, some of the purchases will be information items that can also be shipped over the same communication links. But the majority of the items will be physical ones requiring transportation from a manufacturing site to a warehouse and then to the consumer's address. Thus, it is fair to say that transportation is the last leg of electronic commerce. The likelihood that it also will be a customer of information marketed electronically makes a discussion of transportation even more appropriate.

There is yet another reason for devoting special attention to transportation: Many of the challenges in transportation, particularly the movement of people and goods in a congested transportation system, are common to transportation of other things, such as pieces of information over wires and airwaves. Thus, some of the optimization procedures used for congested transportation systems may be the first approximations to appropriate models of optimization for the crowded communication systems.

Transportation accounts for about 11 percent of the gross national product of the United States—approximately $800 billion. It has had a unique position among industrial activities in the United States. For many years it has been the beneficiary of the Highway Trust Fund, which is derived from the federal gasoline tax (12 cents per gallon, which amounts to $13 billion annually). This fund financed the interstate highway system, which has been a prime driver of commerce in the United States, and in principle it is available for continued improvement of the transportation infrastructure. It is generally accepted that we are reaching the end of the period of seeking such improvements through construction of new highways, and the time has come to strive for improved use of the available roadway network. The improvements are necessary in order to allow the handling of continuously increasing volumes of traffic over the existing transportation networks worldwide. It is certainly no secret that many parts of these networks are terribly congested during long periods every day, particularly in major metropolitan areas.

Concern about the deterioration of transportation systems has been building up over the past few decades. Transportation has been targeted for a drastic restructuring through the use of advance computer and communication technology under the label Intelligent Transportation Systems. The idea is to use advanced technology to improve the utilization of the existing roadway network by such measures as minimizing contention for the use of roadways, reducing the deleterious effects of accidents and other incidents, and eventually even increasing the through-put of transportation links through automation.

In what follows, I outline a likely scenario of evolutionary developments in the transportation domain that may lead to an advanced transportation infrastructure by the year 2008.

Intelligent Transportation Systems The development of Intelligent Transportation Systems (ITS) has been underway in the United States and abroad for well over a decade. In the United States, it received a particularly important impetus from the signing of the Intermodal Surface Transportation Efficiency Act (ISTEA) in December 1991, at the end of the last year of the federal program that created the interstate highway system. ISTEA was to be the beginning of the next phase of development of the transportation infrastructure, involving the improved use of existing facilities, with ISTEA providing seed money, but not sole funding, for achieving this improved use. Since the signing of ISTEA, the US government has funded many projects in the ITS area, including the development of a national ITS architecture, many demonstration studies, and an ambitious project aiming at producing a demonstration of an Automated Highway System well before the end of the millennium. ISTEA was the beginning of a sustained effort by the US government to improve the national transportation system through the use of high technology. ISTEA and its successor acts are expected to provide $45 billion over 5 years for the improvement of the transportation infrastructure, with $500 million allocated for the development and demonstration of ITS technology.

The promise of ITS is based on the concept of using advanced computer and communication technology in vehicles and in the roadway infrastructure to drastically improve the operation of transportation systems. The need for such improvement is evident from data showing the deleterious effects of congestion. In the United States, the estimated the cost of delays due to congestion is $46 billion in urban areas and $76 billion overall, and this is likely to increase as much as fourfold in a decade unless something is done to reverse current trends. Accidents and degradation of air quality are other deleterious effects of congestion. The situation is even worse in more congested parts of the world, such as

Japan and most European countries. ITS is seen as a means for drastically altering this path toward continued degradation of the quality of life.

The concept of ITS encompasses all modes of transportation and addresses the needs of all users. However, it is clear from the course of its development thus far that the deployment of ITS will depend on the ability of various sectors of the economy, including the transportation industry and consumers at large, to assume some of the costs of deployment on the basis of actual and perceived benefits.

The goals of ITS have been defined by ITS America, a national consortium of industrial, academic, and governmental organizations promoting ITS and serving as an advisory body to the US Department of Transportation, as being the following:

improved safety
reduced congestion
increased and higher quality mobility
reduced environmental impact
improved energy efficiency
improved economic productivity
a viable ITS industry in the United States.

ITS was defined by the Federal Highway Administration as comprising 29 services listed in table 1. Management of railroad crossings was subsequently added, further expanding the scope of ITS and raising the number of services to 30. The list of 30 services conveys the desire to eliminate many of the obstacles to the smooth movement of goods and people caused by traffic congestion, but also by some self-imposed bureaucratic practices. Among the latter, a prime example is Commercial Vehicle Operations, which are currently greatly burdened by record keeping and border crossing clearance requirements.

Overall, ITS provides the ability to understand where vehicles are, to take into account their desired destination, and to help them reach their destinations in the most expeditious manner and with the least contention for the use of roadways. A trucking company is, of course, a prime candidate for services such as monitoring of the location of cargo and equipment, providing navigation assistance and route guidance, and providing en route information, but the same services are needed to various

Table 1
ITS services.

___

Travel and traffic management
Pre-trip travel information
En route driver information
Route guidance
Ride matching and reservation
Traveler services information
Traffic control
Incident management
Travel demand management

Public transportation management
En route transit information
Personalized public transit
Public travel security

Electronic payment services

Commercial vehicle operations
Electronic clearance
Automated roadside safety inspection
Onboard safety monitoring
Administrative processes
Hazardous material incident response
Fleet management

Emergency management
Notification and personal security
Vehicle management

Advanced vehicle safety systems
Longitudinal collision avoidance
Lateral collision avoidance
Intersection collision avoidance
Vision enhancement for crash avoidance
Pre-crash restraint deployment
Safety readiness

___

degrees by the truck fleet of a utility company, the vehicles of a distribution fleet, the vehicles of a car rental company, and a host of other industrial and governmental units. Thus, provision of ITS services is a fundamental need of a modern society, and this need will continue to increase as the volume of commercial activities increases. Table 2 illustrates how the various elemental functions associated with ITS are needed, to various degrees, by various industries. That table dramatizes the fact that functions associated with the movement of objects and people are integral to virtually all the essential industries of a modern society.

ITS in all its glory is not going to be installed overnight. Budgetary constraints, safety considerations, and other factors will affect the deployment of various elements of ITS. The following scenario for the evolution of ITS services is based on a realistic assessment of the possibilities.

State and local government entities currently responsible for delivering traffic management services will continue to invest in improvement of these services through the development of advanced traffic management systems, including coordination of freeway and arterial traffic control, and improved incident management. These services, coupled with electronic toll collection, will provide the first elements of ITS without a substantial increase in the budgets of traffic management authorities.

Managers of commercial fleets, in conjunction with public service providers, will develop Commercial Vehicle Operations services aimed at improving the productivity of this important transportation sector. The commercial fleet sector may also provide the proving ground, and early commercialization, of hardware and software necessary for delivering such services as pre-trip travel information, en-route driver information, route guidance, and traveler services information. This is because commercial fleet managers will be able to realize a competitive advantage from the investment necessary for these services. Private independent service providers may join public-sector agencies in delivering some of the above services.

Collaboration of public-sector and private-sector service providers will bring about the entire set of Travel and Traffic Management services to the general driving public. Improvements in public transportation man-

Table 2
ITS services needed by various industries.

	Tracking	Utilities	Railroads	Distribution	Travel
Vehicle ID	Truck ID	Truck ID	Train ID	Truck ID	Car ID
Cargo/equipment ID	Cargo ID	Equipment ID	Rail car ID	Cargo ID	Car renter ID
Location	Fleet location	Fleet location	Train location	Truck location	Vehicle location
Navigation	High	Medium		High	Medium
Scheduling	High	High	High (freight)	High	Medium
Real-time dispatch	High	High	High	High	Medium
Communication	High	High	High	High	Medium
Route guidance	High	Medium-high		High	High
Traveler information	Medium	Low	High	High	High
Electronic payment	High	Medium	High	High	High
Administrative functions	High	High	High	High	Medium
Collision avoidance	High	High	High	High	High
Safety inspection	High	High	High	High	High
Surveillance	High	High	High	High	High
Demand management	High	High	High	High	High
Traffic control	High	High	High	High	High

agement and in emergency management will bring about sophisticated ITS systems comprising virtually all the ITS services except those involving extensive automation of the driving function. It is generally agreed that the latter will require many years of development and experimentation before any wide introduction becomes feasible. However, various advanced vehicle safety systems aimed at aiding drivers in carrying out their driving tasks safely will appear as a natural evolution of safety features of vehicles.

The evolution of ITS is likely to involve an uneven development of the various services, involving both public-sector and private-sector service providers and stimulated by federal funding. Though the eventual integration of all these services into an overall system is both desirable and likely, it is not necessary at the outset. There are opportunities for improving the transportation scene by providing many of the 30 services selectively, attracting users on the basis of direct benefits.

By 2008, commercial uses of ITS will be well established on the basis of the financial benefits derived from them. Trucking and distribution fleets and bus fleets will avail themselves of the full range of ITS instrumentation, including such gear as Global Positioning System locators, onboard navigation aids, digital data communication, and built-in computers. This will allow operators of commercial vehicles to automate many of the clearance and scheduling procedures and thus to substantially increase their productivity. In addition, it will allow them to make use of information from public-sector and private-sector information providers aimed at mitigating the impact of traffic congestion.

By 2008, the use of ITS services will also have reached a large percentage of the commuting public. ITS-enabled vehicles will be able to make use of the full range of ITS services (figure 1). Traffic movement in any particular region will be managed by a Traffic Management Center (TMC), which will be communicating with other TMCs in order to exchange information useful in coordinating traffic flows between TMCs. The entire ITS complex will be as much a system of mobile distributed intelligence as a transportation system.

Vehicles will be able to locate themselves accurately within a few feet, using GPS backed up with dead reckoning (incremental evaluation of position based on a previous estimate and on measurements of driving

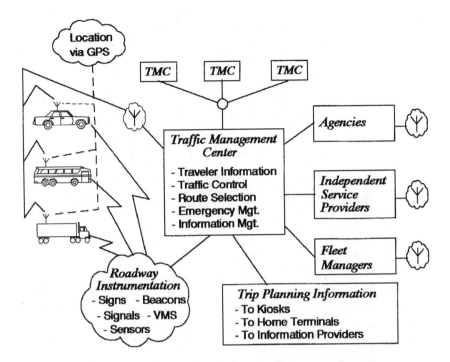

Figure 1

and steering movements). Vehicles will be able to communicate with the regional TMC and, as needed and/or desired, with independent service providers. The concept of service providers other than public-sector authorities is strongly supported by the US Department of Transportation, which sees it as a means for bringing in the private-sector resources in order to accelerate the deployment of ITS. The concept presents unknown, but potentially vast, business opportunities for the private sector, involving the marketing of the new resource of our times, information. Much information is even currently available, which never reaches those who could benefit from it. Examples are weather and pavement condition information collected by traffic authorities, as well as detailed traffic measurements. It is expected that ISPs may obtain such information, process as needed, and pass it on to user subscribers. ISP may even take over some or all the functions of a TMC if privatization trends in this area follow current optimistic expectations. Finally, fleet

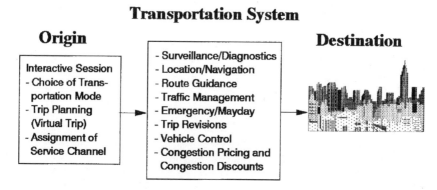

Figure 2

managers and agencies involved in the movement of goods and people will also be networked into the system in order to carry out their functions in real time.

All users will have a User Profile which comprises characteristics of both the users and the vehicles they operate, such as the following:

Onboard instrumentation
  onboard computing
  onboard databases (e.g. digitized maps)
  communication capability
  user interfaces (e.g. voice, display)
  driver-aid equipment available onboard (e.g. adaptive cruise control)
Personal characteristics
  regular commuting destinations
  route type preference (freeways versus side streets)
  preferred user interfaces

Before setting out on a trip, the users may enter modifiers to their profiles, then plan the trip aided by inputs from the system in addition to information available at their home base, onboard their vehicle, or even at a kiosk operated by a service provider. Users may even go through a "virtual trip" simulation, playing out what a driver sees during the trip, in order to familiarize themselves with features which can provide bearings. This trip planning process will take into account the topography of the area as well as the historical records of local traffic, and any information available about current traffic conditions. At this trip planning stage, a user may negotiate a service channel (SC) through the system. The SC will be a suggested trajectory through the system reserved for a specific user, which specific arrival times at various points along the trajectory. The SC will be compatible with the fairly accurate estimates of expected traffic patterns which the TMC will be able to produce on the basis of information it will receive from both infrastructure sensors and the users of the system. The SC will include a suggested departure time and route to be followed for optimum execution of the trip. The concept of a SC may appear to be as one involving relinquishing one's freedom of choice, but it is not. First, we may note that the system in effect assigns a SC to a user even in the absence of a negotiation such as described above. The SC is the movement in time and space that a user is destined to follow once she makes a choice of departure time and route. We may even observe that users in effect attempt to purchase an improved SC when they choose a toll road instead of a side street. A negotiated SC based on accurate real-time information will improve the driving experience of every user.

In exchange for receiving a SC, the user will agree to comply with the route assigned by the TMC. This will hardly be a sacrifice, since this route will most likely be the best one available. To further induce compliance, participating users may also be given a "Congestion Price Discount" if Congestion Pricing is implemented along their route. Congestion Pricing is a variable toll, increasing with anticipated congestion, which is beginning to be used in heavily congested areas around the world, in order to discourage drivers from overloading an already heavily loaded area.

Once a user enters a vehicle into the traffic, the vehicle will become an object of surveillance as well as an agent of surveillance, to the extent that it can transmit information to the TMC about road and traffic conditions. It is neither necessary nor expected that all vehicles will be able to transmit as well as receive information, although automatic transponders will be available for this task. Even a partial use of traveling vehicles as probes of traffic conditions will improve the surveillance information available to the TMC. On the basis of this surveillance, the TMC will adopt appropriate algorithms and strategies for the deployment of traffic in the area, in a way that minimizes the inconvenience to the users caused by contention for roadway space and delivers to them the assigned SCs. Total integration of ITS services will allow the coordination of traffic control signals for actual rather than assumed traffic streams, improving the efficiency of the overall system and smoothing the flow of traffic. The assignment of SCs will allow prevention of congestion over much of the space and time domains of the traffic system. Route revisions will be implemented in response to emergencies such as "incidents".

"Mayday" functions will be an integral part of the system, activated automatically, without the intervention of an incapacitated driver if necessary. Finally, by 2008, some experimentation with devices taking over control of some driving functions will be deployed. The main emphasis will be on driver aids to accident avoidance, such as devices which take over control of a vehicle which is headed for a longitudinal or lateral collision. In addition, the current versions of cruise control will be supplanted by "adaptive cruise control", allowing a driver to latch a vehicle into a platoon of vehicles by making it follow another vehicle, instead of setting a fixed cruising speed, with the driver retaining the responsibility of steering, together with override capability on the longitudinal movement.

Full automation of the driving functions are not likely to show up on highways, although demonstrations of such capabilities will be carried out under federal funding. Such full automation, known as Automatic Highway Systems (AHS), are pursued for three reasons: improved safety, increased highway capacity, and convenience to drivers. It is the first two reasons which are likely to drive the development of automated highways, since they correspond to measurable financial benefits. The improvement of safety would result by first aiding and eventually replacing a human driver in cases of impending accidents, with automated devices providing improved sensing and timeliness of reaction compared to human drivers. The improvement of throughput is possible through elimination of the limitations of a human driver in safely following a dense driving pattern. For example, a human driver requires at least one second before reacting to any stimulus from a vehicle in front. Overall, a human driver has a difficulty maintaining a headway (time-spacing between cars), smaller than two seconds, corresponding to a throughput of 1,800 vehicles per lane per hour. Automation can, in principle, increase throughput by a factor of 2, 3, 4, or more, by decreasing headways by these factors, assuming that vehicle characteristics can be made compatible, and administrative arrangements, including legal ones, can be worked out satisfactorily. It is generally accepted that operation of AHS is not likely to be in place before at least another 20 years. However, it is possible that some degree of automation may start being introduced by 2008 in operating critical, expensive, traffic links such as bridges, tunnels, and certain overloaded sections of freeways, for which the cost of automation is rationalized by the prohibitive cost of replication.

The deployment of ITS will require investment by the users as well as the traffic management authorities. In fact, it is generally accepted that users will bear the greatest percentage of required investment in ITS gear, perhaps as much as 80 percent. However, this investment will be justified by a vastly improved driving environment for all users.

Delivering sensible advice to drivers is a real challenge that will make or break ATIS, the traveler information services of ITS. Many knowledgeable transportation specialists have observed that the worst possible ATIS scenario is telling people just that traffic is horrible ahead, a fact they probably already know. An even worse implementation of ATIS would deliver information that users eventually find unreliable, leading to alienation and non-compliance.

Reliable information to travelers requires accurate modeling of the traffic movement which can deliver accurate extrapolation into the future in estimating such parameters as expected travel times between points on a network. The state of the art of traffic modeling is of mixed quality. On one hand, there is a multitude of bad models based on inappropriate modeling of the properties of traffic links, ignoring the unidirectional influence of traffic, limited only to influence on upstream vehicles. Such inappropriate modeling has led to the "discovery" of paradoxes and other extraneous lore that litters the transportation literature. On the other hand, some sensible modeling of traffic movement during periods of congestion has been contributed by traffic theorists, including this author. It is based on the notion that during congestion what constrains the movement of traffic is the existence of Throughput Limiting Points

(TLPs). TLPs arise either along a traffic link because of an incident or other change of lane capacity, or at the convergence of two streams discharging into a downstream link with capacity insufficient to serve all the traffic. The movement of traffic in a network containing one or more TLPs is a store-and-forward movement, with traffic stored upstream of TLPs until it can be discharged. Techniques for optimizing the traffic movement in a store-and-forward network have been developed, and can be used for estimating with sufficient accuracy travel times between points of the network. They can also be eventually used in assigning service channels to users in a way that minimizes contention for the use of roadways. It is only with such proper consideration of the behavior of traffic that ITS will fulfill its promise of improving the quality of life for everyone.

The deployment of ITS is not proceeding as fast as its most avid proponents would like, and probably not as fast as it should. The main reason is that the perceived benefits by potential users are not compelling enough to induce them to make the necessary investments in ITS. To be sure, some navigation equipment has been sold to the most affluent among potential users, or to Japanese motorists who really need it because of the inadequacy or road markings in Japan. But large scale investment in ITS is still lagging.

The Internet may hold the key to accelerating the deployment of ITS, by providing the means for early marketing of traveler information services. Here is the scenario: Traffic management authorities must collect information about traffic conditions in order to do their job well. Additional information is collected by companies such as Metro Traffic, or Shadow Traffic, and broadcast over the airwaves. The information obtained by traffic management authorities is generally unavailable to travelers, while the broadcast information reaches a few, but in a hit-or-miss fashion. Some of the information is beginning to reach the Internet in the form of color-coded diagrams of traffic conditions, as is the case in Seattle, for example, through the good services of the University of Washington. Additional information of possible use to a traveler may be available from other sources. For example, various agencies provide current, even real-time, information on availability of ride-sharing opportunities. In addition, bus companies are increasingly able to provide real-time location of their buses, in addition to their scheduled location, and they are beginning to post such information on the Internet.

The time has come to collect some of this information, package it, and make it available to travelers. However, in order to make this information really useful and usable, some improvements in the utilization of the Internet will be needed.

In the short term, PASHAs can be used to accelerate the deployment of ITS. In the long term, PASHAs can become an integral part of many ITS services.

The short term application of PASHAs will be to have them collect from the Internet, as well as from any other sources accessible by a computer, information useful to a person planning and carrying out a trip over a transportation network. The PASHAs will process this information and deliver helpful suggestions for a trip, both at the planning stage and en route. Information of this kind will be useful to commuters and businesses alike. Business which can use such information directly in their operations are obviously those operating fleets of vehicles, like truck and bus companies. Other businesses are those engaged in distribution, car rental companies, and also companies operating a fleet of service vehicles, such as utility companies. And in the final analysis, most of the items sold over the Internet, other than information, must travel to their destination, and so all businesses are indirectly affected by the efficiency of the movement of goods and people. Specifically, here is how PASHAs can help travelers.

One of the core functions of ITS is the provision of timely advice to travelers which would allow them to plan and carry out their trip with the minimum discomfort and inconvenience. First, they would be able to plan their trip by choosing the best of several available transportation modes, and then they would be able to move from their origin to their destination by making appropriate adjustment to their routes dictated by current traffic conditions, including non-recurrent events such as incidents which have been recognized as causing the bulk of delays in most major metropolitan areas.

The deployment of ITS has been delayed by the lack of funds necessary for the optimum deployment of requisite technologies. The use of PASHAs can allow delivery of two important services to users for a small investment. The services are *pre-trip travel planning information* and *en route traveler information* (particularly concerning incidents, coupled with advice on recommended incident avoidance action). The former requires only access to a computer at the origin, while the latter also requires an onboard communication link and the ability to estimate the location of a vehicle with sufficient accuracy in order to identify the relevant incidents and traffic conditions.

The three functions of the agent in rendering service in this case are defined as follows:

input preparation   Information useful for making travel decisions is currently unevenly available around the country. However, there is a growing trend to use the Internet in order to disseminate information which is either currently available over the radio, or can be obtained from the traffic and public transit authorities. It is very likely that this trend will result in wide availability over the Internet of information concerning public transit schedules and current performance, ride-sharing availability, traffic conditions, and other relevant information such as weather and road surface conditions. The information available over the Internet is currently, and will probably be for the foreseeable future, disseminated in various forms including text, images (frequently color-coded), and diagrams. One of the necessary functions is to reduce all this information to an input form appropriate for the use of available computational algorithms. In due course, emerging standards will simplify this task considerably.

computational enhancement   This is undeniably the most important step in the process of traveler information services. The translation of raw information concerning traffic conditions into accurate estimates of travel times across a network is still not a very well developed practice. However, advanced algorithms are becoming available which can yield, among other things, the following important information: Given standard measurements of traffic volumes obtained with traditional traffic sensors, we can derive an exact estimate of the number of vehicles along sections of the roadway between sensors and an accurate estimate of expected travel times between various points on the network, over several minutes in the future, based on currently available information concerning traffic conditions and incidents, augmented with historical information concerning traffic demand in the area served by the network. Using these algorithms, the agent of a particular user will obtain personalized information concerning available options of trip-planning as well as adjustments to a trip dictated by real-time information. For example, trip-planning information can be obtained while a traveler is getting ready for a trip, allowing for timely adjustments to a travel mode, route, and starting time, aimed at minimizing contention with other travelers. If a traveler decides to drive his own vehicle, the computational enhancement phase will continue to provide timely advice concerning recommended changes in the trip plan due to changing traffic conditions. It is anticipated that information en-route will be transmitted by voice which is the most acceptable communication type in such a situation.

decision making Because of the nature of this application, most decisions will be left to the user, with the agent providing advice in the most concise and intelligible form. However, the agent may be given the responsibility of initiating contacts for the purpose of such actions as registering for ride sharing, obtaining a public transit ticket if necessary, and notifying friends and associates of the progress of one's trip.

Dissemination of the information by the PASHA can be done over a computer terminal in the form of text and graphics, before the start of a trip. En route, the user may leave the PASHA in a stationary computer and receive the information, as needed, over a suitable communication link such as a cellular phone. Alternatively, the user may carry along an Internet-enabled portable computer hosting a PASHA. In any case, the information would best be disseminated in the form of voice instructions, to minimize interference with driving tasks, but it can be coupled with visual information such as simple graphs. A PASHA's natural language processing capability will include text creation, after which a text to speech conversion is a natural extension. Current text to speech conversion produces voice of rather cavernous quality, but human quality is attainable well before 2008.

Use of PASHAs for delivering traveler information services can accelerate deployment of ITS, obviating the need of immediate large investments. When advanced ITS deployment is in place, some of the services of PASHAs described above may be provided by independent service providers, who may use varieties of software to provide them. This does not mean that PASHAs will retire. Rather, they will evolve into new capabilities enabled by ITS deployment. For example, a future PASHA will act as a driver's agent in negotiating the assignment of a service channel, electronic payment of any related fees, and so on. The PASHA may continue to reside in the user's computer, or it may use guest facilities of a large server on the site of a traffic management authority. It will continue carrying out its function of pre-processing the information received from the system on behalf of its master and presenting to the master what is needed for an optimal decision in a timely fashion.

There is a significant role for PASHAs in the commercial sector as well. One example may be the tracking of critical shipments by PASHAs. A PASHA may act as the personal agent for the distribution vehicle, or even for a particular shipment. It will monitor the movement of the shipment and the traffic conditions along its route, calling for action if the delivery begins to depart significantly from schedule. If it determines that the shipment is about to miss a critical deadline, it may initiate an alternate delivery from the same supplier or a different one. Once more, the profit motive of a commercial operation will justify the development and use of sophisticated PASHAs, spearheading their use in transportation. The trucking industry employs 9 million people in 360,000 companies in the United States, generating gross revenues of about $400 billion through shipments of 5.5 billion tons of freight, using 4 million trucks. The trucking business is growing at 6 to 9 percent yearly. In recent years it has devoted an increasing percentage of its effort in just-in-time shipments, thus reducing inventories at the receiving end. These volumes and trends speak eloquently for the need of improvements in the management of shipments, such as those that PASHAs can provide.

Epilogue

It has been often said by proponents of ITS that the technology for its deployment is all there, and that all we need is a plan and the necessary funds in order to make it happen. The statement is largely true when it comes to hardware, but it falls short of being perfectly true concerning the software and algorithms that will be needed in order to make the deployment of ITS successful. Some of the groundwork for effective surveillance, timely incident detection, and dynamic allocation of roadway capacity to competing traffic streams has been laid, but much work remains to be done before reliable ITS can be deployed. Intelligent agents in general, and their PASHA variety in particular, can play an important role in accelerating progress in this area. They provide a capability for modular deployment of intelligence, and they can be constructed in a modular fashion themselves, taking advantage of current advances in object-oriented programming.

Transportation is but one area in which PASHAs can have a significant impact. A multitude of human activities can benefit from the use of PASHAs as intermediaries in mobilizing technology for the service of humans. PASHAs can improve access to this technology for everyone. Even more important, they can broaden the population of users to include many who today shy away from the use of high technology because of its less-than-friendly nature. Perhaps PASHAs can even help humanize technology somewhat. In any case, they hold promise of giving a considerable boost to the deployment of the electronic marketplace.

III

Impalpable Wealth: The Economy Set Free

6

Work Remade: An Electronic Marketplace Inside the Corporation

David Braunschvig

Remember all the talk about the relationship between productivity growth and real gains in purchasing power? Easily one of the least objectionable ideas of business economics, this relationship is also the most elusive and difficult to translate into specific measures suitable for public or private sector initiatives. Yet the application of methods from the emerging sector of electronic commerce to the inner workings of the corporation provides a glimmer of hope, responding to managers' concern that improvements in information and communication should be indeed enabling factors, not ends in themselves.

Now made possible by open standards and supported by intranets, communities of transactions within and among companies are changing the way people relate in the workplace, promoting significant productivity gains. Transactions in the workplace include, but are not limited to, monetized exchanges. They encompass agreements between individuals or groups to conduct initiatives that have a direct impact on a firm's ability to increase the quantity or quality of its output.

And the meaning of "workplace" is expanding as we watch. Transparency is increasing not only within the corporation but all along inter-corporate lines—manufacturing, distribution, and sales—crossing barriers that only a few years ago looked like international frontiers. Until recently, inter-corporate relations have too often been the business of specially assigned functionaries, usually with only a secondary knowledge of real corporate needs; now, the work can be done cooperatively between the people who should work together—and if we are to compete with rivals whose assumptions about process integration were not shaped

70 years ago by snail mail, bad long-distance telephone service, and railway timetables—it is about time.

In turn, companies will be rewarded with valuations commensurate with their ability to put the infrastructure in place and manage the right incentives to support these communities. This could well be the opportunity of last resort for mature economies challenged by companies from younger, hungrier countries and cultures—short of the protectionist temptations that crop up occasionally, that is.

Electronic Commerce in Perspective

Electronic Data Interchange (EDI) services, the first applications of electronic commerce, were aimed at automating pre-existing relationships between suppliers and corporate customers, mostly in support of the procurement function of manufacturing industries. Since its inception more than 20 years ago, EDI has hardly met the promise of a technology that proposed to generate significant gains in productivity: currently, only about 100,000 companies use some form of EDI, often under pressure from trading partners.

Arguably, one of the causes of this disappointment was the absence of common standards for EDI despite the numerous but ill-coordinated attempts by governments and industry coalitions in the United States and elsewhere to agree on protocols. The Internet's open infrastructure has lifted this constraint, yielding new prospects for a spectrum of electronic transactions involving not only economic agents with existing trading relationships but also companies attempting to develop new commercial links. General Electric Information Services, a leader in EDI, announced in late 1996 that it was teaming up with Netscape Communications to make possible Internet-supported, business-to-business transactions, joining the ranks of parallel combinations such as the MCI-Digital-Microsoft entente.

The vitalizing force of free markets is their incompleteness: existing weaknesses are exposed, to be met with different approaches. For example, the unnecessary overheads of the processing aspects of insurance and banking will go down under competition from outfits taking a more streamlined approach. This will create new opportunities for efficiency (or simply supply) to meet the challenge of new entrants and new processes in these areas. With the Internet and intranets in place, international comparative advantage is going to work not at the level of bulk goods but at the level of individual initiative. A bacteriologist in Lübeck who needs to analyze data on different strains of *E. coli* need only buzz Bahawalpur; a comptroller in Muncie puzzled by anomalies in Pacific Rim sales can get them clarified from Dhaka. Immigration and emigration become movements of tasks, not of bodies.

The prospect of an exponential expansion of the trading universe has generated an excitement as great as, and possibly more sustainable than, the sunrise enthusiasms of the Internet per se. Global commerce is a logical extension of the Internet's ideal of instant universal access. Thanks to electronic transactions, global commerce can fulfill the promise of simultaneous, international access and considerable net economies for both producers and consumers because of disintermediation of traditional distribution channels.

Moreover, electronic commerce can impart to itself an authority resting upon its much-vaunted—if not yet remotely realized—economic prospects, positioning itself as a more pragmatic rendition of the visions awakened by the first generation of the Internet and by the informality of its services (chatting, "browsing," content downloading, etc.). Few business models have proved resilient enough to outlive early investors' enthusiasm for these prospects; most business models have been driven more by fear of missing a great opportunity than by any adequate capacity to analyze or cost it.

Meanwhile, a second generation of Internet applications has emerged, narrower in reach but deeper in effectiveness. These tend to focus on the internal environment of the firm, capitalizing on the realization that the corporate environment offers closely-knit communities and a willingness and an ability to pay for services far exceeding those of other communities, e.g. voluntary associations.

Accordingly, the emergence of intranet services, which can be dated to early 1996, represents prospects for many applications that seem more commercially tangible than Internet-based applications. Following the pattern of Internet businesses' focusing on narrower targets, we must clarify the issue of whether electronic commerce applications can be applied to exchanges of information and judgment between individuals within and among corporations, and not only to monetized transactions between economic agents.

Communication, Information, or Transactions?

Of course, the idea of empowering employees with information technology is hardly a novel proposition. The concept of "groupware" is well established, and not only in the world of corporate information technology. Groupware, whether supported by a simple LAN-based configuration or by a more elaborate intranet environment, is simply another instrument for sharing information and facilitating communications among co-workers.

There has been vigorous debate as to whether our service productivity is really stagnant and to what extent information technology enables, is neutral toward, or impairs productivity growth. Regardless of the answer, enough evidence exists to substantiate the fact that, as they migrate to the desktop, IT "solutions" contribute very little to an individual service worker's effectiveness in getting things done with his colleagues.

The current reality of everyday office life is an overload of email and a plethora of information sources, hardly clarified or made rigorous by the introduction of workgroup technology and filtering devices—each enforcing new unreconciled interfaces. Indeed, there are indications that Web browsing and emailing in the workplace are often viewed as distractions and even as misuses of corporate resources.

This suggests that current groupware applications can wash the most focused users of the services ("masters marked," as Goethe says, "by their powers of renunciation") onto the sandbanks of the information sea precisely because they will not surf. So should we expect to witness an anti-IT backlash from an emerging constituency not of neo-Luddites but of back-to-basics zealots?

Perhaps in order to avert this risk, companies have been curtailing, controlling, and managing the incentives associated with electronic communications. In 1996, Computer Associates, a leading supplier of enterprise software products, started shutting down its corporate email services for four working hours every day. Why? One of the company's executives said simply "It causes people to be more thoughtful."[1] Similarly, SmithKline Beecham, a classic example of a research-based firm that should be ceaselessly striving to encourage internal collaboration, is quietly fining employees suspected of generating excessive email traffic.

Managers are increasingly mindful that improvements in information and communication are at best enabling factors, not ends in themselves: a firm's performance should not be measured by its internal information flows, nor can professional services and employee incentives be correlated with the total megabits of email sent or received. Ultimately, a firm's success is measured by its contribution to shareholder value, which derives from its ability to generate revenues and profits and to sustain growth expectations. Since firms do not operate in a vacuum but achieve these results by effecting transactions with other economic agents, shouldn't the primary focus of technology be to facilitate these transactions ?

To put it simply: corporate IT managers have long realized that knowledge alone is not of itself power, but only more recently have they drawn the corollary that effective use of knowledge is not a function of its abundance and may in fact be just the opposite. A corporation succeeds by using information effectively—the more effectively it uses information, the less it is distracted from its economic mission under the pretense of increasing or improving information flows. The challenge is to leverage the Internet infrastructure to extend the application of electronic commerce to transactions that enhance the corporation's performance, achieving measurable benefits for its users.

Beyond Collaboration

The spreading grasp of the potential and limitations of IT in the workplace is hastening the advent of collaborative applications. The evolution of technology-enabled corporate environments may be schematized in three stages, as table 1 shows.

In the first half of the 1990s, the advent of connectivity standards made possible point-to-point communications on a large scale in the matrix of a corporation.

In the first stage, end users used the Internet to take giant steps (more often than not in questionable directions) and were ecstatic; very soon, they were painfully hung over. The perception of dysfunctionalities

Table 1

	Stage		
	Free-form	Structured	Transactional
Examples of applications	E-mail Browsing Content downloading	Calendering Scheduling Coordination	Incentive-based and results-oriented individual actions and group tasks
Mainstream introduction (vendors)	1992–1995 (early Lotus Notes, Microsoft, Netscape)	1997 (Notes 4.5, Navigator 4.0, Office 97)	1999+
Aim	Connectivity	Cohesiveness	Productivity
Issues	Dysfunctionality	Intangible results	Measurement

resulting from the free-form nature of this type of connectivity is the basis of the demand for more structured collaborative environments.

In the second stage, applications that were meant to facilitate the initiative of an individual "knowledge worker" within the group or groups to which he belongs were generated. These applications are designed to enhance the coordination of tasks, the tracking of initiatives, and the production of steady standards that can be used to expedite workflow.[2] Such promises lay at the core of Lotus Notes and of similar applications that only recently have been fully integrated in their standard offerings. More structured environments designed for the deployment of collaborative applications represents a significant improvement over the earlier tools, but even these environments still aim at increasing information efficiency rather than establishing their usefulness to the material outcome of the owners' and consumers' objectives (i.e., services that have a direct, measurable impact on performance).

It is to meet the very practical test of performance enhancement that transactional environments have been developed. In this third stage, information technology is deployed to support transactions—operating processes, not just the pingponging of information—between individuals and groups, within and among firms. For instance:

• Managers in different procurement divisions of a manufacturing company combine to design and implement a procedure that produces large savings for the company.

• R&D and marketing managers launch an initiative that leads to the rollout of new products.

• Line managers develop methods to expand output with a smaller corresponding increase in costs.

• Customer service personnel coordinate an initiative to improve the quality of service that results in higher customer satisfaction and increased sales.

To be sure, the scope of such tasks varies substantially by sector and type of enterprise, and the examples cited above embody obvious guidelines that any reasonable manager would emphasize. Yet it is the current availability of shared networks and customizable applications that lends credibility to the idea of a more decentralized organization in which individuals and group spontaneously undertake productive initiatives (the much-touted "virtual corporation").

Creating a transactional environment includes, but goes beyond, optimizing the flow of work in an organization, a well-charted area of management sciences (see the definition in note 2). Traditionally, workflow management addresses productivity improvement, assumes a better understanding of tasks undertaken, and relies on the application of information technology in support of a more effective deployment of resources—not only a communications enhancement device. Workflow optimization has usually been used in the context of corporate downsizing and thus tends to focus more on reducing the denominator than on increasing the numerator of the productivity quotient.[3]

The application of groupware technologies, such as Lotus Notes, has indeed led to effective improvements of productivity by reducing the costs associated with transactions processing—the most often cited examples being the mortgage approval cycle in commercial banking and the underwriters' process in insurance. Connecticut Mutual, for example, is known to have improved productivity through "workflow compression" (in this case, by collapsing its underwriting process). This requires breaking down tasks in ways and for purposes not dissimilar to those developed by Frederick Winslow Taylor decades ago. Approaches targeted at service functions, mostly developed in the 1970s and 1980s by US management consulting firms, applied these principles of cost control to administrative tasks.

Yet workflow management approaches still have shortcomings:

• They tend to focus on the denominator—the existing resource base, as most tightly defined—of the productivity quotient. As companies reap the benefits of corporate downsizing and learn to rely on their core competencies, they are becoming more sensitive to the question of how to increase the productivity *numerator*—that is, to augment the output or improve its quality by better leveraging the firm's current resources. Approaches based on workflow management seem to be naturally tailored to act on the denominator and thus might not be best suited to promoting the expansion or enhancement of outputs, all other things being equal.

• They rely implicitly on "command-and-control" management and on a linear vision of how to improve productivity. Tasks are formulated by internal or external specialists, analyzed[4] from their own idiosyncratic perspective, and mandatorily imposed on the "production process." However, in most real-life business situations the internal environment works itself into interplays akin to a market, with agents bargaining and compromising, rather than into a military organization with a hierarchical structure.

The objective of workflow management is to use information technology to improve means and enlarge the choice of ends, not just to manage information more efficiently. Having said that, I must add that if it operates simply on its basic tenets of focusing on cost reductions, and if linear decision flows are assumed, it can offer only narrow assistance outside the more hierarchical structures discussed above.

Over the last decade, the organization development experts have prayed the unending mantra of "process" to the point that this concept has seeped into our consciousness as a fact of the life of corporations, much as certain terms of Freudian psychology have gradually become accepted as proxies for self-perception; indeed, they have become parts of the psyche (or of the organization) even when they did not exist there before.

But what if the understanding of the "process" by which we get things done were often not only too complex to describe and "collapse" but also irrelevant to the goal of achieving a more productive organization?

Ironically, the model for a human organization still ideologically governed in the late 1990s by social-democratic ideology may be the for-profit corporation, inspired by its central planners—read, its organizational designers. A real boost in productivity, driven this time by the quotient's numerator, assumes an environment where negotiated transactions between free agents, subject to rules and incentives, prevail over mandated tasks because they maximize their productive capacity: the numerator's growth potential is likely to be greater than the capacity for contraction of the denominator.

Technologies of real-time electronic exchange—which transcend commerce because their marketplace is one of ideas and processes in general, regulated by overall response as well as by economic rationality—offer the means to go beyond the workflow paradigm and implement within the organization an internal market for transactions, which we think of as a workplace. Though the term "workplace," like "store," is actually archaic, a workplace is where human beings are brought together to work; but in the conditions coming into existence, physical adjacency or proximity are obviously not a prerequisite. The difference between information-oriented, process-oriented, and transactions-oriented methods is illustrated in table 2.

To be sure, attempts to facilitate transactions between corporate citizens precede the advent of Internet and intranet technologies. I recall my

Table 2

	Environment		
	Workgroup	Workflow	Workplace
Examples of applications	Collaborative information sharing (see stages I and II in table 1)	"Downsizing," "rightsizing," OVA, AVA, other cost-focused methods	Relationships between groups and individuals facilitated by technology and incentives
Result	Enhancement of information and communications	Process optimization	Marketplace for transactions

first professional experience in a multinational consulting firm, in the early 1980s. An announcement of a new assignment was posted in each location and each business unit at inception, serving as an internal Request for Qualifications (RFQ) to recruit an in-house consulting team of consultants best suited for the job on hand. Naïvely responding to some of these RFQs, I often found out that a team had already been assembled, that specific knowledge of the client's situation was required, or that the project was on hold until further notice. After a few attempts to respond to these announcements, I came to the realization that the project leader was quite comfortable relying on a team composed of trusted individuals, even if their qualifications were not optimal for the project. This RFQ system proved to be mere lip service to collaboration. Its gradual phaseout in the late 1980s signaled the failure of the organization's ability to leverage its human assets; it also confirmed that trust, not relevant knowledge, is often the determining factor in a highly unstructured production process such as a consulting assignment.

The RFQ blind alley was attributable to the adoption of fax technology, which facilitated simultaneous postings over widespread realms of activity. Could the use of more sophisticated, technology-enabled, collaborative environments, such as those emerging in the late 1990s, have cut channels for critical path information flows and kept information from flooding all areas, relevant and irrelevant? Because such environments facilitate the repeated execution of transactions involving the same participants and because they promote trust through renewed experiences, one could assume so. Yet it is doubtful that even the most natural and seamless environment would, in effect, support the dissemination of intra-corporate transactions without encouraging corporate citizens to participate by means of appropriate incentives. The fact that no rewards or penalties were associated with engaging in or abstaining from the RFQ process was probably at the root of the demise of the system cited above.

Requirements for Developing a Workplace Environment

The right incentive scheme is certainly a determining factor for the successful implementation of an internal marketplace for transactions. Other factors include determining measurable units for transactions, managing the internal transaction marketplace, providing tools that enable employees to evaluate and self-regulate the transactional environment, and ensuring the interoperability between intra-corporate and inter-corporate transactions. As I address these requirements, I will review the promise—and the limitations—of pilot projects or corporate ventures that are the prototypes of form, function, and "feel" for the next generation of corporate environments.

Identifying Transaction Terms

Workflow approaches have correctly stressed the need to define discrete tasks that can support a measurement of outcomes. Systematized components of overall transactions (e.g., a sales referral, a quality-enhancement initiative, a collaborative R&D breakthrough, spontaneous individual inputs to the management of a manufacturing process) must be defined a priori in order to create a measurable basis for transactions. The more these units are based on industry-wide standards, the more likely they are to be sustainable.

By an interesting paradox, this seems to be happening more comprehensively on the inter-governmental scene than on the inter-corporate one. A decade and a half ago, major conferences drew up new, simplified professional languages, such as Airspeak and Seaspeak, to avoid catastrophic ambiguity in the world's transit lanes. Morse Code will be phased out by early 1999; France and the US Coast Guard have already signed off. These processes were urgently driven by considerations of safety and efficient use of facilities—all convergent factors. The possibilities of divergent improvement have yet fully to possess the imaginations of those who must open up to them. Indeed, the Internet flourished initially because it enabled scientists to argue things out faster and to draw more deeply upon information. When corporate management (broadly defined) picks this up, things should start to happen very fast. Companies (mostly in the service sector) have already started to establish nomenclatures and protocols that can provide the basis for a commonly agreed definition of task spaces, which in turn should facilitate the development of application protocol interfaces (APIs).

An initial list of protocol categories has been developed by an association of US-based companies. Over 100 major corporations formed the

Workflow Management Coalition in 1993 to establish standards for APIs applied to workflow products. Five key areas are being developed:

process definition (definitions for workflow icons and tools for development of a common workflow)

process interoperability (standards that allow diverse workflow products to share and interact with each other)

tool invocation (standards for calling third-party tools such as email, document imaging, and applications)

client work list (a standard method for presenting work to a secondary process or end user)

status and management (standard reports for collecting workflow data from audit trails)

In addition to process-driven tasks that force themselves upon us, such as those above, less tangible contributions to value will increasingly be considered as transaction-oriented tasks. In particular, the trend toward a less centralized corporate structure is consistent with the need for groups and individuals to anticipate the fast-changing markets in which they operate. The introduction of a new generation of prototyping methods provides the means for them to develop perspectives on how a particular initiative (for a new product or service, a market introduction, etc.) will fare in a future market and in a competitive environment.

Agent-based simulation tools can enable corporate citizens to express their views on how an initiative can develop into a marketable product. An employee originating an initiative could be allocated the equivalent of a "phantom option" associated with a project designed with these simulation tools. The value of this option would depend on the outcome of the implementation of the project. The options could be broken down into components and traded for services by employees.

Once the tasks have been defined, the quantification of the measurement units must be developed—not a light task, but certainly a fascinating one. It is no accident that, to date, electronic commerce has centered on monetized transactions: Once the thorny issues of access, reliability, encryption, and co-optation of participants have been dealt with, the commercial prospects of currency-based electronic commerce seem obvious. Instead, most intra-corporate and inter-corporate transactions are not monetized and therefore are difficult to measure. It could well be that, over time, the value of a particular transaction results from a market-based appraisal by the user community.

The ultimate objective of a transactions-oriented internal marketplace is to contribute to the productivity of the enterprise. I argued above that there is ultimately a greater payoff associated with increasing the numerator of the productivity quotient than with decreasing its denominator, and that the ability of a transactions marketplace to increase output by better leveraging a constant expenditure of inputs is at stake. And growth in "output" certainly comprises more than a quantitative increase: qualitative improvements, shorter time to market, and competitive positioning should also be considered as desirable outcomes.

Among the pilot cases illustrating this point, that of the Baylor Health Care Management System, a four-hospital, 2000-bed not-for-profit organization in Dallas, stands out. Since early 1996, the BHCMS has been using Metro, a browser-fronted workflow tool from Action Technologies Inc. In a few months, the BHCMS managed to cut the time it takes to negotiate pharmaceutical contracts from three months to three weeks.[5] Although in this instance the initiative appears to be an experiment in technology deployment mandated by a company's corporate management, it is a prototype of an application for which specific incentives could be designed to encourage a spontaneous development of such initiatives in a transactions-based environment.

Managing the Transaction Marketplace

One of the most difficult tasks for the managers of an internal transactions marketplace is a political one: how to define the boundaries of the profit centers within the corporation. In a traditional "command-and-control" organization, rivalries between groups have a way of becoming intense when the rewards each group can derive from an initiative are mostly symbolic or subject to value judgments by superiors. The high degree of interpersonal tension in a transaction-oriented organization where the link between performance and reward is more transparent than in other sectors (for instance, sales-driven service industries) is all too well known: alliances between individuals and groups develop much more intensely in a unstructured corporate culture than in a more predictable process-driven environment. The prevalence of spontaneous alliance-building initiatives would argue for a significant emphasis by corporate managers on defining the "rules of the game." As in other aspects of life, the objective of this game is both to produce and to relate to others. In particular, conditions for associating with and disassociating from others would have to be spelled out in greater detail than in today's prevailingly hierarchical organizational cultures in order to avert corporate "balkanization." Like all marketplaces, the internal corporate environment is likely to be worthy of respect inasmuch as its regulatory system is perceived as balanced and trustworthy.

Another issue pertains to the internal management of recourse, mediation, and arbitration in the event that differences of opinion or claims formulated by employees or groups arise within the organization. The parallel with the legal systems is obvious here. A transactions-oriented environment is likely to transform the scope of the internal counsel function that has been present in corporations for decades, and this will require much more scrutiny in order to promote fairness and transparency (or at least its appearance).

The prospective role of management as a builder of infrastructure, a provider of regulation, and a facilitator of mediation in a transactional environment seems to emerge from this scenario. Yet management can and should do only so much if it is to avoid second-guessing its corporate citizens with invasive oversight. Fortunately, corporate executives can benefit from technologies originally developed in support of electronic commerce to assist employees with the means for evaluation and self-regulation.

Providing Tools for Evaluation and Self-Regulation

Profiling

Arguably, without an understanding of "who's who" that goes beyond the directory of an organization there can be no incentive to transact beyond a small circle of colleagues who are in close physical proximity or who share obvious commonalities of interest. Recent advances in Internet commerce are making this challenge less daunting.

Filtering devices enable individuals to gain access to what interests them. Symmetrically, these devices define profiles that enable individuals to be "understood" by others more accurately. For example, in 1996 and 1997 Firefly Networks Inc. developed applications that support the spontaneous creation of communities of interest in which participants can be drawn to one another on the basis of their preferences. Application of these technologies to the corporate environment should greatly facilitate discovery within the organization.

Mapping

The ability to understand an individual's actual role (not just his official function) is crucial to communication and to transaction. As interactions increasingly become supported electronically, the quantity, directionality, and relevance of a relationship can be calibrated and represented visually to resolve the information into specific rivers of most applicable usage to individual participants. This should enable a user to address his transaction queries to the most relevant protagonist in the organization.

For example, in the mid 1990s IBM started experimenting with a mapping technology that tracks the intensity of collaborations between employees and departments. Note that collaboration goes beyond flows of communication to encompass qualitative measures of joint initiative development. Figure 1 illustrates the discovery process of an individual in the market planning division of a New York location who seems particularly well connected to other employees, departments, and regional offices.[6]

Trust

Another emerging application of electronic commerce is the rating of individuals on the basis of their trustworthiness. For example, in 1996 Network Development Associates developed a product ("Net Deva") that helps participants to recommend "leads" and enables them to rate the validity and the trustworthiness of the agents making the requests.[7] How to establish trust is increasingly at the center of electronic transactions. Originally viewed narrowly as the key ingredient of financial transactions (such as those developed by the payment authorization

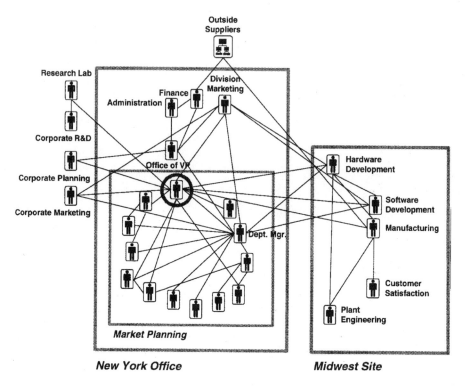

Figure 1

companies Cybercash, Digicash, and First Virtual Holdings), its scope is expanding to all types of transactions.

In 1996 the non-profit Electronic Frontier Foundation developed (in collaboration with various firms) a program called "e-Trust," which is aimed at disseminating labels that characterize the degree and type of disclosure and usage associated with a particular communication or transaction. Figure 2 illustrates three types of labels proposed by e-Trust in support of different usages.[8]

In 1997 e-Trust was still under development, but a similar type of labeling could be used in a corporate setting to enhance the degree of confidence employees can place in a transactional environment.

Managers can provide their employees with technologies that enable them to "profile" their tasks, map their operational areas, and promote reciprocity of trust and understanding. Had the e-Trust protocols been

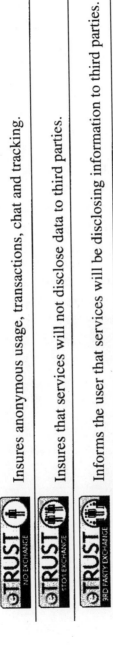

Figure 2

available 15 years ago, the mishaps experienced in the failed dissemination of an internal RFQ system (see above), which resulted mainly from deficiencies in the building of trust among employees, might have been mitigated. Of course, these techniques are not likely to be adopted unless other companies—suppliers, customers, and partners in the production process—embrace them.

Ensuring Interoperability between Intra-Corporate and Inter-Corporate Transactions

Inter-corporate networks (also referred to as extranets) leverage the growing connectedness of intranet infrastructures, and applications that cater to several corporate environments need to be consistent with the configuration of the diverse intranet environments they need to harmonize. Here I will review a few applications that can be structured to serve point-to-point or point-to-multipoint transactions.

In 1996, in an early extension of EDI to intranet environments, the Bank of America and the Lawrence Livermore National Laboratory implemented a payment system that relies on a processing configuration common to both organizations.[9] Though this is simply a conventional application of transactions technology to payment processing, one can easily imagine its extension to other types of transactions. Figure 3 illustrates the transactions flows within and across both organizations.

When a service provider wishes to address the specific requirements of several customers, it must develop a point-to-multipoint system that complies with their intranet configuration. This is the case for the growing number of intranet services that are being deployed in the late 1990s. Examples include health benefit administration services such as those provided by Healtheon, and 401(k) management applications supported by products developed by 401(k) Forum or Rational Investors. Another example is Microsoft's plan to include in its basic offerings applications supporting travel transactions integrated into an intranet environment. Microsoft executives have claimed that such applications will become standard "within the next three years."[10]

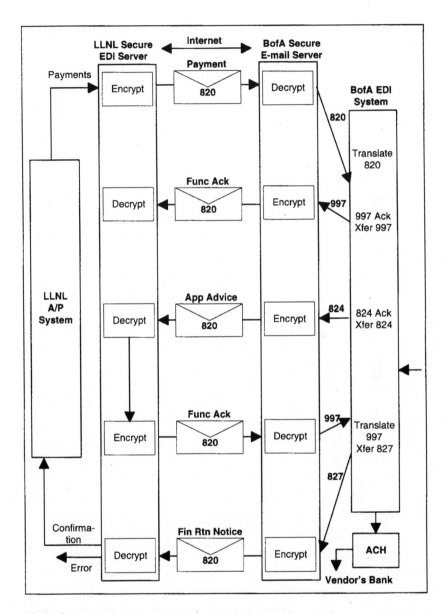

Figure 3

Inter-corporate transactions are likely to expand significantly over the coming decade, and we are witnessing a growing number of applications that link suppliers and customers with common environments. Extranets and extensions of intranets among trading partners will increasingly incorporate shared protocols, not only presenting functional characteristics (such as description and transactions authorization systems) but also featuring other aspects of collaboration (such as filters, profiling, and agenting technology).

Dissemination

One explanation for the apparent lack of effect of IT investments on service productivity has been that the time required to implement applications in the corporate environment is substantial, exceeding that of other productivity-enhancing technologies (such as mechanized transportation in the nineteenth century). This can be observed in managers' perceptions of how groupware actually contributes to productivity. In a recent survey,[11] managers rated the productivity contribution of workflow management (a category roughly corresponding to the second stage defined in table 1) at 5.8 on a scale of 10; they rated email at 8.5 (figure 4). Rather than take this as an indictment of groupware, we should interpret it as an indication that the implementation of structured collaboration is not yet satisfactory from a user's perspective: applications still must be improved to reach an acceptance commensurate with that of the first generation of collaborative applications. Is the adoption of true transactions-based applications likely to meet even more resistance? Perhaps. Word processing and email were hard enough to come to terms with efficiently. So great a change as that embodied in workplace environments requires a new understanding of the relationships between corporate citizens—more specific, an acknowledgment by executives that the information-crowded corporate organization's progressively less hierarchical and structured environment requires that their role as "managers" be more akin to the role of regulators than to that of military leaders. This is the standard consequence, even in the military, of having to rely on people to get the best out of themselves without instruction.

What seems probable is that the organizations most likely to embrace workplace applications are those that have been deploying groupware

Group Productivity
Effectiveness in improving group
productivity on 1-10 scale

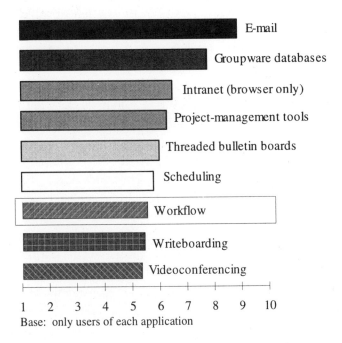

Base: only users of each application

Figure 4 (Source: *PC Week*)

technologies and those that recognize that creating collaboration and
intensifying it where it exists (e.g., between design teams and testers) is
a defining aspect of their corporate culture. In the professional advisory
services sector (which, as I noted above, is an interesting test case in view
of the unstructured nature of transactions), the leading companies offering technology advisory services (e.g., Andersen Consulting), or management consulting (e.g., McKinsey & Co.) are likely to be early adopters
of workplace applications. The primacy of these companies in their
respective sectors would imply that transactional environments could
contribute to increasing the tiering between the top companies and their
peers. This suggests that already dominant companies are becoming even
more dominant as a result of their integration of productivity-enhancing

transactions-based processes. This hypothesis is also consistent with the "winner take all" theory of the dissemination of technology in advanced economies, which has been asserted by several economists. Paul Krugman contends that "just as the physical-capital-using technology of the Industrial Revolution initially favored capital at the expense of labor, the human-capital-using technology of the information revolution favors the exceptional (and lucky) few at the expense of the merely intelligent and hardworking many."[12]

Other observers contend that the dissemination of IT applications does not necessarily have lopsided effects. A survey[13] undertaken by the Wharton School of Management suggests that the earnings of production workers increase by more than 3 percent annually when managers double their use of computers, and that only 50 percent of that increase can be attributed to upgrades in the workers' skills. Thus, it could well be, after all, that "all boats rise" in a transactional environment—but some will definitely rise more rapidly and smoothly than others.

What seems certain is that the demand for transactions-oriented applications within and among enterprises that respect the free-form nature of relationships is becoming more vocal and more imaginative, and that should lead to a significant market opportunity. When can the trickle of pilot projects and experiments noted throughout this analysis start swelling into a wave of commercial applications? Three categories of events must occur in order for workplace applications to enter the mainstream:

intranet dissemination   Once a critical mass of companies start relying on intranet infrastructures, the demand for using them for "more than email" will spur the supply of well-designed transactional applications such as the ones described above.

adoption of common standards and protocols   The advent of applications developed in the context of electronic commerce should accelerate the integration of these applications into the internal corporate environment—much like the existence of open Internet standards led to the development of intranet applications in the mid 1990s.

change in organizational cultures   Empowering employees to transact within and among corporate boundaries could be a tricky challenge for managers, because it also assumes a redefinition of their role. Obviously this will not happen overnight, but a few success stories are required to establish the feasibility of, and the opportunity resulting from, the adoption of these applications.

Though I cannot say how long it will take to dissolve the third constraint, I believe that before the end of the 1990s a large number of marketplace environments will be in place.

Valuation Implications

Like many similar discussions on the substance, form, and timing of the future deployment of IT applications, this one gets to a point where the real question goes from "what" to "so what." As Raymond Aron once put it, "modern history is a steady alternation of progress and disillusionment." I emphasized at the beginning of this analysis that the goal of transactions-oriented technologies is to have a significant, measurable impact on the productivity of the enterprise. One would expect this to be their net effect as their dissemination moves from the category of interesting experiments to that of processes of history—probably toward the end of this decade.

But is productivity increase destined to be a generally desirable idea appealing to writers of annual reports and organizational consultants, or can it have an impact on how companies are valued? Clearly this depends on the criteria used for valuation, and we know that valuation exercises are subject to fashion. Over most of the three decades that followed World War II, investment managers seemed taken by the idea that a company's dominant position, often backed by large-scale activity and an acknowledged brand, was the key driver of its value. The top-rated companies according to these criteria (the "nifty fifty") were the staples of investment portfolios deemed "reliable": it seemed that only these firms could command the market power required to generate the profits rewarded by higher valuations.

In the mid 1980s, the unassailability of dominance as the main criterion of valuation was increasingly questioned as a number of corporate "sacred cows" seemed to be challenged by Asian competitors or by startup firms. Though market power and brand positioning were never completely abandoned as criteria of valuation, other parameters gained more appeal: a company's ability to generate earnings in the future seemed increasingly important, particularly as the development of the

NASDAQ and of technology-related companies accompanied the growth of the capital market as a whole in the early and mid 1990s.

Many of these companies did not generate net earnings. However, since investors were seeking to capitalize on their expectations, they were content to rely on the available measures of growth in performance, as indicated by cash flow or even revenue. For emerging sectors, such as biotechnology or Internet services, valuations were based on cascades of interdependent assumptions linked to a future hypothetical epoch, such as government approval for a drug or achievement of critical mass for a communication network.

The market ran to extremes embodied by expectations-based valuations that characterized the first generation of Internet initial public offerings in 1995; however, only two years later a "return to basics" is emerging with a renewed emphasis on earnings generation.

For example, US cable TV companies had been valued since their inception on a cash flow basis (i.e., without deducting expenses associated with interest, taxes, depreciation, and amortization) under the assumption that capital spending demands would eventually reach some form of limit and that high barriers to entry stemming from technical and regulatory factors would guarantee them oligopolistic rents. With competition emerging from satellite and telecom operators, and with industry consolidation requiring large financial outlays, these assumptions seemed less plausible in the second half of the 1990s. As a result, a growing number of institutional investors rely on measures of *free cash flow,* which deducts interest and capital expenses, for their valuations.[14] In the case of online service companies, the transition is an even more dramatic one: from a revenue-based model to an earnings model.

In this context, the adoption of initiatives promoting a company's productivity growth should appeal to the investment community's increasing sensitivity to a firm's capacity to generate earnings. Methods that measure a company's ability to leverage its resources (human, financial, or technological) in order to expand its output while controlling its use of inputs could be used alongside growth-driven valuation approaches. The perspective of the coming decade will be transfigured by productivity measurement, as illustrated in figure 5. For example, productivity-driven valuation approaches could be developed to address the

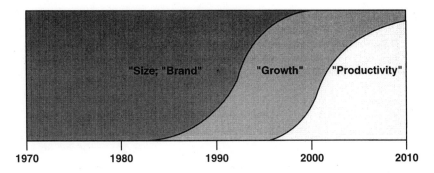

"Size; "Brand" · "Growth" "Productivity"

1970   1980   1990   2000   2010

Figure 5

following question: Given revenue growth expectations of X percent for company ABC, what is its potential to generate earnings? A broader measure known as "total factor productivity analysis" would focus on the productivity of employees and technology, in addition to the productive use of the company's financial resources—value implications correlating with expected productivity gains.

The value generated by a community of transactions within a company is likely to be commensurate to the quality of the workplace environment, as defined previously, with a particular focus on the resilience of its networks, on the depth of its information resources, on the tools made available to its employees to conduct intra-corporate and inter-corporate transactions, on the incentives (positive and negative) for its employees to transact, and on the managerial oversight and "regulatory" dispositions governing the internal market for transactions. As a result, corporate finance professionals, fund managers, investment advisors, and individual investors might end up spending much more time than they now do assessing the internal systems (technical and managerial) of the enterprise as drivers of productivity growth, of earnings potential, and therefore of valuation.

Transactions-Based Communities: A Contribution to the Comparative Advantage of Mature Economies?

The emerging focus on productivity, in the context of electronic communities of transactions in the workplace, appeals particularly to companies in economies now approaching the margin of their present efficiencies and facing increasing competition from foreign players in domestic markets and abroad. Throughout this century, American companies have enjoyed advantages resulting from the commercial environment in which they operate, including the size and scope of the US market, its openness, relatively benign government interference, and the strength of its innovation engine.

Though these advantages remain, one cannot ignore the fact that technological innovations of production processes are adopted abroad with increasingly short lags, often in Southeast Asian countries and occasionally in Europe, potentially threatening the position of American manufacturing companies. Continental European economies, for their part, must deal with much more serious problems, such as a high level of protection of employee benefits which, in the absence of productivity gains, result in an apparently intractable spiral of unemployment and low growth.

American and especially European economies seem to have difficulty addressing the need to leverage their human and technological resources with higher productivity growth. The comparative advantage of mature economies should be bolstered by the advent of communities of transactions enabled by the dissemination of open standards of information technology in the workplace, and their recognition in the financial community as drivers of valuation.

Notes

1. Marc Sokol, quoted in *New York Times,* April 27, 1996.

2. Workflow may be defined as the deployment of information, data inputs, queries, approvals, requests for exceptions, originated in the various work groups that make up the organization. See Thomas Koulopoulos, *The Workflow Imperative* (Van Nostrand Reinhold, 1995).

3. The quotient I refer to throughout this analysis should be understood as the total factor productivity ratio of outputs to inputs. Factors include labor, "technology," and "capital" (itself an increasingly complex category).

4. With methods known as Overhead Value Analysis (OVA) or Activity Value Analysis (AVA).

5. Ellis Booker, "Intranet Workflow Tool Speeds Firm's Decisions," *Web Week* 2, no. 15 (1996): 31–34.

6. Source: *Release 1.0*

7. Reported by Jerry Michalski in *Release 1.0,* November 19, 1996.

8. Source: e-Trust web site, January 1997.

9. Source: *E-Comm,* January-February 1996.

10. Greg Slyngstad, Microsoft Travel Business Unit general manager, as reported in the *Financial Times,* November 25, 1996.

11. Rusty Weston, "Group Pay-off, " *PCWeek,* September 30, 1996: E1.

12. "Not for Ordinary Folk," *Red Herring,* January 1997.

13. Cited in *New York Times,* May 11, 1996.

14. See Susan Pulliam and Mark Robichaux, "Cash Flow Stops Propping Up Cable Stocks," *Wall Street Journal,* January 9, 1997.

7

The Virtual Countinghouse: Finance Transformed by Electronics

Daniel P. Keegan

We are not here to sell a parcel of vats and retorts . . . but to negotiate the possibility of becoming richer than the dreams of avarice.
—Samuel Johnson, "Prospectus for the Sale of Thrale's Brewery"

David Kincaid had just been awakened by a buzz from the personal digital assistant he had left at his bedside. He had switched off all the other communication monitors, but had forgotten that the network could now call his PDA. As he stumbled into the bathroom, David looked at the PDA's screen. He was immediately struck by the first entry: "Saturday, October 20, 2008. After months of negotiation, the giant satellite communication company Orbcomm has finally agreed to guarantee the UN's debt."

"Now," David whispered to himself, "the expansion plans in Laos can go through. We're going to have a deal!"

David was the chief financial officer of Global Ventures, a diversified company with offices in Chicago, London, Frankfurt, Mexico City, São Paulo, Beijing, Tokyo, Seoul, Sidney, and other major cities. Laos meant better product distribution throughout Asia, but the project had been on hold for almost two years because the country's premier couldn't get funding for a new airport. The UN, after taking over the World Bank, had promised to lend the needed money, but only if the UN could overcome its debt problems. With the UN's help, Global's Laos strategy would soon pay off.

The company had already simulated most of the financing scenarios. Monday would be soon enough for action. At the moment, David had other matters to think about. He had agreed to lecture at MIT-Fudan, the university created in 2005 when the Cambridge and Shanghai schools agreed to merge. The talk was coming up, and it was time to prepare for it. The dean wanted a lecture on the new trends in finance. There would be real people in the audience, not just images peering from a wall-size screen. Well, yes, the students in Shanghai would be seeing his talk later because of the time difference, but David would be able to see the fidgets of those physically present and to look into their eyes as he spoke, adjusting his tone and other aspects of his delivery accordingly.

What had changed about finance, and what would the future of finance be like? David decided to record his thoughts on the PDA:

Accounting Will Always Be With Us

"Sixteenth-century Spanish explorers must have been required to report the treasures they found to King Philip V. No one listed accountants in the ships' logs, but they must have been aboard. Similarly, we can assume that stewardship reporting, in some form, will never disappear. Even if there is no other impetus, governments will look to the creators of wealth for a certain share. Taxation will always be with us, and accurate financial reporting will be demanded. No amount of computer processing will change that.

"But information technology profoundly changes finance, not only in the way transactions are accumulated and reported but also in the very structure of how business is conducted. The technologies that shaped today's business environment have been evolving even faster since the late 1990s than before. Among the reasons are the decreased cost of hardware brought about by advances in microprocessor speed, the ubiquitous nature of intranets and the Internet (he power of which has been enhanced by broad use of fiber optics, satellites, personal computers, and other communication technology), artificial intelligence and object-oriented programming (which allow us to reuse computational modules in the creation of complex application systems), the almost universal use of common operating systems designed by Microsoft, highly developed database managers and vastly improved Internet languages (which appeared after Java), the convergence of media, data, and voice communication into a common presentation framework, and the continued improvement of enterprise-wide transaction-processing systems that are now becoming industry-wide."

Financial Control and Integrity

Finance Is the Language of Business; Double-Entry Accounting Gives It Integrity

"Think of your audience," David said to himself. "The Fudan students apparently have a compassion for history. They will want stories from the past to illustrate the present. I should mention Fra Luca Pacioli's contribution of double-entry bookkeeping. After the lecture, the students might use their networks to research the city-states of medieval Italy to learn more. Double-entry bookkeeping began there, well before Pacioli was even born, but the monk recorded how it worked in his book *Summa Arithmetica*.

"Double-entry bookkeeping *was* a monumental discovery. Pacioli's accounting has never been esteemed as highly as Gutenberg's printing, but it too has survived fairly intact for five centuries. I'll develop that theme; it helps to explain why the expected travail associated with instantaneous, global financial transactions has never happened. Perhaps I can even obtain an electronic view of the book from Harvard's Baker Library and start by having the lecture room's screens display some pages, bringing into focus the precise Latin script of this forgotten priest.

"And how do I explain Pacioli and finance to the engineers from MIT? Isaac Newton? Something about every force having an equal but opposite force? That's pushing it a little! Actually, the engineers won't have to be tempted into the subject. Finance is an analytical exercise, one that the engineers will have already grasped because they were trained in the economic tradeoffs of product design."

Newton did, he reflected, have some relevance to electronic commerce in the twenty-first century. Every accounting transaction had two sides; essentially, it was recorded twice. Therefore, even if some group could penetrate the network, they would have trouble covering their tracks. Everything had to be in balance. So he addressed his PDA, which he knew would automatically structure his speech.

The Integrity of Financial Transactions

"In 2008, significant integrity is associated with the reporting of financial transactions. With a few notable exceptions, there have been virtually no significant breaches of the security of accounting transactions, and even in the exceptional cases the principle of accounting redundancy has provided clues. In my own company, Global Ventures, if a customer were able to delete information that he owed us money, our inventory balances would look strange. If an employee were able to increase his rate of pay, our liabilities would seem too high. If a customer changed our sales price, our margins would look too low. Of course, there are many ways to manipulate the records, but control over access—and transaction integrity checking —provides other lines of defense.

"When I was an auditor, 12 years ago, we worried about this problem. The Internet was in its infancy, and electronic commerce was beginning to blossom. We had all heard of 'agent software'—a term, it seemed, that was more written about than understood. Despite these misgivings, we felt the idea had promise. We auditors could develop electronic agents and loose them on the network to report suspicious transactions—a large transfer of funds to Switzerland, for example. But once we developed such a software tool, we quickly found that anti-virus programs could easily be modified to eliminate our agents. These anti-virus programs were particularly devastating to our efforts until we perfected our techniques.

"In the interim, we looked at the nature of financial transactions and concluded that they were self-policing. Even if an individual could simultaneously delete an amount he owed and the offsetting inventory balance, the company's vendor payments would look out of line. If he could get to the vendor's files, the supplier's inventory would look strange. It became clear to us that even the most imaginative thief would have a daunting task of keeping everything in balance, to keep us fooled.

"We then turned our attention to new auditing techniques and developed software to look at the reasonableness of computer balances—a sort of heuristic approach drawing on statistical probabilities. At first, we used these tools during the recurring audit and then, if necessary, followed up on seemingly strange account balances by tearing apart the individual transactions. There was always a trail somewhere in the file if we knew where to look. Eventually companies began to understand what we were doing, and they asked us to sell them our software so they could self-audit their files each day. Several hackers tried to disable these programs (or, worse, modify them), but we found a way to download newly encrypted versions on a random basis. And we armed each version with new anti-agent routines that stood guard until they could be rotated in the next few hours. Eventually the profession caught on to our approach, but not before we added several points to our auditing market share."

Vapor Companies

"Double-entry bookkeeping, agent software, and sophisticated probability routines helped auditing enormously. So did plain old password control. Stolen identities and vapor companies were problematic. There were many ways to get hold of credit card numbers, change the mailing addresses, and use the cards to run up large balances. The credit histories of unsuspecting people were thus shattered. This stopped being so easy on the Internet once providers began to communicate total charges electronically at the end of each day, rather than waiting to prepare month-end mail statements.

"In-store purchases were another matter. Personal identification numbers helped here, but even today we don't have this matter completely under control. Thumb scanning is probably the ultimate answer. This approach crossed over from the military to the commercial world around 1999. Hospitals were the first enterprises to use it, wanting to make sure that they were wheeling the right person into the operating room. Once businesses saw how useful it could be, thumb scanning spread rapidly. Costs have fallen dramatically, but we still don't have an effective way to cross-match thumbprints around the world.

"A decade ago, 'vapor companies' were a much bigger problem than stolen identities. It was easy to set up a vapor company. Any lawyer in the United States could do it for about $500. An enterprising swindler could do it himself if he wasn't afraid of sending a little paperwork to the state and to the Internal Revenue Service. Once a company had a federal identification number, it was alive. Next, you deposited a few dollars in a bank account and sought credit. After these steps, you could engage in all manner of mischief, especially if you were patient, paid a few bills on time, and sought higher credit limits. Neither internal nor external auditors could detect this practice very well until the unpaid balance became so large that it caught someone's attention.

"Eventually, some enterprising organization became the de facto certifier of new companies. To become listed on the certification Web site, a company had to submit properly completed documents, including a letter from a reputable accounting firm. Every organization's funds manager checked the Web before his company would grant more-than-nominal credit. Despite repeated attacks, this Web listing was impregnable, and today it is the standard certifying agency throughout the world. I wish Global had come up with this—we'd have minted a fortune."

Protection of Intellectual Assets

"Of course, protecting intellectual assets is much more difficult than protecting financial transactions—especially now that networks are easily accessed. There is no longer any need to photographing documents with a spy camera. If you are inside the company, you just access the right database—one containing suppliers' prices, new products, costs, bidding strategies, and the like—and instantaneously send it over the Internet to your fellow conspirator. Database password control and encryption help here, but the real breakthrough began when the outbound Internet communication programs started to scan messages for key words. Today, in many big companies such as Global, you need specific electronic authorization from the security specialists before such documents can be transmitted. I expect this practice to spread quickly."

The Changed Nature of Business Information

"Computers have revolutionized business. That large, expensive device that found its way into the corporation during the 1960s to compute the payroll and write checks has become an essential tool of management, extending corporate headquarters' reach to all aspects of the organization, to all parts of the world, and to all of the company's customers. However, even with the changes in technology, business still centers around the shareholders—the individuals and institutions who have invested money and who expect rewards. Still, businesses *operate* very differently in 2008 than they did in the past."

Elimination of Barriers to Entry
"In the late 1990s, corporate financial staffs were at the pinnacle of success. They were needed to coordinate everything, and everything was changing. During the 1960s and the 1970s, the manufacturing base of the United States was profoundly influenced by the automobile industry, which was big and profitable. However, in the early 1980s the US auto industry found itself with aging capital facilities, cozy union relationships, barely acceptable product quality, and an uncertain future. Foreign automakers (especially Japanese ones), which once had competed with US automakers more on the basis of price than on the basis of quality, soon become a major force shaping the US auto industry and its suppliers, and eventually *all* US manufacturers. This competition, coupled with the oil crisis of the mid 1970s, caused one American auto company to go bankrupt, another to have a brush with death, and a third to spend $80 billion on new plant and equipment.

"Despite cries for protection, the political climate of the United States tilted toward freer competition. One by one, competitive barriers started to be eliminated in other industries, such as telecommunications, airlines, and banking. A ripple effect was felt throughout the US economy. Companies downsized, improved quality, paid attention to the customer, embraced technology, and went offshore to find better returns. Already quick to divest, merge, and partner, they became faster in developing new products and services.

"By the middle of the 1990s, US companies had transformed themselves into quick-changing powerhouses and were expanding worldwide. The elimination of entry barriers made businesses retool themselves and become efficient."

The Changed Nature of Finance
"As companies changed, so did their senior financial executives. The chief financial officer and his staff became much more than 'green eyeshade bookkeepers.' CFOs often sat on the board of directors, they were party to every major corporate decision, they thought more globally, and they

Keegan

became chief architects of the company. Spreadsheets arguably did more to change finance than any other innovation of the time, unlocking analytical power and putting it in the hands of even the most recently hired staff member. As routine aspects of the company's accounting process were taken over by computers, the CFO became a financial strategist.

Imagine the monumental task that it must have been in the 1970s to bill, collect from, and reconcile the accounts of 50,000 retail customers. That all changed thanks to technology. In 1997, for instance, Sears billed 26 million people per month. Consider the paperwork matching required to pay 30,000 vendors for myriad shipments—another retailer, in 1997, processed 24 million invoices annually, having perfected the use of electronic data interchange to pay bills efficiently. Think of the payroll department of a company that had more than 600,000 employees—in 1997, the computers of an automotive company assimilated mountains of data and electronically deposited funds into its employees' checking accounts, or sent them checks if the employee desired such nostalgia.

"Despite these advances in technology, in many companies the financial staff was second only to the field sales staff as a percentage of administrative expenses. The CFO's staff was a ready target for personnel realignments. Therefore, outsourcing abounded. Those who remained spent proportionately more of their time on matters of competitive importance, not on the processing of transactions. The books closed without travail, and the financial staff assisted the operating managers in plotting the company's short-term future. Every important decision was based on an analysis of its financial consequences—a task readily completed by the financial staff, aided by the relatively cheap computing power of the day."

Key Performance Indicators

"Rapid information was both a blessing and a problem for most businesses in the late 1990s. It was easy to get lost in data. Therefore, organizations turned their financial staffs loose to define the company's 'key performance indicators' (KPIs)—the few items of information that would motivate everyone to achieve the company's goals. The idea of 'data focus' quickly swept through industry after Bob Kaplan, a professor at Harvard, published a seminal article titled 'The Balanced Scorecard' in *Harvard Business Review.* Kaplan galvanized thought concerning the need for businesses to concentrate on what was important.

"KPIs were more than just historical compilations of financial metrics; they were dynamic, and they were predictive of future results. They treated time to market with the same reverence as gross margin. They extended throughout a company's value chain, from product initiation to customer satisfaction. They were focused on the attainment of goals set internally or with an understanding of the best practices of other companies. Using graphics, they included commentaries by their keepers about what was going well and what wasn't. They separated information from data.

"Technology made it possible to compile such information efficiently. Increasingly, data, graphics, words, and even voice could be recorded together and accessed as needed. In the past, pages of operating reports had been sent to executives for review and analysis, sparking endless telephone calls to find out what was really happening. With the convergence of technology and the ubiquitous network, the operating manager could report key indicators in a compact and meaningful manner.

"Companies could still have all the data they wanted, but key performance indicators were focused *information.* Just by having a quality or customer-satisfaction metric in place, top management communicated its vision unambiguously to the lathe operator and the customer service clerk, who could deliver results. The measurements served as probes into the company, blinking red, yellow, and green about goal achievement. The measurements were the architecture for the company's information technology plan, showing what was important to monitor. And the measurements harmonized the horizontal and vertical organizational structure of the company, a structure that had to exist simultaneously for the organization to be successful."

The Organizational Dilemma

"During the 1990s, all manner of books were published on the organizational dilemma. How, these books asked, could a 'stovepipe,' hierarchical, military-inspired organizational structure cope with the vertical, cross-organizational, boundaryless nature of worldwide logistics? Many believed that companies had to reorganize around processes, shedding their hierarchical structure. But, as one chief executive officer told me while I was researching this matter, 'then I'd have even more stovepipes that wouldn't interact. *Except, they'd be lying sideways.* Leave the organization alone to evolve in its own manner.'

"Key performance indicators simultaneously tracked all parts of a matrixed organization. They brought information over the network to executive management's attention no matter how the company was organized. In fact, the organization's structure was changing so rapidly that it didn't even make sense to publish it. Its pages were obsolete before the laser printer could stack the new organizational chart in its tray.

"Eventually, as the KPIs became stable, there was less checking to be done by the corporate staff. The KPIs themselves, incorporating comments from their keepers, found their way to what used to be called 'mahogany row.' Executive management could then get a direct understanding of how the company was operating—achieving its goals and implementing its strategy—without the usual filters and biases of the headquarters staff."

More Data, but Focused Information

"There weren't that many key performance indicators. There were only a few things in a company that *really* mattered. Were customers happy? Were new products getting to market on time and on budget? Were product and service quality up to standard? Was intellectual capital increasing? Were facilities, machines, and people well utilized? Were employees satisfied and productive? Was market share increasing? Were capital expenditure plans being executed effectively? Was the company doing its part to help the environment? Was R&D looking at the right sciences and technologies?

"Most of the KPIs could be put in place quickly. The company's underlying systems already provided much of the information. All a company required was proper formatting into a graphical structure, a database to house the KPIs, and, most important, commentary concerning problems and actions. KPI reporting energized a company more than any other management technique. It rewarded individuals for executing strategies and for building shareholder value. At first the rewards were psychic, but as the process became stable higher amounts of compensation were tied to goal achievement.

"The balanced scorecard–key performance indicator approach took on even more importance when public accounting firms began to review the data for integrity, issuing reports to management on the information's accuracy. Eventually the CFOs of many companies started to share their KPIs with the investing public, showing how executive management was discharging its stewardship responsibilities. We began to call this 'value reporting.'"

Public Reporting
"This evolution has continued. As you know, in 2008 no company would consider publishing an annual report that didn't include KPIs and commentary from executive management about the company's success. The report contains information carefully tested for integrity and presented so that it can be compared to similar information on competing companies. There's still a letter from the chairman that paints a happy face on everything, but the fact-based reporting of key performance indicators helps the investors understand if the happy face should really have a frown.

"Most of the KPI information isn't in real time. It is a careful compilation of what happened during the reporting period, including whether or not the company generated any profit. It provides a permanent, not a fleeting, record of events. That's not to say that KPIs are useless in predicting the future. What could be more important to future cash results than whether we are getting our new products to market on time?

"During informal reporting periods, managers can, if they wish, view the last hour's results on their screens in full color. However, such inquiries are done more often by the corporate staff than by executives. The latter expect the keeper of the KPI to be on top of the situation; the keeper has been empowered to do so. Micromanagement began to atrophy by the end of the century, and most of the micromanagers with it. Strategists took their place.

"After all the attempts in the late twentieth century to put a terminal on the CEO's desk and give that person an 'executive information system,' only to find that a pot of geraniums would have been less expensive and more useful, we finally have something helpful. But we have found that a little carefully crafted information is better than a fusillade of data."

Shareholder Value

Financial Reporting

"Let's return to the late 1990s once again to see how technology has shaped financial thinking. There had been an increasing recognition that, with few exceptions, investors could rely upon published financial information to provide reasonably accurate information about corporate earnings. The worth of assets and the ultimate valuation of the company, however, was problematic.

"These matters vexed the external auditors. Routine things in finance were getting easier and therefore less appreciated. In the 1960s, the sheer magnitude of effort required to close the books had been monumental. Computer processing was in its infancy, transaction systems were often unreliable, and offshore communication was expensive and slow. Ensuring that a company reported accurate information required superb planning, an inquisitive mind, a facility with arithmetic, and supreme patience.

"As companies built more reliable information systems, however, the mind-numbing compilation work started to diminish. But new types of transactions—the use of derivatives, joint ventures, and monetization of assets—required new standards of external financial reporting that absorbed the time offset by this increased availability of information. While one could argue with the necessity for all these standards, nevertheless the accounting profession met this disclosure challenge, and effort was redirected away from the compilation of data and toward its reporting. The company's internal financial staffs did likewise.

"But by the late 1990s all this was taken for granted. High-quality external financial reporting in advanced countries was the given, not the exception. While the services of an external auditor could hardly be considered a commodity, even competitors in the profession were finding it difficult to differentiate themselves from one another. The natural consequence, they feared, was that price would become the differentiation. I was with an accounting firm during those years. We began to realize that 'The Street' was changing our lives, and we had to reposition external reporting.

"Virtually every developed economy had The Street. In the United States it was called 'Wall Street.' In the UK it was 'The City.' In Japan it was 'Kabuto-Cho.' 'The Street' was a shortcut name for capital traders. These were the individuals who influenced the investment of pension, mutual, and individual funds. The people on The Street, using what were then considered sophisticated communication networks, were seeking investments with a tolerant but varying degree of risk—investments that would maximize the capital supplier's wealth."

Investor Accounting

"On any day there was an enormous amount of money circling throughout the globe. Individuals in the United States and Europe were beginning to understand that the social safety nets that their governments had put in place years before were beginning to crack. They began to save more for retirement, because they could no longer be certain that the government would take care of them as they aged. Therefore, they poured money into the financial markets."

David stopped for a second and thought to himself: "Global is in the portfolios of many of the world's major funds. It may sound a little strange coming from me, the chief accountant, but I actually think about the hard-working people who depend on us for cash as they retire. They've given us their money and asked us to be cautious with it. People, not investment bankers, are our stockholders. We work for them. 'Shareholder value' is a sanitized, abstract term of business. But the words come to life when I mentally look these people in the eye each evening—and as I review Global's closing share price. Fortunately, we've done well for them so far."

He went back to outlining his lecture.

"The objectives of The Street had not been ignored by executive management in the late 1990s. On one hand, the management of an underperforming company risked being replaced when the ire of the investment community had been aroused. On the more positive side, at least in the United States and increasingly in Europe, executive compensation had been tied very closely to stock performance. Unsurprisingly, companies were increasingly seeking to understand the factors that affected shareholder wealth.

"There was a growing awareness that earnings per share was only one touchstone to be considered by management—and perhaps not even the most important one. The Street might punish a company whose short-term earnings fell below an anticipated amount by dumping its stock into the marketplace and thereby decreasing the company's share price. But often a second look triggered buy orders if the company's fundamentals still looked favorable. The Street quickly dismissed externally reported financial information below operating earnings. It concentrated, instead, on the longer-term driver of shareholder wealth, cash flow. As one investment analyst put it, 'Cash is fact, EPS is an opinion.' He was reacting to the judgmental conventions of accounting that influenced earnings such as pension fund accruals, LIFO calculations, depreciation alternatives, deferred taxes, and the like.

"And The Street was becoming more sophisticated. Previously, an investor who became disenchanted by a particular company simply sold his stock and put his funds elsewhere. In some cases, however, The Street might have such a large position in one particular company that such an action would depress the stock price and harm the investor. Instead, there was a growing trend for large investors to be activists, pressuring management to become more proactive in achieving stockholder wealth."

Book Value and Market Value

"Another indicator of the sophistication of The Street was that non-liquid assets were held in little regard. Did it make any sense in the late 1990s that the average market value of Standard & Poor companies was 3.1 times their book value? Any relationship between book and market value seemed purely coincidental. All the work done by internal and external accountants to report the historical cost of a company's buildings, capital equipment, and land did not reflect the organization's real economic worth. That was not to say that investing was unimportant; in fact, companies like Global were spending record sums. What had diminished in important was all the historical accounting for assets.

"The market was probably right about fixed assets. For many companies, long-term assets were more of an albatross than a competitive weapon. Investment analysts considered, for example, the value of a nuclear generating station. Not much, most would conclude; even though it might be recorded on the books as ten digits of past investment. What about steel plants? What about buildings? For many companies, hard assets did not have much significance. They merely represented a historical deduction from funds otherwise available to the stockholders."

Cash Flow as King
"The real driver of wealth was the amount of cash that could be provided to the stockholders, either through dividends or because the market approved of management's reinvestment of this cash. In this later case, The Street would increase the company's share price.

"We began to fathom the actions of The Street. A new body of knowledge that we called 'shareholder accounting' was rapidly emerging. It was nimble, it was unshared, it was not fettered by regulatory pronouncements—and it was practiced by The Street. Shareholder accounting dealt with long-term cash, the funds that would come into the company's door at some future date. Hence, finance had to become more future-oriented, embracing future cash flows as one of the company's key performance indicators."

Financial Modeling and Scenario Assessment
"Technology had become a ubiquitous part of our daily lives, bringing rapid information from everywhere in the world. Our networks had unleashed endless possibilities for amassing databases useful in setting strategies and in projecting scenarios into the future. In the 1950s, only the rare graduate of a prestigious business school had ever heard of present-value calculations; by the early 1990s, such algorithms were available in the library of any inexpensive spreadsheet. Consequently, an individual, working alone, could complete in an hour an analysis that once would have required weeks of work—or, more likely, would not have been undertaken at all. This meant that the expense of scenario assessment would continue to fall dramatically. The natural thought,

therefore, was that the cost of business would go down. Perhaps. But more likely, we thought, sophisticated analysis would become commonplace as companies looked for newer strategies to maintain or enhance shareholder wealth.

"We looked at risk management as a dramatic example. Two decades earlier, only the most knowledgeable financial services companies fully understood what were then the rudimentary techniques for hedging, arbitraging, going long, and going short. By the late 1990s, virtually every major organization had to be aware of risk management in order to protect its financial position. Business was global, conducted in multiple rising and falling currencies. Commodities could be bought on the spot market or on the futures market. Acquisitions and mergers depended on financial leverage. And all these matters were influenced by the time value of money. Most of these 'plays' would not even be possible without a computer; net spreads were far too complex for manual computation.

"Similarly, pricing, logistics, engineered products, lot sizing, and revenue tracking were becoming real-time endeavors aided by the computational abilities of cheap computers. Long-term business success depended upon correct actions *at the margin,* not on average, we concluded. Historical financial information had become much less relevant. It was an interesting check on past decisions, but it told little about the future. Inevitably, then, it was reasonable to expect that historical financial information would continue to diminish in importance—it would be of interest, primarily, to tax authorities, as a jumping off place for additional analysis, and to confirm or deny the expectations of investors."

Residual Income

"At the same time, companies were flirting with notions of economic value, a residual income concept rebirthed from the writings of nineteenth-century economists that stated: 'For a business to be viable, it must, in the long run, cover all costs, including its cost of capital.' Remember, in the late 1990s American companies had just gone through a difficult period of downsizing, and European companies were in for the same. Japan saw this change coming but was trying to stave it off with mercantilistic policies. Cost reduction had been the dominant theme of businesses for a decade, but ways to increase revenue were barging into business thinking.

"The notion of economic value added appealed to American companies for six reasons:

If they could increase their share prices, managers would share in this wealth creation.

If business leaders could grant shares to employees, these associates could also be rewarded for creating shareholder value.

The era of cost reduction was about over. There wasn't much more water in the sponge to wring out. Attention had to be placed on the revenue lines of the income statement, not the cost lines.

There were still some opportunities to reduce working capital through technology if everyone in the company concentrated on

The worldwide nature of business was increasing the complexity of taxation.

To bring about future wealth, companies would have to start investing again. They would need the cooperation of the capital markets—and the capital markets were looking for return.

"Soon there was a renewed interest in the drivers of shareholder value. Modeling software built within a company or provided by companies such as ALCAR began to emerge. These software tools allowed an analyst to decompose a company's financial statements and assess the impact of management's actions on the price of a share. In a blinding revelation of the self-obvious, these models showed that a company's share price could be enhanced if its revenue increased, its costs decreased, its taxes were lowered, its working capital was minimized, and its capital expenditures were managed.

Investment Was the Key to the Future

"But there was more to the story. The scenario-assessment tools permitted simulations of alternative strategies and alternative investments. They demonstrated one very important fact: a company's share price was most influenced by how long the organization could deliver cash. The models said 'Invest for tomorrow as you live for today.'

"These financial modeling tools did so in a compelling manner. They discounted future cash flows back to the present, showing today's effect on shareholder value of a cash flow that might not materialize for years. This was a powerful revelation. The models demonstrated that, while a company's short-term earnings might decrease today because of a management decision, the future cash flows of this decision would significantly enhance today's shareholder value. In other words, The Street was correct when it quickly dismissed EPS as the primary metric of company value. Management began to inch away from short-term earnings and, instead, to share information about major decisions concerning cash flow with investment analysts, accompanied by the opinion of an independent accountant."

Disclosure of Shareholder Value Actions in Published Financial Information
"It is for this reason that you began to see, toward the end of the twentieth century, a Statement of Shareholder Value Improvement in every public company's annual report; you see the company's non-secret KPIs; you read the company's commentary on these matters in the 'Management Discussion and Analysis' section of the report; and you see the auditor's opinion covering several of these matters. Value reporting couldn't be done without technology, the calculations are too complex."

How Finance Works in 2008

The Role of the Chief Financial Officer
David thought he should tell the students about his current job. He had joined Global as the controller, having spent 12 years in public accounting, and he had been admitted to the partnership. He enjoyed public accounting, and he never would have left that field had Global not promised him a shot at the CFO position and dangled stock options before him.

Auditing
"Among other things, my responsibilities include relationships with our external auditors. Public accounting is not significantly different than in the past, except that its scope has increased substantially. Auditors are empowered by regulation to offer an opinion on the 'fair presentation'

of external financial statements. To do so, they test the company's accounting processes to assure themselves and management that these are functioning sufficiently well to ensure the reasonableness of published information. Usually, they do this in conjunction with the company's own internal auditors. To sign an audit opinion, an individual must be a Certified Public Accountant who has demonstrated knowledge of accounting principles by completing university course work, by working on the job for some time, and by passing a challenging examination.

"Occasionally an auditor will find fraudulent transactions. However, most of the auditor's time is spent in testing the controls around systems to ensure that frauds or unintentional errors cannot be accomplished without detection. Because of the various rules of disclosure, an auditor also works with management to present information for the investor considered relevant by the various standards boards and governmental agencies who oversee the profession and the capital markets.

"Much of what used to be called fieldwork by the auditor is now done electronically. In agreement with management, the auditors, from their own offices, can access the company's financial databases at random and apply statistical routines that will highlight unusual activities or strange account balances. Additionally, the auditors have modeling software that they use to project the 'expected' financial statements at least a year in advance. When the actual results are significantly different, the auditors take additional steps.

"In the past, the auditors would review financial processes to ensure that they were working properly. Though this is still done, the line between financial and non-financial processes has become blurred. Therefore, the auditors periodically look at our non-financial business activities to help management understand whether the data being provided is reliable. Two years ago we had them review R&D, last year it was our process for capital expenditures, and this year we'll have them review customer service. Of course, every year the auditors look at our network and transaction security.

"Periodically, the auditors produce informal reports to the CEO and to me, with suggestions for improvements, giving us a chance to correct any problems they noted. Often, we share these reports with the board of directors when they are particularly insightful. Because the auditors now look into a wide variety of business issues, their staff today consists of scientists, engineers, information technologists, marketers, and regulatory and personnel specialists, as well as accountants and tax professionals. They assemble teams from throughout the world as needed.

Global Responsibilities

"While still in public accounting, after being admitted to the partnership, I was assigned overall responsibility for Global's audit. My role then changed significantly, because I had to understand the far-reaching dimensions of the company, not just its financial accounting. I met with the audit committee of the board periodically in private session. With management absent, the board members expected me to speak frankly about any accounting problems that were bothersome.

"Additionally, I traveled with executive management to many far-flung parts of the world and began to see the company's foreign operations personally. In this way, I gained great respect for the company, and management began to feel that I could be of some value as an internal employee. In fact, Jack Clarke, Global's former CFO, thought I might be a good replacement after his retirement. So they asked me to join them.

"Today, Global operates in almost every part of the world, with our major strategies directed toward Asia. By 2020 we expect that there will be more even middle-class consumers in China than in the United States and Western Europe combined. It is clear that companies such as Global can help shape the economic well-being of many countries, a responsibility we do not take lightly. The nation-state is diminishing in importance with the increase in worldwide electronic commerce, being taken over by trading blocks. Our revenues, for example, exceed the GDP of all but the 56 largest countries in the world.

"I travel about half my time—less than before. Teleconferencing has fulfilled its promise. I wish, however, that we could synchronize the world's sleep patterns so I didn't get calls at 3 AM. The time-shift programs of the network help a little. They record the previous night's video messages for review during my normal work hours, but there's always a 3 AM emergency somewhere."

The Language of Business

"Once on board as Controller (I became CFO later), I found out that it is one thing to audit the financial systems of a complex company but something entirely different to run them. The financial effect of every company action lands on the desk of the controller—or, more technically correct, in the company's general ledger. I had learned in school that finance is the language of business, but I didn't know how many people spoke it. Everyone in the company wanted to talk to me, usually about an error in their budget or their personal expense account.

"Let me talk about a company's financial database, its general ledger. When I joined Global in the mid 1990s, many software vendors were inventing new and better ways to present information on request. They had pretty well convinced the world that all problems of the general ledger had long since been solved—and, even if they hadn't, they were strictly an accounting matter that could be deferred while the company did more important things. Global's general ledger had been in this state of deferral for almost 20 years. I knew this from auditing it, but the implications had not sunk in. While the application's record lengths had been changed over the years, I could still find the unmistakable trace of its monthly batch-processing heritage."

A Repository of Financial Data

"The general ledger was the source of the company's important financial information; it was the repository of financial history. Had I been smart enough to call it a data warehouse, its problems would have immediately attracted attention, but 'general ledger' seemed anachronistic. A general ledger is not a thing unto itself; it is connected to everything else. Computer specialists follow with great interest the findings of neuroscience, the study of how the brain works. There are transmitters from one brain cell to another, providing a vast and complex network that allows us to see, to remember, to think, and to communicate. A company's general ledger is similar. It can lodge cost rates, financial history, investment plans, and accounting interrelationships. With only a bit of hyperbole, I call it the company's financial neural network.

"Because the general ledger is so interlinked with other systems, you can't solve its problem without addressing billing, payroll, payables, fixed assets, and Lucifer's bestowal—the scourge of humankind—cost accounting. To know the cost of a car, you have to know the costs of the bolts that hold the bumpers in place, the steel that makes up the bumper, the transistors that go in the radio, and the castings that go into the transmission. Each of these may be bought at different times and at different prices, and one must summarize them all to know the cost of the final vehicle. The complexity of this problem has helped to make the stockholders of computer companies wealthy over the years.

"Like many cost systems, Global's was so fragile and so patched with add-on code that the information technology staff dared not touch it. I wasn't enough of a technician to argue with them, but in my heart I knew that our cost system's record lengths correlated precisely with the 80 columns of a punched card.

"In my first month on the job, I had my secretary cancel subscriptions to 31 computer journals, each proclaiming the joys of advanced technology and how it could support better executive decisions. I was loath to admit it, but I just wanted a general ledger and a cost-accounting system that would let me sleep at night. The wonders of executive decision making could wait."

Integrated, Enterprise-Wide Software

"So I did something, and it worked. Enterprise-wide software solutions, such as those provided by SAP and Baan, had caught the imagination of many companies. This software had been designed from the ground up to handle all the transaction-processing needs of a company in an integrated manner. Such a system promised that you would never again have to worry about connecting accounts payable to the cost system. They worked in unison, built so that various business processes would mesh seamlessly with one another. If, for example, we received some inventory, the receiving module of the system would update our on-hand balance and tell its sister module to expect a bill from the vendor. Similarly, the general ledger would be posted immediately with entries to the payable and the inventory accounts.

"Even with the help of outside consultants, it took us 18 months to install the system in the United States. We all held our breath at the end of 1999, when we pressed the Go button. There was no way to implement parts of the system individually because of their integrated nature. If the new system didn't work, we were in serious trouble. But it worked!

"I had joined the company to be an architect of its future, and the here-and-now nature of enterprise-wide software didn't quite fit my mental self-image. Yet I'll admit to a sense of accomplishment. In time, as we used our networks more fully, the system became interlinked throughout the world."

Technology Continues to Change How We Do Business

"Today, 2008, is just as interesting as when I joined Global years before. The falling cost of processing power is still changing everything. Last year we placed an article titled 'Assets Are Talking Back' in *Accounting Now,* a financial trade journal. The article has been worth its weight in gold. We now make indestructible, plastic-coated integrated circuits with telcom and geographic positioning capabilities for $2.68. The whole thing is no bigger than the anti-theft device that used to be attached to items in retail stores: about 2 by 4 centimeters. We program them with an ID number, a service date, and depreciation routines. We permanently glue them to each of our premium-line night sensors at the plant. As a sensor goes out the door, we supply the programmed codes to our customers. Then their night sensor assets can call in periodically to tell where they are, how much of their cost should be depreciated, and whether they are scheduled for maintenance. We have almost 30 percent of the world's market for night sensors, and we plan to stay ahead of the technology curve. We expect the price of the IC devices that we are making will be under a dollar within two years. Then we'll build them into almost everything we make. Eventually, we'll sell the ICs themselves as others duplicate them. (There's no way to obtain patent protection.) We hope to have a cost advantage, because we developed them first and we have economies of scale.

Pricing

"We're coming along pretty well with our pricing algorithms. Scholastic philosophers debated for almost four centuries about what was a 'just price.' They finally gave up when economists decided that the best definition of a price is what a thing sells for. But the philosophers are back, and they all seem to work for Global. Now they are called 'market-clearing specialists' or 'pricing gurus.' It is incredible how complicated we've made things. In order to price something, we must first consider what it costs. That depends on where we make it, the price of the raw material on the day that we bought it, and the currency of the country that supplies the components.

"Oh, yes, there's that matter of value-added taxes levied by each country involved in our product logistic process. Global, like most companies, has consolidated its manufacturing and distribution processes to bypass high-tax countries, but there is only so much we can do.

"Then there's the problem of allowances and discounts to the retailer. If the retailer buys more than 2000 night sensors in a year, we rebate some percentage of the purchase price. There is the complexity of register-scanned sales credits: a frequent-flier mile to the purchaser, a coupon rebate to the store, and an additional advertising allowance to the chain. When all this is done, we add a markup that we hope will leave us some profit after we clear all the year-end rebates.

"Actually, I am pleased with what our pricing analysts are doing, even though I chide them regularly to keep it simple. Using our networks, we tailor a pricing plan that meets our customer's needs and, thereby, increase their loyalty—while maintaining a level of profit for us. Once the plan is established, our networks can monitor it effectively even though there might be a different plan for each major customer. Occasionally I'm tempted to try some type of definable, standard pricing approach to take complexity out of this process. I know, however, that our buyers' monitoring programs will pick up this change very quickly, and I am afraid that they might play us off against our competitors. At present, the one thing that seems to work in our favor is that even the retailer doesn't really know what it's really paying for an item. The chain has to go through the same calculations we do. Our prices are the beginning point of the retailer's cost accounting, and Lucifer visits them too.

"The complexity of customer-tailored pricing is one of the reasons that this matter has never been outsourced. We would never let Internet software take over our pricing work. It is too proprietary."

Investment Management
"Our investment banking subsidiary—now, there's a company that knows how to use networks. It has done a fantastic job of analyzing the shareholder value drivers of most publicly traded companies, factors it holds in its database. The subsidiary monitors every stock trade on each of the major markets and, using simple statistical variance bands, can spot trends almost immediately. We know that management will buy back the company's shares when their price drops below 'value.' We get there first.

"There isn't much margin on each play, but the dollars add up. Sometimes, when the company hesitates, we'll buy heavily and try to get control. However, this is getting rarer, because there is so much public information about shareholder value in the Reuters database that a stock rarely sells at a deep discount. When a company does sell at a low price, something is amiss. That doesn't bother us much, because when we get stuck with a loony investment we know how to turn the company around. Actually, we obtained many of our now-flourishing subsidiaries in this manner."

The Finance Organization

Contraction of Size, Addition of Responsibility
"My organization is actually very slim: financial analysts, technicians, merger specialists, treasury staff, measurement experts, software support people, and investor relations people, mostly —and plenty of tax specialists. When I joined Global there was a large financial staff, but we outsourced most of their functions and redirected the staff's work into much more important worldwide matters."

Accounts Payable
"After we installed the enterprise-wide system, we found out that, even with up-to-date software, we couldn't do some things as well as others could. It started with the electronic bill-paying network. We programmed our computers to send our raw material receipt data directly to the telcom's clearing bank, and our suppliers sent their corresponding invoices to the same place. Most bills were paid immediately, and at first

this was to me a source of some concern about float and our payables days. Paying bills rapidly decreased the interest we could earn on our excess cash. Interestingly, however, our suppliers quickly picked up our payment speed and reduced their prices accordingly; at least they did so when we asked them to.

"It took a while to get everything synchronized. There were discrepancies between our electronic records and those of the supplier. These had to be manually researched. Pretty soon, however, we found that many of the kinks were in our procedures, and we straightened them out. There was also the problem of small purchases made on the spot in every part of the company (for supplies and the like). But we issued debit cards with varying spending limits and eliminated the trivial paperwork. After a while, there wasn't much for the accounts payable department to do, and it shrank to nothing. Most former members of that department have become cost analysts."

Billing

"The same thing happened with our customer invoices. Off to the telcom they went. Oh yes, *our* customers also noticed that their payables days were decreasing. Our accounts receivables went down to six days, but our product margins decreased by almost a point when our customers asked for price reductions because of *their* quick payment. All this reminded me of how frail traditional financial measures had become in the electronic marketplace. Past ratios don't mean much any more. Our billing and cash posting departments have also disappeared."

Purchasing

"Purchasing didn't report to me, but this department diminished in size once we installed our new enterprise system. The computer previously alerted the purchasing department that it should release orders for steel and other raw materials. We wondered what would happen if we went around the purchasing middlemen and sent this information directly to the steel distributor. The answer is that we would have had three years' worth of steel in our warehouses. Fortunately, the vendor's computer picked up our unusual order pattern and alerted someone to call us. Again, there were some procedural matters that we had to fix.

Now, however, things are working pretty well—we simply have one of my analysts monitor the purchasing operation periodically. Global no longer has a purchasing department listed in any of its internal telephone logs. There is still the need to identify potential vendors, but the product designers take care of this. My staff follows up on any electronic snags."

Payroll
"The payroll staff hasn't gone away, but we've folded those that are left into our Human Capital department. The accounting part of payroll became a snap once we eliminated labor distribution.

"Some of you might not know what 'labor distribution' means. Eons ago, in the 1930s, factory labor was the major component of product cost. As time progressed, many companies established 'piecework' systems in which an employee was paid for how many things he or she stamped, lathed, or assembled each day. Therefore, someone had to record the production of each person and how long it took. Shortly thereafter, accountants recognized that this information would give them a way to know the cost of making things, and the labor distribution system fell under Lucifer's curse. By the 1990s, factory labor had become an increasingly small portion of the company's expenses; smaller than, for example, product distribution. But factory data was also easier to collect. owing to our plant-floor scanning devices and our data networks.

"We killed labor distribution when I received a capital expenditure request for a $14 million add-on to our enterprise system that would beam all this information off satellites and give it to us immediately. Just the thought of that information at my fingertips made my skin crawl. The capital request had great economics; the system would save enough to pay for itself in less than three years. There was a look of astonishment on everyone's face when I asked 'Why should we collect such information at all?' I was violating a basic belief of the day: that all data are valuable and could be archived cheaply. By this time I was a senior executive, however, so I had all the votes I needed (one). Admittedly, we had to rethink product costing a little.

"After labor distribution went away, it became pretty easy to outsource the payroll. My analysts look into our procedures every so often. Payroll

still represents 40 percent of our costs, but research scientists and office staffs rather than factory workers make up the lion's share. Incidentally, I redirected the proposed $12 million capital expenditure and put some of it into our product distribution procedures. I don't know if the third-shift painting line in Cleveland made standard last night, but I'll live with that."

Fixed Asset Accounting, Budgeting, and Internal Auditing

"Fixed asset accounting? Not much to it any more. We have a very inexpensive system that does everything we need. Primarily, the system schedules preventive maintenance and forecasts replacements; accounting is almost an afterthought.

"Departmental activity budgeting? Mostly, the computer does it. We did, however, develop an activity budgeting approach some years ago in which the departmental supervisor not only submits his financial budget but also lists the activities that his department performs. We compile this information each year to determine if the cost of these activities is going up or down. We also consolidate these activities into an overall profile of the company's major processes—for example, customer service—in order to see where we should apply technology. One time we noted there were more than 40 handoffs to process an incoming customer order that required special engineering. That made us come to grips with engineering drawings and part numbers. We now have a sophisticated network that allows our customers to configure the products they want over the Internet. The customers know best what they are trying to sell, and they are in better positions to determine the engineering tradeoffs. We still have to review these orders for production feasibility, but the operation is much simpler. Our activity budgeting system tells us that entering orders is significantly less expensive now.

"Internal auditing has been taken over by our analysts, assisted by our system technologists. I've also outsourced much of this to our external auditors—not only because I came from such a background, but also because the board is less jittery when we receive independent confirmation that our business processes are properly controlled. Our public accounting firm has tens of thousands of people worldwide and can

afford to invest in tools and training to keep them up to date. It is their core competency, not ours, so I get better auditing at less cost."

Taxation

"The tax department has grown during since my arrival in 1997. One of the things that attracted me to the enterprise-wide software package was its ability to compute the added value of an item at each stage of production. The software we purchased came from Europe, and its designers had to address corporate taxation, international tax treaties, and customs duties.

"Now I know how much value we add at each logistical step. Therefore, we have the ability to determine our tax liability quite accurately in every jurisdiction in the world. But, as an unforeseen consequence, the tax authorities can audit us. We used to be able to make broad estimates based on information so confusing that no one, including us, could understand it. I think we got the totals about right, but the amounts due to Kabul, Sacramento, and Paris were broad-brush allocations.

"Actually, we were fortunate to get the system working when we did, because Kabul, Sacramento, and Paris were getting their systems to execute and were beginning to understand where to look. Tax auditing is so lucrative that outsourced tax-compliance reviews have now become a significant commercial activity. Governments are contracting with private firms that will do this auditing for them, efficiently and at lower cost. We think about entering this market ourselves on occasion, but we know that our competitors would never let us see their records. It has to be someone independent.

"We've stood up pretty well to the tax audits. However, I know at least a dozen household-name companies throughout the world that will never get out of the courts. They would settle for about anything just to turn off their legal fees, but they are test cases, picked to scare everyone else into conformance.

"We have some 300 people on our worldwide tax staff, all armed with the latest communication technologies. Even so, there doesn't seem to be any way out of the mess. Every taxing jurisdiction has a different set of laws—rules that keep changing. My parents must turn over in their graves when they hear a good American like me say that we need a uniform, worldwide tax law. Yet, it's true."

Treasury

"Treasury is complicated, because we borrow and invest in every capital market in the world. We have computers that do nothing, 24 hours a day, except keep track of our currency hedging positions and compute the expected outcomes. Let me give you an example. We book an order for Japanese-made optical cutting tools for summer delivery, and we begin making a product in Ireland 6 months earlier. The Irish don't want to be paid in yen, they ask for punts; and when the transaction is all over, we like dollars. If the yen's value against the dollar falls or if the punt rises during the six-month order-fulfillment period, it could wipe out all of our profit. So we 'borrow' yen that we don't have, promising to return it 6 months later when our customer pays us. We 'buy' punts so we can meet the Irish payroll. That locks in our dollar profit except for the interest on the yen borrowing.

"It never really works the way I explained it, because we have about 15,000 transactions like this each day and we don't want to treat them individually. Instead, our communication networks try to balance out our currency exposures. For example, on the same day there might be an order in Ireland for items that will be made in Japan, and then the currency exposure might net to zero. Additionally, we may want to stay in dollars because we expect the punt's value to fall and we'll be able to buy punts cheaper at a later date. If it all sounds very complicated, it is. It's called *currency risk management*. Risk management is a commercial matter that we could never handle without computers and fast networks.

"We moved our treasury department to London in 2003. The United Kingdom had deregulated its telephone industry early and had developed one of the most advanced communication infrastructures in the world. Our treasury department found that it could handle all of Global's work and other companies' risk management besides, so we established confidentiality walls and bought faster networks. Today, we handle almost 30 percent of the electronic risk management commerce in the world, snatching it away from geographically oriented, slower-moving banks. We charge next to nothing per transaction, yet this part of our business is one of our most profitable.

"Treasury is one area, however, that we must monitor very closely—we turn our auditors loose regularly because there is so much potential for disaster. We may have billions of dollars tied up in foreign currencies on any given day. There would be much more, except that electronic commerce is taking some of the delay out of international business—there's less float time. Often, ordering and paying occur almost simultaneously. And if Eastern Europe signs the single-currency agreement our volume of business will go even lower.

"Our risk-management activities are so immense that the central banks of large countries can't let us fail. We'd take down worldwide commerce with us. Just last month, we threatened to unwind our position in one country's currency and de-list it unless the country took control of its printing presses and reduced inflation. The government fell. Our London treasury department braced for some unflattering coverage on the Universal News Network. You know, the usual: 'Have businesses become political entities?' However, there wasn't much we could do about it; we were too exposed. *Fortune* and *The Economist* came to our rescue with in-depth articles about risk management, but they didn't have the audience of UNN."

General-Ledger Accounting

"That covers most of my staff functions, almost everyone else is in scenario analysis. Oh, yes, we have two general-ledger accountants."

Global's Use of Information Technology

Communication

"The speed of communication has been a blessing to medical diagnosis, has helped people learn things more quickly, and certainly has enhanced the worldwide standard of living. Today, virtually every new household appliance contains some type of microcomputer that can be controlled remotely. Businesses are beginning to install wall-size plasma screens in every conference room, not just those of the leaders. These allow worldwide meetings to be held without airplane tickets. And technology has given us intelligent toilet seats for our home so that we can monitor our heart rates.

"But the technologies are not what is so exciting to businesses; it is their low cost. At Global we have an operations review center where we can bring up key performance indicators from any point of the world—and we can instantaneously monitor press releases from other companies. That gives us immediate insight into what our competitors are doing. There are technological advances every day—it looks as if a 3-cubic-centimeter, plug-in, trillion-bit glass cube memory is only about year away from commercial use. The falling cost of technology is revolutionizing business. A few years ago, we could only dream of doing things that are now commonplace. For example, we now use very inexpensive satellite pictures to monitor sugar plantations worldwide. We estimate the probable size of the sugar crop, and we can then hedge our futures contracts more accurately. Each month we record 'our impossible business dreams.' They usually materialize—fast.

"Each business advance feeds on itself. At the turn of the century, we supplied portable computers to our industrial customer sales staffs. Today, these computers are connected by the network to headquarters, and our design engineers can answer even the most complex questions almost immediately from any place in the world. Like others, we also use these communication networks to rush spare parts where needed and to remotely diagnose the failure of one of our products. Today, we guarantee that we will supply a needed part to any place in the world in less than 24 hours. We don't always make it—airplanes still have to confront weather—but even if we have to pay a few penalties, our image of service reliability impresses our customers.

"We have been building a database of components' lives, and we believe we will shortly be able to predict failures quite reliably. Statistical probability software is challenging our historical beliefs about warranty expense. We now believe we can turn this expense into a new source of revenue. We've already begun to pre-position some of our heavier components and some of those with long lead times at customer sites. Soon we'll put smaller components there too. Within a year, we plan to announce an 'absolutely no unexpected downtime' maintenance service. For a yearly fee, we'll service our industrial products machines ourselves, replacing still-functioning components during regularly scheduled field trips before they fail. We anticipate that most of our customers will improve their productivity by about a percentage point, so the price of our service should be easy to justify."

Software

"Software is the real lord of business success. Remember my telling you that our enterprise-wide software was very expensive? The entire project cost us almost $90 million before we were finished. Frankly, it was well worth it. Not only did it make everything mesh better, but the system even knew something about cost accounting. Except for its scope, there was not anything particularly remarkable about this system. It simply did what it was supposed to do very well, and in an integrated manner. What was remarkable was its impact on the organization. There were enough checks and balances in the new system to ensure that transactions would be entered correctly the first time. Therefore, legions of managers who had previously reviewed the accuracy of information and corrected errors could be redirected to more important work.

"Our enterprise software was a resounding success. But real business breakthroughs started with artificial intelligence software. I do not recall any one dramatic AI breakthrough—only small, continual improvements. As computers became more powerful, it became practical to program increasingly complex 'if / then' routines: 'If the customer is in the top ten, then refer the question to the lead service representative.' 'If the employee is new, then execute the fringe-benefit menus.' These 'if /then' routines could be linked together into an effective type of simulated reasoning—for example, 'If the fringe benefit chosen included vacation pay, then execute the vacation pay bank routines.' Eventually, as we tried more sophisticated reasoning, it became difficult to follow each of the program's logic paths to a conclusion—the software could maze through billions of alternatives. It was almost impossible to test new AI systems for accuracy. But gradually, with increasingly sophisticated software and even faster computers, we were able to perfect our applications. We don't actually use the term 'artificial intelligence,' which cannot be defined with enough precision, but we clearly have such applications.

"Today, we won't even look at the financial case for a new business plan if it is not accompanied by a technology plan. We put aside almost 9 percent of our revenue each year to maintain and upgrade our systems and networks. Most of the time, we don't even ask for a complete economic rationalization of a technology expenditure. To Global, computer networks are not there to save money; they are our way of making money. They permit us to monitor customer satisfaction. They allow us to funnel more products through the same distribution chain. They allow us to make more things in the same factory. They allow us to continually update our product offerings. They help us talk to customers even if they are three oceans away. They allow us to do double-entry bookkeeping without travail. They post our metrics on every employee's display screen. And they have helped us to grow into the twentieth-largest company in the world.

"When I entered the business world, we marveled at the falling cost of computer hardware. Now we are seeing this with software. There are inexpensive software modules that can be assembled easily into very complex systems. Object-oriented programming has brought about this cost reduction. For instance, we can buy a client object from a vendor, and replicate it for each customer, and the software knows the typical attributes Global will need to service this customer. The object will go to the Internet automatically and collect data about the company—its annual report, for example. With the annual report, we know the company's financial profile, the names of its officers and directors, its listing market, its operating divisions, and its products. In other cases, the client object will use "wizards" to guide our clerks as they enter other data, such as electronic billing addresses, terms and conditions, product announcements, and distribution locations. What is so amazing is that the master customer object can be purchased for less than $50 and replicated at will. Objects such as these are gradually replacing major portions of our enterprise software. They know how to link automatically with most of the commercially available software in the market.

"Today, there is a program module for just about everything, from blood flow diagnosis to underground pipeline mapping. There is even an object for California business taxes. All my technical staff has to do is download the object from the network and include it in the application that they are constructing. There are services such as those that were provided by *Consumer Reports* and J. D. Power that rate the effectiveness of the objects and their ease of use.

"Today's constraining factor is not the software, not the hardware, not the network. It is human creativity. We still need skilled, imaginative individuals who can research a business opportunity and integrate the technology needed to put the required process in place. Yet there is reason to be pleased: even the grade schools are doing an excellent job of preparing their students for the creativity challenge. A decade ago, we had the first graduates who had grown up with a mouse—the non-furry kind—in their hand. This century, just by playing sophisticated reasoning games at home, children develop abstract logic skills without human tutors."

The Downside of Integration

"Technology has ushered in much that has been very good. But when I get too complacent, I remember what happened at the turn of the century, when a millennium-date routine bug of a utility's computer in upstate New York brought down the Northeast's power grid long enough to disrupt electronic commerce. Because the lights were off at the clearing banks, panicked bank managers throughout the country turned off their ATMs. Consequently, people temporarily paused in their normal buying patterns. Company networks, sensing a decreased demand, backed off of their purchases, and their vendors backed off theirs . . . and the vendors' suppliers, theirs. It took Global almost 4 months to revive itself.

"The computer-commerce relationship was very fragile. Network technology had unleashed endless possibilities for rapid communication, sophisticated scenario analysis, and transaction paperwork reduction; however, the integrated nature of commerce meant that there weren't any short circuits to stop the automatic actions of our systems. There was nothing new about the cascading of reduced purchases throughout the economy. Recessions had always seen this snowballing effect. But the integrated nature of electronic commence added speed.

"We've been taking information technology for granted during this decade. But as we have been building our computer networks, they are having a profound effect on the worldwide economy. A small glitch in some out-of-the way place can create unforeseen consequences, because everything is so immediately linked to everything else. During the millennium year, a minor problem in a small utility's software affected our plants in Missouri. Today, something that happens in Berlin can almost immediately change our production plans in Singapore.

"Still, it is an exciting time to be alive."

David's personal digital assistant immediately converted his speech into print—and got most of it right. David pushed the "send" button, and his text was transmitted to Global's headquarters, where the PR staff would shape his outline into a polished speech, accessing video clips from the electronic library so David would be able to show and illustrate his points on the lecture hall's plasma screens. Fra Pacioli would be proud.

The electronic messages that David received after his talk suggested that the speech had been a success. Several responders noted they had been concentrating so exclusively on the technical aspects of the network that they had lost track of its real-world application. They appreciated knowing about the impact they were making. Several of the students in Shanghai liked the thought that finance is the language of business and decided to learn even more about this subject. Still others related their own millennium-date stories.

But the comment that David enjoyed the best was this: "I plan to study International Taxation next term. It looks like it will get me a steady job when I graduate."

8

Unseen Guardians, Invisible Treasures

Daniel E. Geer Jr.

There is nothing so powerful as an idea whose time has come.
—Voltaire

This essay is about security. A wise professor once described the "four verities of governance" as follows:

Most important ideas are not exciting.
Most exciting ideas are not important.
Not every problem has a good solution.
Every solution has side effects.

It is easy to imagine that security is, by virtue of its nearly perfect mapping to this list of verities, an integral part of governance. And so it is—with privacy as the side effect most central to this essay.

The best current understanding of the natural world is that change comes in short bursts separated by long periods of stability—"punctuated equilibrium," it is called. Change comes to computing in just the same way. Fast forward, if you will, from the very start of computing, and watch the successive waves: mechanical computing engines, then time-shared computers, then mainframes, then distributed computers, and now the leading edge of the next wave.

Yes, each wave solves the problems of its predecessor. The first computing engines were certainly preferable to deriving six-place logarithm tables by hand, but who could afford such devices in peacetime? Time sharing ameliorated the expense of the computer's rarity, but it fostered a general reliance on the computer's availability that made users vulnerable to a single point of failure. Serializing a company's work through the rigid discipline of an industrial-strength mainframe guaranteed bankable throughput, but it obliterated casual interactivity as an option. Distributing networked computers removed many sorts of bottlenecks, but the ad hoc, cloud-like interactivity it required came with (information) asset risk along both the "securability" axis and the "manageability" axis. The recent appearance of universal clients (browsers) and the "three-tier" model eased the management aspect of asset risk, but, if anything, it heightened the communications risk. Throw in the accelerating growth in connectivity and, well, what's next?

Since each wave has put more information in play, it is obvious that the future of computing will have security as a central organizing principle. I cannot recall a moment in computing history when Voltaire's statement that there is nothing so powerful as an idea whose time has come was more obviously attached to a single concept than it is to security today. But being at an historical inflection point makes prediction a challenging task. (Around 1949, John Von Neumann said "It would appear that we have reached the limits of what it is possible to achieve with computer technology, although one should be careful with such statements, as they tend to sound pretty silly in 5 years.")

Buckminster Fuller may well have had it right when he said "I have come to the conclusion that you can either make sense or make money, but not both." It is on this interplay that the future of security hinges. The series of compromises between individual and vested interests is still modifiable, and I hope that this chapter will enable the reader to participate in that design process from a position of fact. While it would be easy to write an essay of plausible sanguinity, that would be of little service.

Security

What It Is
"Security" has the vernacular dictionary definition "freedom from risk or danger." It is an ancient concern, little changed except for details since humans banded together to purposely modify the probability of having, rather than being, dinner. The means may evolve, but the ends remain.

In this, the reader may guess the first principle: that *security technology is about means, not ends.* The corollary of this principle is that the means should serve the ends. *The measure of any security technology is the degree to which it can be integrated into existing organization*—in other words, the degree to which it serves the existing organization's ends rather than bending the organization to its service.

But little is absolute, however comfortable some of us are with black-and-white characterizations. Security is unavoidably about tradeoffs, and it is in those tradeoffs that the end result is largely determined. What security technology can offer is a kind of decision making that broadens the class of plausible opportunities. In this sense, security technology propagates trust in an untrustworthy world.

In propagating trust, we transfer what we know in one setting to another place where it can be verified. If my spear can kill a jackal, perhaps I may confidently go where a lion lives. If I can provide my mother's maiden name, perhaps you can confidently change the mailing address for my credit card bills. Security technology is an enabling technology, not a disabling one. It makes much more possible than it makes impossible, notwithstanding the propensity of security salesmen to focus on fear, uncertainty, and doubt.

Nevertheless, security technology is interesting only at its margins. Any fool can say "permission granted" all the time; it takes skill to carry "permission granted" right up to the precipice but not over it. What security technology can do is define the margins more precisely so that less and less acreage need be spent on buffer zones.

I define the terms I will discuss below as follows:

authentication the business of proving that a claim of identity is authentic, i.e., that a claim of identity is trustworthy because it can be verified

authorization the (one should hope) formal process of giving access, control over change, or agency to an entity who (one should hope) has already been authenticated

accountability the ability to prove impeccably who did what and to whom

integrity the property of a message or a stored file which implies that the information has not been and cannot be changed by a hostile third party

confidentiality the property of a message or a stored file which implies that the information has not been and cannot be exposed to a hostile third party

non-repudiability the property of a message which implies that the author of the message is unable to disavow authorship.

With security technology, each of these words corresponds to a state of nature that can be obtained at the price of a tradeoff between risk and benefit. This is not a new idea. Banks do not verify every signature on every check. They establish a cutoff where the probable loss equals the cost of detection; checks below this amount are not signature-verified (the cost of verification exceeding the probable loss), and checks above this amount are always verified (the probable loss exceeding the cost of verification). The skill of the implementer of security technology is in adaptively balancing the cost of protections to the cost of risks avoided.

All these characteristics begin with authentication: who you are. This "who" can be individual or it can be a synthetic name (a "role" identity, if you will). All the other characteristics follow variously, but the question of who you are in the sense of your personal identity can be accomplished in only three ways:

what you know (e.g., a password)
what you have (e.g., a passport)
what you are (e.g., your fingerprint).

The idea of a what-you-know system is familiar to anyone who uses a computer, that of a what-you-have system to anyone who wears a badge. Sometimes the two are combined; for example, an automatic teller machine combines what you have and what you know. What you are is properly known as *biometrics*. Already, physically secure facilities everywhere use fingerprints, palmprints, voiceprints, or retinal scans. In 10 years, non-biometric identification will be quaint if it exists at all. The public's appetite for convenience and companies' fear of penetration will drown out any worries over having your physical characteristics online.

A few more definitions:

threat the possibility of getting into trouble, i.e., the possibility of entering a state where some information asset is compromised

attack the means by which an opponent achieves the threat, i.e., the means to get the victim into a kind of trouble favorable to the attacker.

What are the risks of a networked computing environment? The threats that confront any information-centric organization are exactly three:

unauthorized release of information
unauthorized modification of information
unauthorized denial of access to information.

Note that each of these threats begins with the word "unauthorized." Indeed, the dictionary defines the computer science version of the word "security" as "the level to which a program or device is safe from unauthorized use." Security is exactly equal to control of authority. If we are to get anything right, we have to start from that premise.

Yet categorizing threats is like categorizing disease symptoms; it's necessary but not sufficient. Threats are accomplished by attacks, and there are passive attacks (eavesdropping) and active attacks (message fabrication). There are numerous species and subspecies within those two genera, but their fundamental duality is as follows:

Passive attacks cannot be detected; therefore they must be prevented.
Active attacks cannot be prevented; therefore they must be detected.

If eavesdropping on message traffic, reading private files, or recording conversations matters to you, you must, a priori, prevent the corresponding passive attacks, because you cannot detect them in progress. Conversely, if false claims of identity, misappropriation of credentials, modification of messages in transit, or intentional delay of communications matters to you, you must detect it in progress, because you cannot prevent it a priori. In other words, security technology exists to detect modified messages (broadly defined) and to prevent eavesdropping on messages (also broadly defined). For both cases, we have one and only one tool: cryptography. The central terms of cryptography are the following:

cipher   an algorithm controlled by a key (a secret)
encryption   the application of a cipher to data
decryption   the recovery of encrypted data

Encryption is about keeping secrets: you keep a secret of your own, and so do others. When two parties want to communicate, they use their respective secrets to satisfy each other of their identity and their authority, and they may also establish conversation-specific secrets. This use of secrets to establish a claim of identity or authority has a long history. The term "password" comes from military usage, where it means, specifically, "a word authorizing the utterer to pass, a secret of admittance." This repeats my contention that all security technology is about propagating trust. Perhaps redundantly, I mean propagating trust across boundaries—for example, across an untrustworthy internetwork, between two unrelated corporations, through a national frontier, or by way of a courier. Irredundantly, security technology does not create trust—creating trust is, and must remain, outside the scope of security technology.

Because we base all security on the keeping of secrets and because the keeping of secrets is really all we know, the strength of a security technology is proportional to the strength of its underlying cryptography, whereas the strength of a security system is proportional to the inescapability of its application. This echoes the premise, stated above, that the quality of any security technology is measured by the degree to which it can be integrated into the existing fabric of the organization. The more "the security system" impedes the way people do their work, the more likely they are to try to work around it. If they can work around it, there is a combination of false confidence and pervasive temptation; the more they can work around it, the more likely a security breach will be. In that sense, the best security systems are undetectable as well as inescapable.

An important characteristic of any security system is *containment*. A ship has good containment when it has an arrangement of bulkheads and compartments such that no one hole will sink the boat. A security system exhibits good containment when an outright breach of one part of the system does not materially advance the attacker's ability to breach another. It is important to think big here; a security system means not just the security technology underneath, but the policies, procedures, and individuals that live among them. Security breaches are more about outcome than about methods.

Public reporting on security breaches is always spotty, so what we know about them is incomplete and biased. Nevertheless, an executive of an organization must worry about both tangible losses (e.g., diversions of the organization's resources) and intangible ones (e.g., loss of the public's faith and confidence in the organization). While the garden-variety cracker might have little real opportunity to inflict tangible losses, he can certainly inflict intangible ones. In fact, the real cost of a breach is measured not in dollars but in trust. (In one sense, a misuse of security technology propagates trust, too; it just propagates it out the window.)

It is tempting to imagine that "private enemy number 1" is, say, a teenage sociopath with money to burn, time to kill, and more smarts than self-control. This is a delusion. A person with skill, determination, obsession, and resources may be able to break into some arbitrarily complex computing facility or another, but that is not the point. A lone wolf is rarely the problem; internal breaches always dominate. What is an external attacker's first measure of success? Gaining the credentials of an insider. Therefore, a competent internal security regime moots external threats as a side effect. The one exception is when the lone wolf wraps up his rare skill, keen insight, and personal obsession into a program and posts it for an army of tasteless clowns to use.

The kinds of secrets we can keep are cryptographic "keys"—just numbers. There are two great families of cryptographic systems:

symmetric (secret-key) cryptosystems Two parties share a common secret key before communicating.

asymmetric (public-key) cryptosystems Each party has a two-part key and shares one half with its counterparties while keeping the other half hidden.

And there are two more terms worth knowing:

key distribution how keys are created and moved to where they will be used

key revocation how compromised keys are recovered or at least invalidated.

Symmetric and asymmetric cryptographic systems are more alike than they are different. In particular, just as all security systems are about propagating trust, all cryptographic systems are about distributing keys. The secret-key systems, because counterparties must share a conversation key before initiating information transfer, require an online, on-demand key-distribution service with which each party has a relationship in advance. In other words, the fundamental cost of secret-key cryptography is the cost of secure, low-latency, on-demand key distribution, but this mandatory pre-conversation exchange means that key revocation has zero marginal cost (the service just refuses to issue a fresh secret). By contrast, a public-key system doesn't require any in-advance secret sharing, but before initiating information transfer counterparties must verify that a publicly available key is genuine and current. In other words, the fundamental cost of public-key cryptography is the cost of secure, low-latency, online key validation but key distribution has a near-zero marginal cost. Table 1 summarizes this.

As a simple rule of thumb, *the cost of key distribution plus the cost of key revocation is a constant.* This (the security world's variation on "You can pay me now or you can pay me later") has implications for the places where secret-key and public-key systems ought to be used. Secret-key systems are generally better where prior relationships dominate, where messages may be both frequent and large, and where authority can be revoked promptly—for example, within an organization. Public-key systems are generally better where stranger-to-stranger communication is dominant, where messages may be valuable though rare, and where the costs of revocation (checking) can be borne as a tax on transactions.

Here is a final set of terms, the first of which you've seen before:

non-repudiability the property of a message which implies that the author of the message is unable to disavow being so—i.e., proof of authorship

digital signature the electronic equivalent of india ink on bond paper—the electronic mark that delivers non-repudiability of a message

public-key certificate a letter of introduction that binds a name to a key by way of the digital signature of an authority figure.

Digital signature, straightforward with public-key cryptography, makes electronic commerce possible. Digital signature and digital signa-

Table 1

	Secret-key systems	Public-key systems
Key distribution	High cost	Low cost
Key revocation	Low cost	High cost

ture alone can extend the concept of contract to the exchange of bits. Though the details are largely besides the point, you should understand that in a secret-key system you and your counterparty can be completely assured that your conversations are private, that your messages are received as sent, and that each of you is indeed who he says he is. In a public-key system, you and your counterparty have the same availability of confidentiality, integrity, and authenticity, but, in addition, should you have a falling out, you may be able to convince a judge of who said what and to whom. You pay for this with a modest loss of efficiency.

There is, of course, a lot more detail that matters, but this is good enough. You now know how to talk about the future.

What Will Be

Security is the central organizing principle of human society. Those who can deliver it answer "Who's in charge here?" on their own terms. Even though more than half of the people now living have never made a phone call, the information society is redefining the sophisticated parts of the world, and the rest will follow as they always have. The terrible beauty of electronic expression is that its cost of duplication and transmission is nil. Security in the information society is about how to bound flows of information that otherwise answer to no physics.

Vested interests are waking to the idea that the power which grew out of the barrel of a gun, the bankbook, and the concentration of useful arts has become vulnerable to information-centered power. In consequence, the information-security steering wheel has many more hands on it now that which way it is pointed is important. Technical progress accelerates; there is no shortage of horsepower to go with that steering wheel. In his book *The Art of the Long View,* Peter Schwartz says that even futurists consistently underestimate the effects of technologic inputs on the course of history. Let us not do that—we are playing for keeps.

Some changes in electronic information and in the security around it are certain; some are conjecture.

The first change, already here, is the introduction of electronic credentials that have some workable interoperability. Automated teller machines are interconnected in a way that would have seemed exotic a decade ago. Proximity cards can open doors in a company's buildings all over the world. Telephone calling cards work anywhere there's a dial tone. Merchants can "swipe" all sorts of plastic. Some colleges issue a single smartcard for every access-control and commercial purpose. In each case, the lure of convenience and the cost of misuse are balanced against somebody's taste for risk and benefit.

The second change, now well underway, involves fully electronic identities and the credentials to support them. The identities include email addresses, usernames, domain names, and World Wide Web services known only by their universal resource locator (URL). The corresponding credentials themselves are pretty idiosyncratic; conventional passwords dominate, though various hand-held devices may substitute for the well-known human frailties in password choice. As of this writing, "public-key identity certificates" are just beginning to show up in Web browsers; they are of little guarantee as they stand.

The third change, which has just begun, is a redefinition of what an identity is. The 1980s' great paradigm shift to distributed computing delivered "location independence," which might well be thought of as location irrelevance. In an electronic world, one might say "There is no there there"—that it is, as Nicholas Negroponte said in *Being Digital,* a "place without space." A fully wired world has no inherent concept of place in the physical way. "Location" last had meaning when it could be "surveyed and marked off" (as the dictionary says). An electronic identity is equivalently without physical embodiment; rather, it is exactly equal to the ability to control a name by controlling its cryptographic key. I postulate, then, a fundamental change: the boundaries of the future will be overlapping spaces defined neither by their geometry nor their mass but by the cryptographic keys that alone can demarcate the scope of their identity.

Perhaps the best first attempt at re-codifying law to match electronic realities is the Utah Digital Signature Act. As law must reach to issues of proof and conduct among strangers, the unique readiness of public-key-based digital signatures makes them central to what the law can describe and thus enforce. Recall that digital signature can deliver non-repudiability—proof, if you will, of a bit of history. As you should surmise, this proof is contingent on two presumptions: that the cryptographic details are solid and that the owner of the cryptographic key pair keeps the private half truly private. What the Utah Digital Signature Act does can be stated simply: A digital signature is valid if the key has not been revoked. Prosaically, if you don't protect your private-key half, you are nevertheless bound by documents signed using it. This change—likely to presage other laws—illustrates that the cryptographic key is the true identity, whereas your ability to use "your key" is more like the key's delegating its powers to you than the reverse. Ultimately this may be as important to the interpretation of rights and responsibilities as the introduction of legal incorporation in the fifteenth century.

This suite of ideas—that an entity is defined cryptographically, that what can be proved cryptographically is exactly what can be enforced, and that a cryptographic key is valid until proved otherwise—bends us in a direction where our collective intuition is ill prepared. Let me illustrate using a point of current debate.

If a cryptographic system is solid, only knowledge of the key will permit a confidential message to be opened, a digital signature to be made, or an identity to be proved. Thus, one who has access to the key controls these uses and, by proxy, controls the lives of those who depend on the key's sanctity. If we each solely control our keys, gentlemen and thugs will not read one another's mail. If, however, we are required to share our keys with, say, employers and governments, then our keys will not be able deliver the ultimate cryptographic sanctity. This leads to the fourth change: rethinking the tradeoff between privacy and accountability.

There is a continuum between accountability and privacy. Absolute accountability is possible only where there is no privacy. From *Brave New World* to the near-universal promise of divine justice in the end, the premise of absolute accountability is that nothing can be hidden. In counterpoint, the freest people (in the words of the *Oxford English Dictionary,* those most "immune from the arbitrary exercise of authority") are those who have a space which is theirs and theirs alone, both figuratively and concretely. To be absolutely free is to have the option of absolute privacy, whether it is the individual's interest in the nonexistence of "thought crime," the corporation's interest in trade secrets, or the state's interest in keeping secret (classifying) information as it sees fit. It is fair to say that each key creates a sovereignty, and the person who would be free must have the corresponding means to privacy.

Yet societies exist only as a result of compromise, and the spectrum between absolute privacy and absolute accountability is broad. Each historical compromise has picked a different point on the line. As has often been said, what is wonderful about a small town is that you know everybody, whereas what is awful about it is that everyone knows you. Military organizations lean so far toward accountability that they can care little for privacy. Frontiersmen of every era have sought freedom and have soon found that to be left alone it helps to be out of reach. In the information society, what will be the right tradeoff?

It is complicated, this question of what is the right tradeoff, but there is no question that some answer will be derived and that it will have downstream consequences. If we lean too far toward accountability and too far away from privacy, we may risk liberty itself. If we lean too far toward privacy and too far away from accountability, civil order may be threatened. At the time of this writing, not even in educated America does an informed electorate exist, and it is impossible to imagine that one will anywhere exist before this tradeoff is rebalanced.

History tempts us by posing the same question over and over again. To paraphrase Benjamin Franklin, "Those who would trade liberty for security deserve neither." To quote Thomas Paine, "The price of freedom is eternal vigilance." To quote Esther Dyson, "Encryption is a powerful defensive weapon for free people. It offers a technical guarantee of privacy regardless of who is running the government. It's hard to think of a more powerful, less dangerous tool for liberty." To quote Simson Garfinkel: "Privacy could be the crowbar that finally splits the classes apart for good. We already have the financially rich and financially poor, and the information-rich and information-poor. But we may soon add the privacy-rich and the privacy-poor. And that could be the biggest threat to democracy yet."

The fifth change is far off, but I believe it to be inevitable (and to be an opportunity for innovation in both technology and commerce). This fifth change is to make security and privacy into commodities that can be parts of the fabric of daily life, much as the complexity of telecommunications infrastructure is, for the public, reduced to a touch-tone keypad. Already there are glimmers of this. For example, many urban supermarket chains in the United States now offer the holders of "affinity cards" discount prices on groceries. If you let the chain correlate your purchases across and among shopping excursions, you will be granted 5–10 percent off at the register. The manufacturers of various products are interested in knowing who you are, now that this is feasible. I submit that this is an isolated but legitimately auction-based estimate of the price of privacy: privacy at the grocery store costs 5–10 percent. Another example: Early online merchants discovered pretty quickly that a "Web mall" is an irrelevancy. The only reason for a physical mall is that the co-location of goods and services draws customers with the efficiency of one-stop shopping. On the Web, however, everything is equidistant. Merchants quickly figured out that instead of co-location as a drawing card, they could find out a lot more about their customers than they could in real life because they could track the customers as they went through the Web store, correlate the visits, measure whether tailoring the visual "catalog" to your last purchase encouraged impulse buying, keep your order status in plain view for you to inspect, and so on. In other words, we have here a different sort of convenience-privacy tradeoff: the customer gets better service because the merchant knows him better. The improvement in service is bought with the loss of privacy, or the price of privacy is poorer service—your choice. One more illustration: Thousands of electronic discussion groups once thrived on the Internet with neither palpable administration nor participant self-identification, but then information highwaymen discovered that the cost of dumping advertisements down the pipe was so low that money was to be made with a return rate as low as 0.001. (Apparently, the percentage of gullible fools is greater than that.) An avalanche of "spam" destroys a free channel, but some have been reborn as ever-so-lightly censored pay channels. The cost: your money, your name, and your taste in subscribed channels. The benefit: the service of being left alone, at least with respect to the "spammers." The risk: that your privacy service is corruptible.

In their technically compelling paper Privacy-Enhancing Technologies for the Internet (CompCon 97, University of California, Berkeley), Ian Goldberg, David Wagner, and Eric Brewer show that only pseudonymity and anonymity provide real privacy, largely because only cryptographically enforced identity hiding provides a technical guarantee. Pseudonymity is interesting in that it can be a self-supporting commercial service: you can pay for pseudonymity in that you can pay for agency. Celebrities have long relied upon faceless agents to do what they, as well-known individuals, could not do. They have paid for privacy, and only the perfidy of an agent is likely to breach the containment wall. In an electronic world, cloaking the true identity of an individual is certainly a service worth paying for. and most Internet service providers have a goodly fraction of accounts that, except for billing data, reveal nothing about their holders' true identities. It is not coincidental that, from the outset, celebrities preferred CompuServe to its competitors because it had a policy of keeping all usernames pseudonymous.

Anonymity, a variant on absolute privacy, is harder to accomplish, for to be truly anonymous you must have conversation only by the most indirect of means. Already there are "dead drops" where anonymous counterparties leave messages for others to pick up if only they have the key by some other route. Will strong anonymity be commonplace in the information economy? Probably not, but an analog—non-traceability of payments—may be.

A sixth change may be merging what we know from ecology into what we know about security. Some advanced researchers are already pursuing the identification and repulsion of computer viruses. There is so much to learn here that it is hard to predict, but we must believe ecology's lessons that only diversity of species guarantees selection of the fittest, that self-healing redundancy is a good idea for basic encodings, that an infection of the immune system epitomizes "an ounce of prevention is worth a pound of cure," and that there is no such thing as an unalloyed advantage.

Commercial Concerns

Electronic commerce requires electronic payment mechanisms. Payment mechanisms are probably more numerous now than they will ever be again. At the time of this writing there are more than thirty distinct methods, each seeking a place in the sun. Each payment system is actually a security system; each has the problem statement "speedily move authentic, authorized, integrity-protected, confidential, non-repudiable messages over an untrustworthy medium between counterparties who need share no prior relationship." Each word of that problem statement needs precise definition before a system can actually be engineered. For example, "authorized" can mean "carrying two signatures," or "self-authorizing" (like cash), or "having a delegation chain wired into it," or "provably logged in a repository." Besides any pre-existing market dominance their sponsors may enjoy, what distinguishes each of these payment systems is what distinguishes any security system: the degree to which it can be integrated into the existing commercial fabric.

When Gutenberg invented movable type, the only customers were the monastic "amanuenses" (literally, "slaves of the hand") who copied books. They had evolved special marks and abbreviations which, to an extent, lessened the manual labor of copying. To print books acceptable to such customers, Gutenberg had to duplicate all these marks even though the existence of movable type meant that they were no longer as useful as they had been. By extension, any new technology must first duplicate a function before it can replace it. Thus it is with payment. The world's means for moving money, for clearing transactions, for translating among representations, and for profitably allocating risk must be duplicated before they can be reworked.

Moving money is relatively simple: construct a message that says "A pays B," cryptographically sign it, and send it on its way. To give it a transactional semantic, change the delivery method to ensure acknowledgment of receipt and strict ordering of effective times. What varies are the details of integration. For example, Open Market offers a payment system for Web commerce that cleverly uses the URL to carry not just page-location information but also invoices and payments, so that a merchant can use the Internet as conveniently as the credit card swipe box. Cybercash offers an electronic wallet that is closely analogous to the wallets we are all used to carrying. The Financial Services Technology Corporation sponsors an electronic analog of an ordinary paper check. Stored-value cards are already in use worldwide—all that remains is to hook them up to the Web. Digicash offers an electronic analog of cash.

The last example, Digicash, is perhaps the most interesting. As with ordinary cash, the various transactions between bank and account holder, buyer and seller, or merchant and bank are not anonymous; however, banks that dispense Digicash cannot correlate it with merchants' receipts, and there is no requirement for dispensed cash to be turned in to the bank after each transaction. In other words, Digicash is cash as we are used to thinking of it, only better. In the United States, many more personal payments are made in cash than by other means, though many more dollars move in non-cash payments. In most other countries, cash dominates both in frequency and in amount. Regardless of where cash is used, handling it is expensive in terms of labor; Digicash is much less expensive, as it is completely machineable and it doesn't wear out. It also crosses borders, so surveillance is not feasible—and therein lies the obvious debate. I predict that the absence of a sufficient private economic demand for electronic cash will largely sideline it, but that 10 years from now sophisticated people will mightily regret the passing of the kind of money that was backed, but not surveilled, by a government they then controlled.

Micropayment schemes are likely to proliferate over the next decade. Micropayment has a strong draw for information vending: it is the only way to introduce metered use to an otherwise unstructured world. Notwithstanding the public's affection for all-you-can-eat pricing, the commoditization of the Web both on intranets and on internets guarantees a metered-use pricing model. It is this applicability that makes micropayment inevitable by supporting private currencies that clear outside the existing financial networks. Management information services departments everywhere will embrace micropayment as a means of reinstituting chargeback. Every merchant who wants to give frequent-purchaser benefits will want to issue scrip redeemable at his or her store. Digital's clever "Millicent" even permits middlemen and their customers to buy and sell scrip while clearing scrip purchases in the conventional way.

Whatever form of micropayment one uses, it will be cryptographic at its core. Unless a "bank note" is signed, there is nothing to attach its value to its issuer and no way to prevent duplicate spending of the same note. Because one of the aims of micropayment is its suitability to sales of very low value, micropayment, of all the cryptographic security mechanisms discussed here, is likely to push hardest on the fundamental axiom of engineering: "fast, cheap, reliable—choose two."

Visa, Mastercard, and American Express have agreed on a payment scheme known as Secure Electronic Transactions (SET). This is the most ambitious implementation of public-key cryptography yet planned, and yet it is little more than an automation of the credit card swipe box—with one exception: a SET payment hides from the bank what the customer bought and hides from the merchant how the customer paid. The cost side for Visa or any other credit card association is fraud, and some of that fraud is by merchants. Hiding the credit card number from the merchant improves the association's bottom line, since a "technical guarantee of privacy" for the card number precludes that sort of merchant fraud. However, merchants want the credit card number in order to track customers and to handle disputes, so the privacy component may not actually be implemented widely enough to matter economically. Visa's early statement that absent sharing the credit card number with the merchant they could pass along a 0.5 percent discount rate savings can be turned around to describe the price of that particular kind of privacy. Were it not for Visa's market dominance, I would hardly imagine that SET had a chance of adoption.

The closest integration of electronic security with payment is that offered by smartcards. Though implementations vary, I will use the term "smartcard" to mean any electronic device in a form compatible with your pants pocket that stores something of security-related value to you. Think back to the basic drill with public-key cryptography: a key pair, the public half of which is published (like a number in the phone book) and the private half of which is kept really, really safely. I suggest that the only way to accomplish the latter is by means of a device which you can put in your pocket but which will not threaten your security if you lose it: a smartcard.

Of course, the smartcard is only one half of the hardware needed—you also need some sort of reader to put it in. To be really useful, smartcard readers need to be universally present anywhere your identity might matter, but putting them into computer keyboards and tying them to Web browsers is a giant first step—one that is already well underway.

The smartcard of 2008 will have your private-key half and your thumbprint; you'll turn the card on by incidentally touching it while inserting it into a reader. Anything transactional in nature, such as getting access to some resource, buying something, or changing some data somewhere will be authorized via the credentials on your card. Whether these are identity credentials or capabilities, the card will be the container. The only question is: Is that private-key half something to which only you have access, or is it on file with the gendarmes? Nearly all corporations and many governments maintain that they cannot let their subjects have secrets, so the smartcard may not be yours alone. Nevertheless, your smartcard will create (and hold) unique keys known only to you, because you will want to be able to issue credentials to others, delegating to them the ability to act in your behalf in circumscribed ways. For that, the smartcard in your pocket will be not only a client of security services but also a provider of them.

This issue of delegated authority will drive much of the technical elaboration of security. At stake here is not only the expression of authorization but also the circumscription of contractual liability. There can be no commerce without contract and no contract without recourse. In order for delegation-enabling security technology to spread, it has to generate revenue; however, because protection of any sort is mechanically inefficient, protection is a tax on productivity. Why not put that tax where it is easiest to put any tax: on transactional exchanges? In other words, we will pay for security via transaction taxes (whether in money, in time, or in privacy). Since interface standards promote vendor-neutral interoperability, technical means to express liabilities and means of recourse in the same language we use to express scope of authority will flower. I predict that in 10 years identity certificates will be used about as birth certificates are used today, but that delegatable authorization certificates will be used as often as we now use cash. In fact, I predict that delegatable authorization certificates will tend to supplant cash.

These variations on security technology are, as ever, necessarily cryptographic at their core. Only cryptography can offer proof that a warning was read before a license was exercised. Only a digital signature by a trusted third party can transfer risks from one to the other or undeniably envelope the transaction in insurance. Only cryptography can establish logs that will stand up to adversarial inspection. Only cryptography can delineate territory in a world without borders.

A Vignette

How might all this play out in "ordinary" life in the year 2008? Consider this fictional vignette.

Biometric devices born of the Human Genome Project can keep track of your location at all times merely by sniffing your DNA out of the air. You are in constant contact with everyone who knows your name, and only the global computing infrastructure arbitrates the difference between knowing your name and not. Names are the ultimate coin because security technology is merely a way to take actions based on identity, and identity is only a name. You might have several names, some known only to one group of colleagues and some only to others. These names denote privileges, some of which, because of the increasing powers of prediction born of the genetic science, are as heritable as a gene itself. ("You can't go there; you have a genetic weakness to exposures you would receive.") In 1997, only the very poor or the very rich never carried keys or money; in 2008, they are the only ones who do. The poor do so because they are not part of the electronic "First World," the rich because opting out of the dominant system has always been the prerogative of wealth. Voting is so convenient and ordinary as to be casually worthless, and the free market has led to opinion registration—that is, a vote is, like everything else, a secure binding between a name and an object of desire. Network traffic is taxed in much the same way freight once was, with occasional spot inspections serving the same sort of purpose (criminal interdiction, data collection, confirmation of other information) but with an instantaneity that begs for a judicial system quite different from the ponderous old one. Existing sovereign powers hold on more through reliance on a secure global positioning system than by any other means, but they are largely dependent on "trusted third parties" for anything connoting proof in the electronic sense. Nearly everything is auctioned, and the principal function of government is to extend to nearly every sort of transaction the kind of protections against runaway markets that only stock markets enjoyed in the 1990s. Taxes on consumption are based on legitimated auctions, the only ones where third-party recourse is still possible. New crimes have been invented, most of them involving the abrogation, hijacking, or sale of authority, and old crimes have passed into the sort of quaint oblivion that ancient English law is full of. Delegation of authority is a common idea, even to non-digerati, and the number of currencies is either zero or a zillion, depending on how you view an economy based on media of exchange that are ephemeral and trending toward grants of authority. Small merchants of non-perishable goods have disappeared, but delivery systems for everything else have flowered spectacularly. The public, well and truly driven by what per-person sophistication in advertising can deliver, is as grateful for the convenience of having all its wants anticipated as is necessary for it to overlook the side effects. Privacy is a privilege, not a right, as governments find themselves unable to enforce what they themselves would abjure, namely the quaint idea that gentlemen do not open one another's mail. Agency, via pseudonymity, has become an analog of and a replacement for privacy, and the relative wealth of the individual is measured in the difficulty of finding out what he or she is really up to.

Conclusion

I am reminded of Arthur C. Clarke's prescient statement that "any sufficiently advanced technology is indistinguishable from magic." Security technology is this kind of magic; even in a location-free, fully wired world, it extends the realm of the possible from absolute privacy to absolute accountability.

Security technology is at its best when it is invisible yet inescapable. It must be simple enough to be transparent, yet it must be effective even where enough booty is available that absurdly difficult attacks become plausible. Because of this tension, security's details will never be understandable except by the very few. The skill that is required to really secure a high-value facility is at least 90 percent of the skill that would be required to mount an effective attack.

Security technology is the glue between our physical reality and the electronic one. The balance of power is inexorably tilting to the electronic. The idea of privacy may someday seem as distant as the fifteenth century does to us in these last years of the twentieth, but surely we live with the effects of the fifteenth century all around us.

Who are we? What can we do? Where can we go? What can we say in confidence and without the chance that it can be twisted by others? What is the nature of proof absent anything tangible? Will the distance between the affairs of daily living and those of the real decision makers grow or shrink? Will history have meaning when all its artifacts are merely bits? What are the issues of identity when authority is delegated in open-ended ways? Is community really to become virtualized? If so, what does community membership mean? Might technological magic outstrip the general population's intuitive grasp and so becomes merely the modern analog of alchemy and witchcraft? Will your identity remain a stable mix of that which is unsaid and that which is perceived by others at a distance? In short, how will our children's lives and those of their children reconcile today's ideas of physical safety, intellectual property, and societal place with a world that need not hold those ideas paramount, if indeed it need attend to them at all? Security has a central role in all of this; please consider it in your enlightened self-interest to closely track its progress and to make it serve our highest ideals.

IV

Getting There: The Tasks and the Visions

9

The Walls Coming Down: Interoperability Opens the Electronic City

Robert J. Bonometti
Raymond W. Smith
Patrick E. White

Every day we see, hear, and read more about the emerging technological marvels that are paving the way toward next century's products and services for information, communications, education, and entertainment. The transformations already unfolding about us promise no less than a fundamental metamorphosis in the ways we manage our lives, institutions, and businesses. The nature and the fabric of economic and social activities are in flux, and the surroundings with which we are so well acquainted will soon be displaced by new socio-economic paradigms. Cyberspace will alter the notions of "community" and "workgroup," and it promises to redefine socio-economic structures, interactions, and influences. An important illustration of these forthcoming changes is represented by the concept of virtual hyperteams—associations of people and their computing environments that are not constrained by their members' distances in time, in space, or in political or socio-economic status.

Computing and communicating are no longer separable, and this suggests that "computication" may be a more appropriate word with which to capture the essence of the irreversible union of computers and communications. Economically efficient computication will fundamentally reshape business processes and indeed the fabric of everyday life in the twenty-first century. The profound implications of ubiquitous computication can already be glimpsed in several early-stage technological precursors that are evident today. Among the early manifestations of computication environments are the escalating speed and diversity of multimedia applications supported by local-area networks, by the Internet, and by network-centric computing architectures[1]; the emergence of unified messaging systems that integrate voicemail, email, paging, and so on; computer-telephony integration (CTI); the proliferation of hand-held personal digital assistants (PDAs) and personal communications services (PCSs); and the advent of interactive digital television systems that rely on parallel supercomputer-class media servers to host programming and interactive content.

The bases for the conduct of economic activities are shifting away from energy utilization, physical transport, and mass production to information utilization, electronic transport, and customization. To distinguish it from the familiar economy of the late twentieth century, the twenty-first-century schema should indeed be called "the electronic marketplace." While "electronic commerce" will be a necessary and essential element of the electronic marketplace, it represents only a subset of the coming transformations.

We are all well aware of the central role that standardization of currency played in the development of modern economic systems. Quantization and monetization of economic value in terms of a standardized, trustworthy, ubiquitous framework have been seminal elements of the foundational principles that underlie modern economies (mechanisms for measurement and transference of value, liquidity, investment scalability, etc.). We believe that interoperability will play no less an important role in creating the electronic marketplace.

Interoperability is so ingrained in our economic activities that we often lose sight of its pervasive significance. Without economic interoperability, what we view today as national economic systems would degenerate into non-competitive, monopolistic "fiefdoms" instead of richly integrated economic sectors supporting robust diversity in the production and consumption modalities of both cooperative and competitive classes of products and services. The complex ecosystem that underpins successful capitalistic societies is, unfortunately, not yet pervasive throughout the world.

When Boris Yeltsin recently visited a large supermarket near Washington, he was struck by the diversity of products on the shelves. He proudly proclaimed that Russia did not support such inefficient redundancy in its economy. For example, why is there a need for seven varieties of green beans to be juxtaposed on the supermarket shelves? Aren't all green beans essentially the same? While politely acknowledging President Yeltsin's observation, a State Department aide pointed out that competition among multiple providers ensures that Americans enjoy the highest quality of goods and services at the lowest cost. And, he further emphasized, our shelves are always stocked.

How will society achieve robust interoperability across the plethora of systems in the electronic marketplace? What is the appropriate business model with which to economically stimulate the provision of interoperability-enabling services?

The primary value-adding service delivered by "common carriers" in the twenty-first century may in fact be "middleware" services. The fundamental basis of high-value competition among providers of telecommunications services will not be connectivity based on physical facilities, as it was during the twentieth century; it will be mid-level and higher-level services that enable interoperability. In other words, the basis of high-value competition in the telecommunications industry is shifting from hardware to software. What we are suggesting here goes far beyond the realm of syntactic intermediation (which is already here in various forms) and into the realm of new and advanced modes of semantic transformations, which we dub "transinforming functionality."

The time constant for physical evolution of large-scale networks will remain rather long, perhaps on the order of a few decades; however, the time constant for revolutionary advancements of software based services and applications will be an order of magnitude faster than this. The telecommunications industry must learn to creatively extrapolate the slowly evolving capabilities of large-scale network infrastructures to support ever more advanced services and applications with middleware "glue logic." Thus, the primary value-creation opportunity for "common carriers" will be the provision of intermediation functionality that facilitates transparent, logical integration of diverse platforms, systems, and services.

The internal network of our economy has been electronically based for quite some time now, as illustrated by transactions between the Federal Reserve and its member banks and by various other bank-to-bank transactions. But the vision of an electronic marketplace extends to a ubiquitous end-to-end electronic infrastructure supporting commerce, marketing, information services, delivery of "information products" (news, electronic books, entertainment, reference and educational materials, government information and services), and financial and investment services (including banking and portfolio management). Among the key components of the enabling "middleware" services underlying this infrastructure will be interoperability engines, which will perform syntactic and semantic intermediation and service integration.

How Do We Invoke Interoperability Today, and How Good Are We?

Today there are two major perspectives on interoperability in the information age.

The first perspective emphasizes the interworking functionality that allows messages to transit different physical transmission and networking environments. We are all aware of the Internet's power to accomplish this feat. The Internet is not a monolithic network, nor is it controlled by any one entity. Rather, it is a loose (i.e., non-centrally controlled) global conglomeration of diverse networks that possess the power of internetworking by virtue of their adherence to the powerful and widely used family of protocols known generally as Transmission Control Protocol/Internet Protocol (TCP/IP). The interoperability represented by today's Internet can be considered "low-layer interworking," since it is concerned with the lower four layers of the conventional protocol stack. (Our references to protocol layers are with respect to the seven-layer OSI Reference Model, or OSIRM.)

The second major perspective generally held on interoperability today emphasizes platform-independent computing capabilities. In essence, this aspect of interoperability deals with portability of code across heterogeneous computing platforms. A simplistic illustration is provided by the familiar task of sending email between two microcomputers. If two computers are running identical operating systems and applications software and are interconnected via an Ethernet local-area network (LAN), it is not surprising that a message sent from one is faithfully displayed on the monitor of the other. But things become more interesting as the source and destination systems start to diverge. Perhaps one computer is running one resolution scale on a 15-inch monitor, while the other supports a different resolution scale on a 21-inch monitor. The top three layers of the protocol stack (in particular, layer 6) are responsible for shielding the end user from the complexity of differing hardware drivers and image-generation functionality. Now consider three markedly different computers, and just to make things interesting assume that one is located in Washington, one in Boston, and one in New York. The lower-layer interworking functionality noted above is performed by multiple network elements which establish a logical link between the three computers via the Internet. We are greatly simplifying the detailed story here and avoiding important details such as addressing, hosting, segmentation, and reassembly. Suffice it to say that the Internet accomplishes the delivery of bits from the source machine to the two receiving terminals in such a fashion that the original information content of the message can be recovered. But suppose now that the sending computer was an Intel 200-MHz Pentium-based machine running the Windows 95 operating system, while the destination computer in New York was a Macintosh computer running System 7 on a Motorola 68040 processor, and the machine in Boston was running Unix on a Sun SPARC station. Getting information-carrying bits to flow between these machines is only part of the story. The other part involves significantly different platforms' interpreting and acting on these bits and ultimately displaying faithful, semantically identical representations of the transmitted message. This is the interoperability job performed by the upper three layers of the OSIRM.

Of course, the real world is vastly more complex than our simplified illustration might suggest. For example, browsing the World Wide Web relies on distributed computing functionality in which your client software (the browser) works cooperatively with a distant server to deliver multimedia content to your desktop via the Internet. Interoperability "plug-ins" are often required to supplement your browser's native capabilities by expanding its functionality and/or by facilitating compatibility with extended sets of applications. Similarly, software "patches" are sometimes required when applications are ported to different machines and/or different operating systems.

One of the most powerful and significant paradigms in computing today is the object-oriented software environment. In a nutshell, objects are software entities that meld data and instructions into one self-contained package. The principles of object-oriented programming have fundamental significance for the efficient development of portable (i.e., interoperable) software code.

Whereas some past programming languages, such as C++ and Small-talk, utilized object-oriented technologies, fairly recent developments by a number of major computing firms on a pure object-oriented language known as Java have generated considerable interest and excitement. Java embodies a relatively new approach to programming that relies on instructions' being interpreted at run time, in contrast with older techniques in which source code was compiled into complete machine-executable programs. One aspect of this newer technology is its suitability for use in "applets"—small programs that can be efficiently mapped onto distributed application environments hosted on the Web.

Some firms have extrapolated Java in ways that suggest that a new paradigm of network-centric computing (NCC) is about to unfold. NCC's enthusiasts cite interoperability along with other properties such as low-cost streamlined "thin client" terminals as motivators for abandoning the more traditional base of powerful personal computers ("fat clients") in favor of NCC environments. Time and market forces will determine the outcome of this ongoing competition. Suffice it to say that Java is being heralded as an enabler of cross-platform interoperability for future applications developments. Other fairly recent standards such as the Common Object Request Broker Architecture (CORBA) are enhancing interoperability in object-oriented environments.

How good are we at achieving widespread interoperability today? This is not an easy question to answer, and subjectivity enters the discussion almost immediately. While great progress has been achieved in establishing metrics for the efficient development of software, we are not aware of any widely agreed upon metrical framework by which progress toward widespread robust interoperability can be assessed. As we build ever more complex, diverse, and pervasive computication environments, it may be worthwhile to devote some research effort to developing a metrical framework to gauge interoperability (and reliability) across very-large-scale environments.

Should we expect to see major interoperability improvements for systems and networks in the coming decade? We are not sanguine about this unless more emphasis is placed on the importance of robust interoperability. In fact, there is ample justification for us all to be concerned about the escalating diversity evident in the systems and technologies emerging today. The payoffs derived from the electronic marketplace will in no small way be related to our success, or failure, at achieving widespread robust interoperability throughout the infrastructure.

The Foundational "Infostructure" of the Electronic Marketplace

Our analyses suggest that a compelling vision of the electronic marketplace should incorporate the following elements:

• satisfaction of the "sacred" principles and requirements underlying fundamental societal goals, including universality of service (information anywhere, anytime, at an affordable cost), competitive markets, and multi-level fault-tolerant reliability of the infrastructure upon which the electronic marketplace is based

• unprecedented productivity throughout the societal infrastructure, spanning individuals to institutions

• personalization of information, communications, and entertainment environments

• simplicity of human-machine interfaces achieved via technologically leveraged complexity

• trustworthiness, predictability, and security providing the foundational bedrock for high-confidence environments

• architectural and system schemas that embrace the important and powerful design principles of modularity, evolvability, and scalability

• robust interoperability characterized by seamless integration of hypermedia technologies and information services across multi-modal hybrid network architectures.

These properties of the information infrastructure, or "infostructure," promise to make our lives more productive, educationally enriched, enjoyable, and perhaps less stressful. Productivity enhancements will span the spectrum from individuals (time-management aids, unified messaging) to entire vertically integrated sectors of the economy (health care, education and training resources, manufacturing systems). Speed, efficiency, and cost effectiveness will be promoted throughout the electronic marketplace (from health care records and insurance filings to inter-business electronic invoicing and payments) by widespread data interchange, as well as by semantically agile information and data fusion capabilities. Both humans and their machine-based applications will demand the ability to intelligently effectuate dynamic autoconfiguration of services.

Personalization and customization of information and communication services, from customizable "push" technologies to customer-driven service provisioning, will herald an era of unprecedented ease of use. Intuitive interfaces such as conversational programming will make possible previously unattainable levels of user friendliness. Although the human-machine interface will become progressively simpler and more natural, it is important to realize that the basis for this advancement lies in ever increasingly sophisticated technologies. Much as a professional magician gives the appearance of simplicity to a complex and dangerous act, technology will increasingly be called upon to cloak its own complexity.

As the hidden complexity of the electronic marketplace escalates, system-level survivability and reliability will create stringent requirements for robust fault tolerance and self-healing capabilities to permeate the entire infostructure. Modular, evolvable, and scalable architectures will mitigate concerns about capital stranding, never-ending technological advancements, demographic changes, and other risks that are inherent in the business of very-large-scale networked compucation environments.

Cyberspace today is greatly inhibited by concerns about privacy, security, and authenticity of information. A reliable and trustworthy infostructure is an essential precursor for a viable electronic marketplace. Competition, technological advances, and a legal and regulatory environment conducive to the needs of the new millennium will create high-confidence environments in which the electronic marketplace can flourish.

Interoperability is also essential for a widespread and universally accepted electronic marketplace. Many of the underlying sacred principles and societal requirements for the electronic marketplace, including healthy competition and cost-effective solutions for ubiquitous high-performance services, require an infostructure built upon the principles of interoperability. "Networks" will become hybridized (i.e., supporting diverse layer-2 and layer-3 protocols) and multi-modal (i.e., built upon multiple transmission technologies, such as wireless, optical, and electrical wireline). In other words, monolithic network domains will lose significance and blur together; only the conglomerate "network of networks" will retain a pragmatic identity.

The rich diversity of emerging technologies, exploratory trials, nascent deployments, and novel proto-business models—ranging from transactional schemas for business on the Web to new industries such as local multipoint distribution service (LMDS) and personal communications services (PCS)—suggests that the future will indeed be characterized by heterogeneous diversity throughout the infrastructure.

A New Age Approach to Interoperability

Notwithstanding the many desirable properties that diversity and heterogeneity bring to the electronic marketplace, they present us with the daunting problem of integrating and unifying disparate networks and computication environments. Rather than minimize or eliminate diversity, we should seeks a means of circumventing non-interoperability.

Past and present approaches to mitigating the undesirable aspects of diversity have focused primarily on standardization and regulation.[2] The large-scale public switched telephone network (PSTN) in the United States relies on rigorous standards to seamlessly bridge the many individual networks operated by independent service providers, and to ensure that the many types of instruments attached to the network's periphery are compatible with one another as well as with the technical requirements imposed by the network's architecture. The PSTN is an example of a monolithic network that uses rigorous technical specifications and controls to ensure interoperability across network elements and to guarantee quality of service. One obvious benefit of these standards is that we need not discard our phones and our fax machines when we move from one state to another.

Whereas standardization and regulation have been the primary means of ensuring interoperability, we believe that future generations will leverage technology in new ways that downplay reliance on rigid standards and regulations, at least in the converged domains of information, communications, and entertainment. Early precursors of this trend are already evident in some network architectures. For example, bridges and routers perform limited syntactic intermediation at layers 2 and 3 at the interfaces between subnetworks. Protocol encapsulation and tunneling are being applied to achieve lower-layer interworking. The most robust form of syntactic intermediation in networking architectures today is that performed (primarily at layer 4) by gateways—powerful network elements that can perform intermediation functions such as address translation and the resizing and/or restructuring of packets that must traverse subnetworks built to significantly dissimilar standards.

From Bridges, Routers, and Gateways to "Transinformers"

Notwithstanding the impressive capabilities of the interworking machines that are operating today, it is apparent that they perform few if any functions that require semantic interpretation of the information content carried in segmented form via packets. For example, decimating or aggregating TCP packets in IP datagrams does not require the interworking machine to "understand" or make judgements about the information contained in the packets. Yet this level of intermediation will become increasingly important in the networked electronic marketplace for several reasons.

First, the emergence of interactive computication environments in which humans interact directly with intelligent systems to receive services and to conduct information-oriented or commerce-oriented transactions will require semantic interpretation to be performed by machines, both within the network and at endpoint servers and information appliances. The tasks of discovery, navigation, and search through hypermedia content repositories can of course be accomplished by means of indexing schemes and keywords, but advanced capabilities in the next century will likely be able to directly discover, navigate, and search through hypermedia databases using semantic and contextual interpreters.

Second, logical interoperation of various media forms will require at least some degree of semantic interpretation. For example, a task as simple as using a voice-only interface device (say, a PCS phone in your car) to access information residing on a Web page and expressed as a collection of multimedia content elements would require considerably more than straightforward text-to-speech translation capabilities. How do you navigate to the site that hosts the information you need in the first place, when the sole user interface is your voice? Assuming that you are able to navigate to the target site, how will the information residing in multimedia form there be translated into a logically coherent and complete information flow relying solely on audio, the one media dimension you are currently using? There are ways to perform this trick today—for example, with distinctly accessible stored media versions of the same content (text only, text with graphics and images, audio only, full multimedia incorporating text, images, audio, and video, etc.). However, interoperability constructed with this type of framework begins to look more like an inefficient "Rube Goldberg contraption" instead of a suitably elegant solution for the electronic marketplace. The end state we prefer to envision invokes unique instantiations of stored hypermedia content which are nonetheless addressable by one, a few, or all of the media dimensions in which the information has been coded into its repository. The goal should be to maximize the media dimensionality of delivered information subject to constraints imposed by the capabilities of the accesser's computication platform and the network modalities that convey the information to its destination.

A third motivation for semantic intermediation functionality is the need for integration of hypermedia technologies and information services. This becomes particularly important when the burdensome task of discovering, analyzing, reconciling, summarizing, and acting upon diverse information sources is itself relegated to cyber-automatons. The tremendous potential of intelligent-agent technologies to elevate human productivity to unprecedented heights is only beginning to be understood in a comprehensive fashion. Far beyond "book report" retrieval functions, agent technologies promise to empower us with the ability to electronically "clone" ourselves. Thus, being in two (or more) places at once will no longer be impossible. An electronic clone will become a de facto surrogate capable of representing its creator in knowledge-based decision-making tasks associated with information and commerce transactions within the electronic marketplace.

A rational vision would call for agents to be empowered only with definitively limited powers of attorney. While you may be comfortable with your electronic surrogate buying a theater ticket, only the most technologically fearless among us might consider sending an agent out to purchase a car or a home! What does appear to be clear is that an efficient mechanism enabling agents to be interoperably agile will be needed in the electronic marketplace. Locking all of society into one standard for access to hypermedia databases appears as unpalatable as having to train each agent in myriad protocols and languages before dispatching it on an errand. Not far removed from these impractical approaches is the notion that every information server will be required to be capable of interacting with every conceivable agent that knocks at its door. Though server-based intermediation seems to make some sense at first glance, it too is beset with impracticality.

A fourth driver motivating advanced intermediation functionality is the as-yet-unsolved problem concerning distributed management of quality of service for hypermedia flows that traverse diverse independent networks, which we discuss below.

Analogous to the role which electrical transformers play at the physical layer to conjoin circuit domains with different impedances, we will use the term "transinformation" to connote semantically agile transformation of hypermedia content for optimized interworking of diverse applications on heterogeneous computication devices across hybridized multi-modal networking architectures.

Economic Imperatives for Robust Interoperability

Is interoperability an economically measurable property of the electronic marketplace? If it is, how can we estimate its value? We believe that the economic value of interoperability should indeed be quantifiable. Although we do not present a detailed quantitative model here, we suggest a rough order-of-magnitude estimate to gauge the importance of interoperability from an economic perspective. We first address several qualitative considerations underlying the economic valuation of interoperability. To demonstrate that interoperability indeed possesses economic value, we consider several ways in which economic costs are incurred under conditions of non-interoperability.

Consumers of products and services are economically penalized by non-interoperability. A direct manifestation is the absence of downward pressure on prices exerted by competitive forces in markets where the goods and services have low (or zero) barriers to substitution. In other words, interoperability and standards beget substitutable alternatives, which in turn beget lower prices as a result of competition among suppliers. Consumers also pay an indirect penalty in terms of lost flexibility, portability, and fungibility in the products and services they procure. A somewhat more extreme version of this penalty is the potential for becoming stranded on "isolated islands of technology," with the opportunity cost of forgone alternative choices exacerbated by the high cost of switching to an alternative. This is essentially a technology-based customer lock-in effect. The desirable state of affairs from the consumer's perspective would be technology solutions that are future-proof, at least in the sense of being cost-effectively upgradeable and evolvable.

This point is illustrated by business considerations regarding the provision of consumer equipment. Who bears the cost of obsolescence and churn? Three different business models are evident in today's markets:

• The customer buys and bears the risk of obsolescence and churn. Some examples of this are high-speed V.nn modem technologies, ISDN CPE, and the RF terminals and digital set-top boxes bought by customers under initial marketing strategies in the direct-to-home satellite television industry.
• The service provider provides capitalized items of equipment and bears the risks. One example is the analog cable television set-top boxes provided to customers for a monthly rental fee.
• A middle-ground solution where the customer procures heavily subsidized equipment. Risks are now more evenly distributed. The paramount example of this business model is the marketing strategy for cellular telephone services.

Non-interoperable technology islands can promote macroeconomic distortions as a result of inefficient resource utilization arising from lost economies of scale and scope. There is also a greater tendency toward inefficiencies when otherwise generic and co-specialized complementary assets become de facto specialized assets in environments where there is little or no interoperability. Mathematically, we may expect the economic valuation of interoperability to be a function of the proportional relationship between the number of addressable entities in a fully interoperable environment versus the sum over addressable entities within "interoperability islands." Consider, as a simplistic illustration, an electronic marketplace composed of 100 non-interoperable supplier systems, each supporting 1000 consumers across a total population base of 100,000 consumers. Without interoperation across the disparate domains, the order-of-magnitude metric for value in the collection of "stovepipe" microeconomies is 100×1000, or 100,000; conversely, if all 100 suppliers could address the full population of 100,000 consumers, the valuation metric is

$$100 \times 100,000 = 10,000,000.$$

Thus, the relative valuation of the interoperable electronic marketplace with respect to the non-interoperable case is a factor of 100 (the number of stovepipe domains that became interoperably unified). This should not be surprising; it is, of course, a natural extension and a corollary of Metcalfe's Law (which addressed a single monolithic network environment).

A second-order economic benefit from interoperability throughout the electronic marketplace is the availability of "perfect information" about competitive products and services, which is a theoretical precursor of an efficient free-market economy.

Complementary Perspectives on Interoperability

Euler and Lagrange both made important contributions to the theoretical development of mathematical models for fluid dynamics, but the conceptual framework for their models differed significantly. One approach was based on the perspective of a moving fluid element that is being acted upon by forces associated with the dynamic properties of the environment it experiences within the flowing medium. The other approach treated observable properties of the bulk medium from a perspective "outside" the flow itself.

Analogous to these two complementary vantage points, we can view interoperability in an abstract sense by following a given class of systems as it moves through time or by considering all classes of systems at a given epoch in time. The former perspective emphasizes the dimension of interoperability associated with evolution of the properties of a particular system class over time. This view focuses on the backward compatibility of the system's current instantiation with its predecessor legacy systems, as well as its propensity for forward evolvability based on advancements in underlying constituent technologies. The latter perspective emphasizes interworking compatibility (physical, syntactic, semantic, etc.) among all related classes of systems (say, communications systems) that co-exist at a given epoch in time. In analyzing the role of interoperability in the electronic marketplace and in its underlying information and communications infrastructures, we are concerned with both of these perspectives. For example, we can follow the evolution of the systems that promote transactional liquidity at a point of sale (PoS) in the domain of electronic commerce. The predominant system performing this function today is the magnetic-strip credit card, which is read at a retail PoS terminal and electronically approved for use in the particular transaction. This system's predecessor was a non-magnetic imprint-oriented credit card, which required manual intervention in the form of telephonic query for usage approval. Clearly, the present instantiation is backward compatible with the system externalities of the imprint-oriented generation, as we all have experienced when long delays occur at the checkout counter because the card reader or its network connection has failed, forcing the retail establishment to fall back on the plain old telephone system (POTS) to obtain approval. On the other hand, it is likely that the current generation of credit cards will eventually be supplanted by smart-card technologies, which will (one hopes) retain full backward compatibility but will offer enhanced features, such as improved security and low-cost direct interfaces with personal computers (so that manually entering credit card numbers on the keyboard will not forever plague Internet-based electronic commerce transactions). Ease of use may be improved by future smart-card technologies that will rely on wireless physical interfaces, perhaps using the newly designated unlicensed NII-band spectrum at 5 gigahertz.

Let us extend the credit card illustration to present an example of the "snapshot in time" perspective on interoperability. Considering the present epoch, it is apparent that magnetic-strip credit card systems depend on network externalities, such as the speed, reliability, and accessibility of connections from the remote point of sale to a host computer that handles the approval process. Today's credit card reader must be inter-operable with a number of networking technologies, such as POTS and VSAT satellite systems.

The Nature of Standards: Do Competitive Market Forces Promote or Inhibit Interoperability?

Standards can help to enhance the quality of goods and services, and they can help consumers avoid "technology stranding"[3] and get flexibility and portability in the products and services they choose. Standards promote downward pressure on prices, and they tend to stimulate multiple sour-cing and robust co-marketing of ancillary products and services. For example, microcomputer purchasers today have a wide variety of manu-facturers to choose from, and there is prolific value-adding economic activity by independent software vendors.

Though these motivations for standards make sense from the perspec-tive of consumers of products and services, they are less compelling to producers. Firms can be expected to leverage their distinctive competitive advantages to achieve the highest practical degree of customer attraction and lock-in. In many cases, customer lock-in is an essential element of a firm's strategy, particularly as it relates to aftermarket goods and services.

Over the past decade, W. B. Arthur ("Increasing Returns and the New World of Business," *Harvard Business Review,* July-August 1996) and other economists have emphasized the fundamental importance of the law of increasing returns as it relates to sustaining high rates of growth in technology-intensive industries, particularly software-based industries. Thus we arrive at an apparent paradox regarding the effects of standards on producers of goods and services. Not surprisingly, while it is quite common for producers to recognize the benefits they can mutually derive by freely and cooperatively developing standards, there are also cases where external pressures must be exerted to compel the development of standards. This is the important juncture of the public-policy environ-ment with standards-making activities. Standards-making activities range from those driven entirely by industry and trade associations to govern-ment laws and regulations. The public-sector objectives that foster gov-ernment involvement include the health and welfare of the citizenry, the allocation and coordinated use of scarce resources (such as the electromagnetic spectrum), and the preclusion of monopolistic power by one or a few dominant players in an industry.

A simplified model of innovation and technology development can provide insight into the apparently dichotomous forces that impel both producers and consumers to seek interoperability in the goods and services they exchange. Introduction of a fundamental innovation into an industry generally results in the entry of a number of entrepreneurial competitors as design optimization is hotly pursued. Competition in the early stages of the nascent industry's life cycle tends to be based less on pricing than on functionality, performance, and features (including ergonomic factors). The market is driven by pro-technology, risk-taking early adopters and lead users.

This scenario can play out only so long before several powerful forces lead to establishment of a dominant design. First, a technologically superior instantiation of the new product or service may compel the industry and its marketplace to coalesce around it. Second, one competitor may emerge as dominant not necessarily because its design is the best but rather because that competitor is able to achieve decisive competitive advantage by leveraging complementary assets (e.g., brand equity, marketing and distribution channels, strategic alliances with other vendors). The third force leading to establishment of a dominant design is market demand for "grand unification"—in other words, the market's tendency to gravitate toward universality and consistency in the products and services it consumes. For pragmatic reasons, users demand temporal and geospatial interoperability as a means of attaining economic efficiencies and reduced complexity. (American consumers would not be happy if moving from one state to another required them to replace all their electrically operated devices because the power grids were based on different voltages and line frequencies.) A fourth force promoting standardization is the desire by vendors and service providers to achieve economies of scale and scope. If no single vendor has sufficient market power to attain a "winner take all" outcome in the competitive battles of an early-stage industry, one or more groups of producers may opt for cooperation and coalesce around a compromise design.

These forces compel collapse of the diversity inherent in the early-stage industry. Whatever the major stimulus, barring a unique victor, communities of interest arise to cooperatively (or at least pseudo-cooperatively) embrace interoperability. Often, catalytic forces, such as the influence of standards-making forums and government oversight agencies, are also at work. An oftentimes complex and protracted politicized process then ensues as various factions vie for dominance in the compromise solution. Producers seek to achieve competitive leverage by having their proprietary technology dominate the compromise standard, thereby receiving the market-expansion benefits derived from standardization while nonetheless preserving their competitive advantages in the underlying product and process technologies. Next to outright victory in the battles of an early-stage industry, this outcome is most beneficial to the dominant faction: it reduces their time to market (they are producing product while their competitors are ramping up to implement the newly defined standard), and it speeds their attainment of economies of scale and scope in production processes. This is quite obviously a high-stakes game, and proponents of various competing platforms for standardization are motivated to make political deals with others in the community of interest in order to achieve maximum support for their proposals.

The complexity of the interactions among competing factions and as-yet-unaligned parties introduces inherent delays into the standardization process as compromises and alliances are built. Delay tactics are often artificially introduced into the negotiation process by weaker vendors seeking to achieve parity with their stronger adversaries, or at least to reduce their competitors' time-to-market advantage. The greater the number of competing proposals and the more zealous the participants (i.e., the greater the benefits one may win if one's proposal dominates the new standard), the greater is the probability of fragmentation during the quest for standardization. A well-known example of such fragmentation is provided by the case history of Unix, an erstwhile universal language now available in multiple (non-interoperable) flavors.

By one means or another, a de facto standard emerges. Quite often a standard is formalized and legitimized through its adoption as an "official standard" by one or more cognizant standards-making bodies. The industry then enters the mature middle stage of its life cycle, which is characterized by high volume, evolutionary embellishment of the dominant design, and price-sensitive competition. The market is no longer driven by early adopters, but rather by mainstream consumers. Eventually, the standardized solution to the interoperability quest becomes obsolete as the industry enters the late stage of its life cycle. Newer technologies begin to drive yet another wave of innovation, and the cycle is born again.

Several factors can lead to dilution of the power and effectiveness of a standard. Incomplete and/or imprecise specification of a standard can result in de facto non-interoperability of "conforming" systems defined by excessively broad specifications. Fragmentation of the community of interest, noted above, can also be highly detrimental to a standard's effectiveness. We cited the case of Unix, and there are many other similar examples, including ISDN and, more recently, the apparent fracturing of the community of interest for compressed voice over frame relay services. (The Frame Relay Forum chose G.729 for FRAD products with voice capability; Microsoft adopted G.723.1 because of its compatibility with the H.324 standard for videoconferencing.)

Despite the challenges inherent in standards development, and notwithstanding the several cases we have cited in which the power and effectiveness of a standard became diluted, we want to emphasize that there are also many important success stories, or at least partial success stories, including the alignment of SONET and SDH standards for worldwide interoperability of broadband ISDN technologies and the progress made by the Grand Alliance process in the development of standards for high-definition TV.

We conclude our discussion of standards-making processes with a note of concern for the future. We are all well aware of the tremendous competitive, technological, and economic benefits to be derived from convergence of the communications, information, and entertainment industries. The two primary forces driving the convergence of these industries are the technological ramifications of digital microelectronics and the new laws and regulations that are breaking down the artificially induced historical segmentation of these industries (and, indeed, sectors within these industries, such as local and long-distance telephony). The concern we raise stems from a side effect of digital convergence that may undercut interoperability: the cancerous growth in the size and scope of the respective communities of interest involved in particular standardization domains. One need only attend recent meetings of bodies such as the ATM Forum, the Internet Engineering Task Force, and many other standards-development forums to witness firsthand the dramatic growth in communities of interest. While the time scales for technological advancements and product development cycles are continually shrinking, the increasing bureaucratic inertia of our standards-making bodies threatens to undermine the effectiveness of standards in achieving interoperability solutions in a timely manner. Certainly improvements in organizational dynamics and processes can ameliorate this, but another solution may well lie in technology's ability to save itself.

Desperately Seeking Interoperability: From Digital Esperanto to the N^2 Conundrum

There is actually a spectrum of approaches to interoperability, in an abstract sense. At one end is "Digital Esperanto," a rigid and unique universal language for the electronic marketplace. This extreme solution is neither practical nor desirable for a number of reasons, including its technological intractability and its chilling effect on the advancement of technology. Other concerns include difficult and expensive conversion of legacy systems and susceptibility to catastrophic failure modes that are mitigated by diversity within a network of networks. At the other end of the interoperability spectrum is a nonsensical modality that we call "the N^2 conundrum." In contrast with rigid adherence to the unique protocol of Digital Esperanto, this approach freely admits any and all narrow-domain "standards," including the many proprietary flavors that would arise. Its premise is that interoperability can be achieved in a straightforward manner by translation from any one "standard" to any other "standard." Clearly, the order of complexity required in the translation engine tends toward N^2, where N is a large number corresponding to the plethora of independent protocols and languages. While one may argue that advanced capabilities in processors and dense memory technologies may make this approach feasible, the complexity and the management burden associated with distributed, real-time change control across the many languages in use suggests that technology will not be able to save itself from a Tower of Babel fate if it relies strictly on this brute-force approach alone.

Though even twenty-first-century technologies are not expected to be capable of coping with arbitrary degrees of diversity, we can expect powerful capabilities to be available for dealing with reasonable levels of diversity provided that a meta-architectural control layer is implemented in a morphologically efficient manner. We suggest that the fundamental role for standards in the era of technology-enabled interoperability will be simply to minimize the number of non-interoperable domains to a manageably small number.

What is the most efficient meta-architectural control point in the electronic marketplace? Our thesis is that this functionality is optimally hosted within communications networks, as opposed to implementation in edge devices. There are three main points to be addressed regarding the undesirable properties associated with performing interworking functions at the edges of a network.

First, assigning responsibility for syntactically and semantically agile translation to devices at the edge of the networked electronic marketplace (servers and end-user devices) does not achieve a realistic or efficient solution for interoperability. This is true even if N, the number of non-interoperable domains that must be interconnected, is maintained at a modest value. (Of course, too modest a value brings us back to the problems associated with the Digital Esperanto approach.) The main problem with edge devices performing interworking functionality is that these computication systems become needlessly burdened with expensive complexity.

Even if one assumes that "client-side" terminals will speak only one language (so that they remain compact, inexpensive, and power efficient) and "server-side" network elements will assume the full burden of translations, one arrives at a solution mode that might be technologically feasible but nonetheless is grossly inefficient. For example, if you operate a Web site to support your business, do you really want to be burdened with maintaining up-to-date interoperability drivers on your local server so that no customer will turn away because of a language barrier? This example leads to the second main point: that distributed real-time management of change control at every independent edge server on the Internet (and throughout the networked electronic marketplace) is overly complex and non-economical.

The third point concerns the management of quality of service across independent, multi-modal hybrid networks that lie between the source and the sink of an information flow. We devote the next section to this important topic.

Quality of Service

"Quality of service" (QoS) describes the degree of "goodness of fit" that a network provides in support of the requirements of endpoint users and applications. Although parameters may be specified with respect to sections and elements constituting a network, it is important to recognize that quality of service is fundamentally an end-to-end issue and that it can differ significantly for various information flows coexisting in a network at any given time.[4] Although operators of monolithic networks can guarantee quality of service to their exclusive customers by maintaining network performance parameters within established technical limits, monitoring (let alone controlling) quality of service in the "network of networks" environment is far more problematic.[5] This is a major motivator for "intranets," which are networks relying on basic Internet technologies but operated under the exclusive control of some entity that can, in fact, assure quality of service and guarantee security.

As we progress toward a multi-modal hybrid network environment as the underlying infrastructure for the electronic marketplace, we will be increasingly confronted with end-to-end service-assurance dilemmas. Not only must technical issues be resolved, but new business and legal frameworks will undoubtedly be required. These new models must address the business operating relationships and responsibilities among the many legally independent network entities that must cooperate and interoperate in a technically interdependent manner to enable quality of service to be measured and controlled, in a distributed sense, to satisfy the dynamically changing portfolio of customer requirements. Since end-to-end QoS assurance in a multi-modal hybrid network environment requires dynamically coordinated interactions between underlying network domains, we consider it to be an important issue under the broad theme of interoperability.

Many difficult technical and legal questions need to be addressed. Who bears responsibility for quality of service across diverse, heterogeneous networks? How is quality of service specified, requested, negotiated, measured, and maintained across disparate hybrid networks? What roles must be played by the many interoperating carriers and network operators?

One thing appears to be clear: while end-user hardware and software can be expected to play important roles in resolving the quality-of-service dilemma for multi-modal hybrid networks, the endpoints can only contribute functionality that can be considered necessary, but far from sufficient, in resolving the overall problem. This is the third reason why interoperability cannot be implemented only at the network periphery. Quality of service may ultimately have meaning only at service endpoints, but it must nevertheless be managed cooperatively by all elements of a heterogeneous "network of networks." In order for this goal to be realized, future meta-networking architectures must support real-time negotiation between service endpoints and the collection of (legally independent) network elements. Furthermore, robust protocols for distributed management and control across independent networks must be developed so that the full parametric trade space affecting quality of service can be utilized to best meet the fluctuating requirements of endpoint users and applications.

How to apportion legal responsibilities and liabilities among service providers and network operators must also be worked out. One approach might be to assume that all links via "public" or "common carrier" networks, including all Internet connections, are absolved from any liability associated with QoS degradations—in other words, to apply the principle of caveat emptor to publicly accessible networks. This approach then requires those users with mission-critical QoS requirements to build or lease intranet facilities. Though this solution is appealingly simple, it is doubtful that it well serves the needs of the electronic marketplace to be reliable, trustworthy, and predictable.

Another seemingly straightforward approach might be to require independent network operators to establish upper bounds on parameters that affect end-to-end quality of service for traffic that traverses their network domain. It is not clear that this approach can be implemented in a pragmatic way. Pre-arranged cooperative service agreements may not be flexible enough to deal with rapid fluctuations in the types and volumes of data flows. It is doubtful that such a "static solution" could adequately satisfy the complex and fluctuating quality-of-service requirements of large populations of users, let alone accomplish this while maintaining highly efficient utilization of network resources. Furthermore, the mechanism for apportionment of liabilities across multiple service providers supporting myriad users over many different multimodal hybrid networks would still need to be resolved.

On the other hand, micro-managing the "network of networks" to ensure reliability, security, and quality of service may well prove impossibly complex and expensive. Network monitoring, control, and administration functions (such as billing) would become unwieldy if information flows were managed on a packet-by-packet basis at the interfaces between independent networks. Additionally, the resulting delays introduced to accomplish this might be incompatible with end-to-end delay requirements. These are two of the more compelling arguments for flat-rate billing. The major danger here is that the cost of monitoring, controlling, and administering services may well become much greater than the cost of providing the services.

It will be essential to support a robust hierarchy of guaranteed service classes to satisfy the diverse QoS requirements of the electronic marketplace. In particular, guaranteed quality of service for applications requiring real-time flows of information will be increasingly demanded by people and their applications. A realistic solution must recognize that individual ("monolithic") networks will be fully independent in a business sense and in a legal sense. The myriad elements of these independent networks will be geographically dispersed, physically distributed, and logically segmented, but they must also be intelligently cooperative. The fundamental approach to quality of service must be based on intelligent, cooperative network elements distributed throughout the multi-modal hybrid infrastructure. Collectively, these elements will be capable of supporting a variety of endpoint service requirements.

Another significant concern about quality of service stems from the ramifications of "forced pseudo-interoperability"—that is, transcoding between "lossy" compression algorithms used for voice, video, data, etc. Compression and coding technologies enable efficient bandwidth utilization for information transport and storage. They are absolutely essential to the creation of viable business opportunities for services that would otherwise be uneconomical and/or impractical to provide, such as direct-to-home satellite television. Dynamic channel adaptation (i.e., adjusting degree of compression in response to the changing conditions of a communications channel) may even have some potential as a surrogate for encryption-based access control.

In a monolithic network architecture, high compression ratios can be achieved by means of sophisticated algorithms that are "lossy" in the sense that perfect reconstruction of the information content is not guaranteed. Despite this ominous description, lossy compression algorithms are in widespread use because their benefits far outweigh the side effects (for example, occasional small distortion in a television image regenerated by a video codec from a stream of compressed video data, or equivalently small distortions in a speaker's voice incurred by speech compression). The imperfections in the reconstructed signal are generally small and manageable; however, should a need arise to convert one highly compressed signal into a differently compressed form (due primarily to implementation of different encoding algorithms at service endpoints), the resulting imperfections can be magnified significantly.

The need for transcoding appears to be on the rise, and it may become relatively commonplace in the electronic marketplace. For example, different engineering approaches for PCS architectures incorporate different vocoding (voice encoding and decoding) schemes. While quality of service can be adequately measured, monitored, and controlled for a given architectural platform, the situation is far less benign when a user on one architecture (say, GSM) is conversing with a user on a different PCS architecture (say, CDMA). Another example is the use of different vocoders in various vendors' approaches to enable voice traffic to be carried via the Internet (often referred to as "voice over IP").

Although it is straightforward to calculate the overt economic cost of encoding and decoding associated with hardware and software required in endpoint equipment and/or in network processing elements, it is much more difficult to assess the overall penalties incurred under transcoding environments. These penalties range from degraded but usable service to outright disruption. In its logical extreme, non-interoperability engendered by lossy transcoding environments may be a major contributor to the "digital Tower of Babel" syndrome.

Tearing Down the Digital Tower of Babel

Can technology ultimately save itself from a "Digital Tower of Babel" fate by enabling efficacious bridges to be built between "interoperability islands"? If it can, what are the key technical challenges?

The challenges associated with designing, implementing, and maintaining disparate engines that will bridge non-interoperable environments are exacerbated by the ever-changing nature of the technological landscape. Cross-platform application and service independence such as that provided by Java and related developments is important, but unfortunately it is not sufficient to remove requirements for network-based intermediation.

Components of a Research Agenda for Technology-Enabled Interoperability

This section highlights four representative research areas that we believe are essential to achieving the goal of technology-enabled interoperability[6]: Advanced Directory Services, Active Networks, Advanced Network Management Techniques for Multi-modal Hybrid Networks, and Complexity Theory and Application.

Advanced Directory Services (ADS) are a major element in the quest for interoperable services and integration of heterogeneous distributed computing environments, including network-centric computing. Operating-system hegemony was a key element of the winning strategy in the war for dominance of desktop computing. Similarly, advanced directory services are expected to play a pivotal role in the race for dominance of network-centric and Internet-based or Web-based computing environments. These environments will require rapid, seamless integration of dispersed, distributed applications hosted across diverse, heterogeneous computing platforms.

Directory-service concepts are familiar in many networking environments today. We are all familiar with the numbering scheme and the associated directory used in the plain old analog telephone system. ISDN uses numbering and directory services governed by the E.164 standard. The Internet uses a four-part addressing scheme for IP datagrams.

Asynchronous transfer mode (ATM) networks are using their own distinct cell-based addressing scheme built around virtual path and virtual circuit identifiers.

The challenges motivating further research in ADS stem not only from the greater scale and complexity of the future "network of networks" but also from the need to reconcile the multiple addressing schemes used by the various networking environments across the electronic marketplace. Furthermore, fast and efficient interoperable directory services are essential for distributed computing environments, which are becoming increasingly intolerant to latency. ("Latency" refers to delays introduced by network elements in passing data or instructions from one computing platform to another. These delays can create significant processing bottlenecks and waste high-performance resources such as processor cycles.)

Active Networking has recently become a focus of major research efforts. Stimulated by the Defense Advanced Research Projects Agency, industry and academia have begun to develop revolutionary concepts and technologies for networking. Basically, the concept of active networking blurs the distinction between network communications functionality (switching, routing, etc.) and peripheral computing functionality. Today's networks perform some processing on the packets of information flowing through them; for example, a router may examine and rewrite a portion of a datagram's header—say, to change an address for an intermediate node that will subsequently handle that datagram. But current networks in general do not operate on the contents of data packets, and this is the crux of the concept behind active networking.[7] Active Networks research is addressing critical issues associated with distributed heterogeneous compucation across cooperative, intelligent network elements and peripheral systems, and it is therefore quite relevant to the themes articulated here.

Advanced network management techniques for multi-modal hybrid networks is our third highlighted research area. Present day architects have had at most very limited experience with the notion of distributed cooperative intelligence operating across many independent network environments, and the problem of assuring quality of service in such environments is at best poorly understood today. This is a topic of great importance for robust end-to-end interoperability throughout the electronic marketplace. Many network operators today are implementing network-management schemes under the principles of the Telecommunications Management Network (TMN) standard. Other communities are pursuing advancements such as the next-generation Simple Network Management Protocol (SNMP), which has widespread application in IP environments. While these efforts are certainly important and will impact network management for many years to come, longer-range research needs to be emphasized because of the escalating complexity of our emerging "network of networks."

Complexity theory and its applications hold great promise of helping architects understand and develop management schemas for the long-term future (i.e., beyond the 10 to 15 year horizon).

The Infostructure as a Complex Adaptive System

The concepts and techniques of complex adaptive systems hold great promise for coping with the escalating complexity of networking environments. Much fascinating research has been stimulated and performed by highly talented interdisciplinary organizations such as the Santa Fe Institute and the Ernst and Young Center for Business Innovation. Complexity theory is a marvelous framework with great potential for important applications to network management and to many other disciplines. Though some strides have been made in applying concepts of complexity theory to network management, much more research is warranted—particularly in the problem domain of managing independent multi-modal hybrid networks, which will soon support active networking technologies. The abstract picture we have painted for the electronic marketplace and its underlying information infrastructure is manifestly conducive to treatment by complexity theory.

In a nutshell, complexity theory deals with systems composed of many interacting elements which, although individually obeying relatively simple rule sets, nonetheless produce enormously complicated systems-level behaviors as a result of the myriad interactions taking place. If objectives can be specified for the individual elements, such interactions are describable in terms of the adaptive behaviors of intelligent system elements, or what is more usually referred to as complex adaptive systems behavior. Many fascinating results across multi-disciplinary domains have already been demonstrated from complexity theory. The theory is heavily rooted in biological sciences (including insights into genetic adaptation and the origins of life itself), although it is both protean and eclectic with respect to disciplines as wide-ranging as mathematics, physics, economics, electronics, and even business and industrial process controls.

The complex adaptive systems model is precisely the type of abstraction we have painted for the future "network of networks," in which many independent domains, each hosting many network elements, must intelligently interact to cooperatively assure quality of service to an enormous population of users with dynamically fluctuating service requirements. Individual network elements and edge devices can be treated as obeying a certain rule set for interactions with other entities, and metrics based on objectives "sought" by individual elements can be specified, such as maximizing bandwidth utilization, minimizing the number of lost or corrupted packets, and minimizing latency. This is a rich problem domain worthy of attention by leaders in the field of complex adaptive systems research. If this class of problem is not sufficiently interesting and challenging, an additional level of complexity can be introduced by recognizing that the physical and logical topology of the large-scale network itself (including peripherals) is constantly changing! It is not clear if such complexity is best approached from the perspective of transitioning network states, or if a stateless approach is a more suitable model to adopt.

Reinventing the "Common Carrier" Business Model

What forces are motivating the evolution of the "common carrier" business model from its twentieth-century basis of providing narrowband connectivity to a twenty-first-century model in which it plays a major role in the quest for interoperability in a diverse, heterogeneous electronic marketplace? Telecommunications "common carriers" face an increasingly software-centric basis for high-value-adding strategic differentiation in the future electronic marketplace. The "telco" of the twenty-first century will have to "migrate up the stack" in delivering products and services to sustain appreciable growth and value-creation opportunities. There are a number of forces motivating this transition[8]:

· unbundling (as a mechanism to "jump start" and stimulate local competition)

· reductions in network operating economies of scale and scope due to inevitable competitive share loss and the ever-expanding diversity, complexity, and heterogeneity of network technologies

· competing alternative access technologies and platforms

· migration of intelligence from within the public network to its customers' premises on the network periphery; for example, emerging CTI standards will undoubtedly lead to advanced packet voice functionality (say, voice over IP and voice over frame relay) with enhanced call control features (such as call waiting, multi-party conferencing, call forwarding, etc.)

· the unstable and transient economic phenomenology embodied in today's Internet and related business and regulatory frameworks, such as flat-rate distance-independent pricing (which is suitable and efficient for packet networks but not for circuit-switched networks such as the PSTN, which guarantees quality of service for real-time services and applications). ESP (enhanced service provider) exemptions introduce the concomitant issue of who should bear the costs for congestive loading of local PSTN switches, which were not engineered for long-holding-time data sessions

· the looming potential for the commoditization of transport itself.[9]

These factors threaten to erode the value of the PSTN as we know it today. This point is understood by the telcos that will prosper in the twenty-first century. They have already begun a process of business diversification and migration to more fertile ground along the industry's value chain. Analogous to the wise strategic reorientation to which Bill Gates led Microsoft in its relationship to the Internet (from discounting the significance of the Net to the "embrace and extend" philosophy), the successful telcos of the next century will experience a strategic metamorphosis away from their twentieth-century roots.[10] Within Bell Atlantic, we have recently been focusing management attention on reevaluating our extant core competencies in light of the major forces of change that are impacting our industry. An element of our strategy in striving for high-performance success in the new millennium involves understanding our current limitations and taking action to build new strengths, while leveraging current corporate strengths that promise to enhance competitive advantages under the new paradigms of the electronic marketplace. Our strategic long-term vision embraces provision of middleware-based services integration as a key element of growth and value creation for our future business as a "common carrier." We believe that a major differentiating element of our near-term strategy stems from leveraging superior technological capabilities to support "total customer care" in its broadest sense. While customer care will assume an important role as a strategic differentiator in the newly deregulated telecommunications arena, we believe that in the long run customer care will become an absolute requirement expected by customers from any serious competitor in the game, and it will become foundational to all other elements of strategic differentiation. Bell Atlantic will continue to pioneer the business and technological transformations which twentieth-century telcos must pursue in order to reinvent themselves.

Currently recognizable players that will compete on the cyberspace battlefields of the twenty-first century include extant network operators such as telephone companies (of all sorts, from local carriers to interexchange carriers and competitive access providers), cable television network operators, satellite system operators, narrowband wireless network operators (cellular, PCS, mobile satellite, etc.), broadcasters, and others. These players will likely undergo significant technological and business-process metamorphoses and may not be recognizable in the future in terms of their current corporate and industry identities.

The technological transformations include the widespread objective to upgrade monolithic networks to broadband architectures capable of delivering the full spectrum of information, communications, and entertainment services. These technological transformations are being fueled by phenomenal rates of advancement in the following areas:

• digital microelectronics, such as ultra-large-scale integration (ULSI) technologies, which continue to increase the number of devices that can be integrated in a single silicon chip for advanced memory, DSP, and microprocessor architectures
• analog microelectronics for radio systems, such as monolithic microwave and millimeter-wave integrated circuits incorporating relatively new

and exotic solid-state technologies (e.g., GaAs and InP heterostructure devices)

• communications theory and engineering techniques, particularly in modulation, coding, compression, multiple access and network-management technologies

• advanced software technologies such as pure object-oriented environments with the power to be interoperable with legacy systems and databases; semantic speech processing that enables conversational programming environments; and operating system advancements such as run-time systems, multi-threading and multi-processing techniques, and parallel processing environments leveraging predictive branching

• optical technology advancements, such as high-speed dense wavelength division multiplexing systems, holographic mass memories, and eventually all-optical networking environments

• advanced power generation and management technologies, such as high-energy density batteries

• flat panel displays that are large, bright, power efficient, and high resolution

• exotic and potentially high-payoff technologies which we are only at the threshold of developing today, such as nanotechnologies, molecular- and bio-electronics, and embedded micro-electrical-mechanical-systems technology.

Graceful, economically realistic, and efficient evolution of large-scale high-performance networks will necessarily take a long time. The challenges confronting network operators and service providers will be exacerbated by the rapidity and impact of revolutionary changes in their underlying constituent technologies, which will advance at rates that are an order of magnitude faster than the rates at which large-scale networks themselves can evolve.

New business structures and processes will also contribute to the changing nature of present-day industries. Mergers, acquisitions, and strategic global alliances are already reshaping the converging communications, information, and entertainment industries. Competitive advantages are being sought by forging both vertically and horizontally integrated strategic business relationships. The pro-competitive regulatory and legal framework, not only in the United States but in nations around the world, is having a profound impact on the business environment. The impact of technology on our industry's business structures and processes is also apparent, and perhaps it is best exemplified today by the quest for viable Internet-based models that will promote electronic commerce and the broader characteristics of an electronic marketplace.

Achieving a robust electronic marketplace will require new concepts that promote "business process interoperability." One example of this important requirement is the need to develop multi-industry integrative mechanisms for efficient billing processes appropriate to an environment in which hypermedia content will be transported across multiple independent packet-based networks that must dynamically cooperate to assure quality of service to end users.

A High-Value-Generating Role for "Common Carriers"

Since providing basic communications services is unlikely to be a high-margin enterprise in the new millennium, where do today's telcos migrate along the value chain to remain competitively healthy? The common carrier of the twentieth century is a well-known and well-understood entity. Common carriers are treated uniquely within the regulatory environment; for example, the prices they charge for services delivered to the public must be authorized as approved tariffs by cognizant federal and/or state government agencies. Common carriers are responsible for provisioning, maintaining, and operating the public telecommunications infrastructure of the nation, and they are responsible for taking the sacred principle of universal service and translating it into reality. The United States would not have achieved its preeminent role as a global superpower if the telecommunications industry had failed in its mission of creating a world-class information infrastructure.

Notwithstanding their past successes, the nation's common carriers are facing new challenges and transformations. Congress, the executive branch (including the Federal Communications Commission), and regulatory bodies in all fifty states are working closely with the diverse set of companies that constitute our national telecommunications sector. These collective efforts will effectuate profound structural and regulatory changes appropriate for the Information Age while ensuring that fundamental public-policy objectives are not compromised. This is an extremely difficult and complex process, especially given the differing interests and business motivations of the private-sector participants and the wide range of political philosophies by public-sector and private-sector participants. We do not purport to have any deeper insight into the ultimate outcome of this process than any of the other players in our industry; however, we believe that change is inevitable and that the eventual outcome will position the United States to continue its legacy of global leadership into the twenty-first century. Along the way, it is quite possible that the essence of "common carriage" may evolve, and we therefore place references to common carriers in the twenty-first century inside quotation marks to emphasize that the complete set of characteristics that these business entities will possess are as yet unresolved. Our analyses support the argument that says, in essence, that technological advancements and pro-competitive regulatory forces can be expected to create an environment in the next century that successfully achieves the goal of making information, communications, and entertainment services available to all citizens and organizations anywhere, anytime, at the lowest economically feasible prices. The plethora of independent multi-modal hybrid networks can be expected to make basic connectivity to the information infrastructure a commodity. Given this observation, as well as the many other business challenges facing telecommunications service providers today, we believe that "common carriers" of the next century will be motivated to seek new growth mechanisms and value-creating business opportunities.

The coming cultural metamorphoses will affect entire industries as well as individual businesses. At the macro level, the value chain will undergo profound changes as the information, communications, and entertainment industries converge and create new strategic business models. At the micro level, individual corporations seeking to stay competitive will have to adapt to the new framework and perhaps strategically reposition themselves along the newly defined value chain.

The importance of interoperability throughout the electronic marketplace has suggested that fertile ground is available for "common carriers." We have argued that along the spectrum of approaches to interoperability, from "digital Esperanto" to the N^2 conundrum, the "sweet spot" lies somewhere in the middle where standards weakly limit diversity and technology-based solutions are practical. We have also contended that "endpoint only" approaches to achieving interoperability are insufficient, and network elements must play a key role in the process.

While most "common carriers" will undoubtedly continue to provide basic communications connectivity services, those seeking more profitable and competitively differentiating positions along the value chain will migrate to software-centric middleware services. Perhaps the major component of value generation in the portfolio of competitive middleware services provided by "common carriers" will be based on their unique ability to efficiently and pragmatically enable robust interoperability throughout the electronic marketplace. Network operators will dynamically offer multiple tiers of service in order to satisfy the myriad requirements of end-users' specifications for quality of service. The "common carriers" of the twenty-first century will drive the interoperability engines that unify and integrate the rich diversity of applications and services that permeate the heterogeneous environments of the electronic marketplace.

Notes

1. For example, desktop videoconferencing capabilities have been united with groupware capabilities.

2. These solution modes are evident throughout civilized cultures, not only in communications and information systems but across most all engineering disciplines as well as in broader social contexts. Technical standards minimize the degrees of freedom among individual entities which must work together in a way that is perhaps somewhat analogous to the concept of the "social contract" (developed by the philosophers Locke, Hobbes, and Rousseau) which stipulated that people surrendered some of the unconstrained freedoms they possessed in a state of nature for the benefits they enjoyed in civilized communal societies.

3. A fundamental logic behind the use of standards is the desire to mitigate otherwise incompatible vendor-specific attributes of a product or service, and to ameliorate or eliminate vendor-specific dependencies.

4. The parametric trade space for QoS management includes variables such as bandwidth, bit error rate, end-to-end delay, delay variability, codec/modem complexity, adaptive session-specific coding schemes, degree of signal processing sophistication, and timing and synchronization requirements of related multimedia subflows.

5. For example, a telephone company providing a dedicated T-1 facility in a metropolitan area (say, for a large business customer) can definitively guarantee

the maximum bounds on end-to-end delays in order to satisfy requirements imposed by the customer's set of applications. On the other hand, if the customer is connected to the Internet, the service provider can no longer guarantee end-to-end quality of service levels because that one network operator does not control, or necessarily even have monitoring visibility into, the many other network domains across which the served customer's traffic will pass. Furthermore, until very recently, the Internet operated predominantly in a connectionless mode, which implied that the end-to-end path through the Internet for a given information flow could change during the course of a session. Thus, as a result of congestion at a router or failure of a communications channel, the IP datagrams belonging to a particular end-to-end session might travel significantly different routes and perhaps arrive in scrambled order. The connectionless Internet model relied on TCP controls at layer 4 to "restore" reliability of the end-to-end service by reordering TCP packets into their correct sequence (regardless of their order of arrival), taking action to correct for lost or corrupted packets, and so on. This approach works quite nicely and in fact achieves highly efficient resource utilization for the network links and elements, provided that the end-to-end service does not have to satisfy a quality of service objective other than eventual delivery of a correct message on a best-efforts basis. For non-delay-sensitive email this is acceptable; for delay-sensitive mission-critical data, real-time flows (such as voice and video), and other traffic classes that do require quality of service guarantees, it may not be an acceptable networking modus operandi.

6. Although we have limited the discussion here to these four chosen topics, we emphasize that relevant communities of expertise must not only develop a more complete agenda, but they should also prioritize that agenda so that the most promising areas of research receive high-priority consideration for funding.

7. For a comprehensive high-level overview of concepts and technologies which the research community is studying under the theme of active networks, see D. Tennenhouse, J. M. Smith, W. D. Sincoskie, D. J. Wetherall, and G. J. Minden, "A Survey of Active Network Research," *IEEE Communications* Magazine, January 1997.

8. Physical plant has served as a primary component for economic valuation of telephone companies during the regulated-monopoly framework characterizing the industry for most of the twentieth century. This basis is rapidly transmuting as a result of a suite of recent regulatory and statutory changes that in turn are engendering business model transformations.

9. Over the past decade or so, there has been much debate and discussion about the potential commoditization of basic telecommunications services (switching/routing and transport/connectivity/access). Some argue that these basic services will be non-differentiable in the marketplace and may be wholesaled by future network operators. While the jury remains out on this issue, it does appear clear that competitive proliferation of these services will quite likely create downward pressures on profit margins. The sea of competing modalities to deliver

basic communications supporting the framework of information and entertainment products and services continues to swell.

10. In a 1996 article titled "The iWorld Future: Strategy for a New Telecommunications Environment," Michael Spencer et al. of Booz-Allen & Hamilton address the transformations likely to unfold in the telecommunications industry, emphasizing the changing business strategies that will be necessary to achieve success in the evolving environments.

10

Paying Up: Payment Systems for Digital Commerce

Stephen D. Crocker
Russell B. Stevenson Jr.

Melissa rushes into her small Manhattan apartment. Ever since she finished classes at Stanford and began her residency at the Gotham Research Institute, her life has been even more hectic than it was on campus. Though she is in her late twenties, Melissa is just getting used to managing a career and her own apartment.

Today is a big day, and Melissa is pressed for time. She has to go to Boston this evening for a meeting tomorrow. She has gotten behind in her accounts, and this morning she looked at a condominium. She looks at her watch and sees that she has 45 minutes to spend at the screen. That will leave her just 15 minutes before the cab comes.

She walks over to the screen and sticks her card into the slot. It greets her: "Good evening, Melissa." She could program in something punchier, as her brother does, but she is more interested in results than style, and she hasn't been willing to spend the time. To her, the computer is just another appliance.

Melissa thinks about ordering the performance of Grofé's *Grand Canyon Suite* she heard on the way home to be downloaded to a recordable CD. She'd rather do that than go to the music store near work, which takes more time and is usually more expensive. But she'll have to do it when she gets back; there's no time tonight.

She turns her attention to email. Sixteen messages, including three vid mails, show up. She left the office an hour ago, and she was afraid she'd be awash in postings by now; sixteen isn't so bad. Two of the vid mails are baby pictures from friends. One looks like a travel brochure but is really an ad for a vacation home. "Fat chance," she thinks as she blurts out "Delete" to make the voice-response unit dispose of the ad. Melissa will look at the other vids later. She has money on her mind right now, but the one piece of mail she really wanted hasn't arrived yet. Nervous, she decides to dispose of regular business. "Money, in and out," she says.

"You have one paycheck and two bills," says the screen. The screen flashes Melissa's paycheck briefly. Paychecks are always deposited automatically, but she can control whether she gets a brief summary or all the details. Melissa long ago got bored with checking each detail of her paycheck.

The bills flash up. Unlike her cousin Laura, who lets the screen pay her bills automatically, Melissa hasn't gotten comfortable with giving up complete control. The bills come in, are compared to her profile of regular expenditures, and are queued up for quick payment. The combined utilities statement is on top. The usual $297.00 for gas, water, electricity, sewage, Internet, and trash pickup. "OK," she says, causing the amount to be debited from her bank account and distributed to the various utility companies. She remembers her dad explaining with some excitement what actually happens behind the scenes. She had tried to be polite, of course, but it had been tougher than usual.

The next bill is Melissa's card statement. She has been sticking her card in slots all over town recently, running up a big bill. She is about to say "OK," but she holds off to see if there's enough money. "Hold," she says, as she moves on to two chores that are really on her mind.

Because she is going to be away all day, Melissa needs to get some shopping started for the big dinner two nights from now. "Groceries, please," she says. Immediately, aisles of food show up on the screen. She orally maneuvers down the aisles, pointing and selecting tomatoes, corn, and everything else she needs. In a few minutes she has what she needs for the recipes she chose this morning, and she has ordered them to delivered at 5:45 P.M. She is glad Federal Express has gone into the local delivery business.

The screen says the groceries will cost $75.82. "OK," says Melissa. In the old days, her dad said, she would have had to use cash, a check, a credit card, or a debit card. She remembers that she actually used all those things, but it seems like a long time ago. Now she just sticks the card in the slot and says "OK." If she needs to schedule the payment, either to conserve funds or because a payment isn't due for a while, all she needs to do is say so. Otherwise, the money moves quickly out of her account and shows up on the other side. Dad sends money to Melissa's brother Andrew that way now, although he grumbles that Andrew seems to need refills a little too often.

Andrew's birthday is tomorrow, and Melissa has decided to give up trying to find an appropriate present and just send him some money, which is what he says he wants anyway. "Web site, Cartoon Cards," she says to the computer, and the home page for the site loads on the screen. She looks over a series of cartoons and finds a card she thinks Andrew will like. "Send number 7 to andrew 12 at pomona dot edu," she says, giving her brother's email address. "Enclose $50. Sign it 'Melissa.'" The screen shows the card Melissa has selected, with her name at the bottom. An "attachment" icon shows that $50 is to be attached. At the bottom of the screen is the message: "This is the card you've selected. The cost to send it is $1.00. Please indicate if you want to send it, change it, or cancel this transaction." Melissa says, "Send," and the screen flashes a large, cartoonish "THANK YOU" at her.

Normally calm, Melissa is a little nervous now. The real estate agent said she would have to close the deal by 6:00 tonight or the condominium would go to someone else. She really liked the condo, and she needs to send $1,000,000 to the agent. She has only $260,000, and she asked the bank for a conventional loan. She gave the bank access to her complete file, not that there was much to see. Why should it take them all day to see that she really did graduate from college and medical school, really did pay her bills regularly, and really did have a job that paid enough? The application screen had done all the computation and had assured Melissa that it shouldn't be a problem, but nonetheless it told her to check her mail later. It is now 5:50.

Melissa's computer makes the sound that suggests a paper envelope falling through a slot—archaic and symbolic, of course, but very welcome. She looks at the new mail and is relieved to see that it is from the bank. She scans it quickly, wondering why all the fine print is necessary. Then she finds the critical part: "Your loan is approved; activate the icon below to accept the terms of the loan and the funds will be instantly available." Too relieved to grumble about "instantly," Melissa double clicks the icon, listens to 5 seconds of the bank's self-serving ad music, and then quickly looks for the mail from the real estate agent. She pulls it up and scrolls to the "commit" icon. "Yes!" she says.

Some wag has programmed quite a lot of fanfare into the icon. A picture of the condo flashes up, followed by some lengthy fine print. "The real estate contract," Melissa thinks. "This is what passes for informed consent in the real estate business. Well, I guess we do the same with patients too." Next comes an animation of a truckload of money moving out of a bank and arriving at a picture of the real estate agent. The real estate agent does a little jig on the screen and exclaims "Congratulations, Melissa!" As he starts to dissolve on the screen, he adds: "The key to the condo has been downloaded to your card. It's all yours; move in anytime." Melissa shuts off the screen, throws some clothes in her overnight bag, and races to catch the cab.

This little scene could well happen in the year 2005. All the requisite technology exists now. The barriers to be overcome relate to organizing and deploying appropriate business relationships, marketing new services, and resolving unsettled legal issues; they are not technological.

The Internet is already affecting commerce significantly, both by making the traditional forms of commerce more efficient and faster and by creating entirely new forms. Those effects are beginning to accelerate, and they will have revolutionary implications. Commerce on the Internet is still in its infancy, but most observers predict that annual commercial transactions on the Internet will be measured in tens of billions of dollars by the year 2000. For reality to come even close to these expectations, the participants in Internet commerce will need payment mechanisms that function as securely, confidently, and efficiently as their analogues in the three-dimensional world.

Electronic payments will receive a substantial boost from the US government in the next few years. After January 1, 1999. under a program known as Electronic Funds Transfer 99, most of the federal government's payment transactions each year, including social security and welfare payments, veterans' benefits, and payments from appropriated funds (and excluding tax refunds), are being made electronically.[1]

Like Internet commerce, electronic payment systems are still at an early stage of development. Several companies now offer basic payment mechanisms that allow purchasers to pay with credit cards, and a few have implemented the electronic equivalents of checks and small-value cash. Many more contenders will enter and leave the marketplace of payment systems before stability and general acceptance of a set of payment mechanisms are achieved.

The number and the diversity of the payment systems that exist or are on the drawing boards reflect the novelty and the unstructured nature of Internet commerce. Those payment systems vary considerably in their approaches to meeting the basic needs of any payment system. Those basic needs, however, are the same in the digital world as in the physical world: security, reliability, convenience, ease of use, ubiquity, and (for some types of payments) auditability.

Electronic payment systems can be expected to evolve as the electronic marketplace grows and matures. Eventually they may include entirely new payment instruments that have no counterparts in the physical world. For the time being, however, most Internet payment systems are likely to be either conventional systems translated to the Internet or systems that function in new ways but still mimic the forms of payment that consumers and merchants are accustomed to using in the physical world.

Payment Systems and Internet Commerce

Realization of the Internet's commercial potential has been slower to develop than many had predicted. One of the principal reasons for this has been the absence of payment mechanisms suited to Internet commerce. Among the barriers facing individuals and businesses are the following.

Limited Payment Mechanisms

The most common method currently used for making payments over the Internet is by credit card. Obviously, this method is available only for transactions between card-holding consumers and authorized merchants. Infrastructures for the Internet counterparts of check payment and low-denomination cash payment have been introduced only recently, and have not been widely accepted.

High Transaction Costs

Credit card payments over the Internet carry relatively high transaction costs, particularly for low-denomination payments. Accordingly, credit cards are likely to prove too costly for low-denomination transactions. For substantial transactions, the average bank fee to the merchant, or "discount rate," for major credit cards is 2.1 percent of the total amount, to which is added a surcharge of approximately 0.3 percent when the credit card is not physically present. To avoid these fees and surcharges, payments between businesses are routinely made by check.

Payment Fraud

Transmission of credit card information over the Internet leaves consumers, merchants, and financial institutions exposed to the risk of fraud from a number of sources. Stolen credit card data can lead to unauthorized charges on accounts, resulting in losses to merchants and financial institutions, inconvenience from the cancellation of credit card accounts, and possible financial liability to the consumer. The relatively anonymous nature of users on the Internet makes it difficult to detect such fraud. Financial institutions, businesses, and individuals fear that electronic checks and currency may also be subject to payment fraud in the form of dishonored or "bounced" checks, forgery, and counterfeiting.

Merchant Fraud

The open, anonymous, public nature of the Internet may allow users to pose as legitimate merchants or as well-known vendors and to collect credit card payments without delivering the purchased goods or services.

Lack of Privacy

Some Internet payment systems may affect the privacy of a transaction in ways that threaten privacy interests.

Unfamiliarity with Internet Commerce

Businesses and financial institutions have been reluctant to adopt or develop Internet payment mechanisms, and government regulatory agencies have been hesitant to enact regulations, because of their unfamiliarity with Internet commerce and their concern over maintaining adequate security and system integrity. This is especially so where the systems do not use existing bank accounts. In addition, merchants and financial institutions are concerned about the financial and competitive costs associated with adopting new technology that may not be accepted by the market or by regulators.

Closed Architecture and Incompatibility

Businesses may be unwilling to be constrained by payment systems that fail to operate across major hardware and software platforms. Consumers cannot conduct business with merchants whose systems do not readily interface with their system. In addition, banks and other financial institutions currently process transactions under a variety of well-established networks and protocols that are extremely difficult and expensive to change.

Inconvenience

Current Internet credit card payment methods generally require consumers to enter their card payment data each time they wish to make a purchase or to establish an account with a merchant. This process is particularly burdensome when effecting small transactions or multiple transactions with different vendors. Minimum-transaction-size requirements and lack of support for payments between consumers or between businesses further limit the usefulness of current Internet payment systems.

Payment Systems and Payment Instruments

How do we get from today's predominantly paper-based payment systems to tomorrow's predominantly electronic ones? To understand this requires an examination of familiar payment systems that most of us think about only when they go awry. Fortunately, they seldom do go awry; the kinks were worked out long ago.

In the United States alone there are approximately 300 billion cash transactions, 60 billion check transactions, and 10 billion credit card transactions per year. Most consumers regularly use cash (including coins for small payments), checks, credit cards, and debit cards (if only to make withdrawals from automatic teller machines). Most also have at least some experience with other, less common payment instruments, including traveler's checks, money orders, transit tokens, stored-value cards, wire transfers, and discount coupons. Another class of things that function as payment instruments are frequent-flyer miles, cards, stamps, and other "affinity programs" that enable consumers to "earn" value to be used for purchasing goods or services. Yet another set of widely used payment instruments includes drafts, letters of credit, and electronic data interchange. Each of these payment instruments has behind it a substantial and often complicated support infrastructure (a "payment system"), without which the instrument would be useless. Even cash, which of all payment instruments we take the most for granted, would be of little use without the US Mint, fleets of armored cars, bank vaults, alarm systems, coin-counting machines, and a variety of other less visible but still important system components. Underlying the commonplace check are fleets of trucks and airplanes that ferry bundles of paper checks to clearing houses, sorting machines that sort and route them, and a complex system of settlement accounting largely operated by the Federal Reserve Board. A credit card transaction now involves, among other things, electronic terminals at merchant locations, complex communication links, enormous data processing operations, and an elaborate system of operating rules established and administered by card associations and credit card companies.

These existing systems are the background against which network-based electronic systems will function. In some cases, network-based systems will merely allow the convenient use of existing payment instruments on the Internet and other computer networks. In some instances, network-based systems will allow or facilitate the creation of entirely new forms of payment instrument—together with, of course, the necessary infrastructure to make up a new payment system. In any event, the transition from today's payment systems to those we have hinted at above will be evolutionary rather than revolutionary.

Varieties of Payment Instruments

The payment instruments mentioned above constitute only a partial list of those in relatively common use today. And many of them come in more than one flavor. For example, there are ordinary checks, certified checks, and cashier's checks. Stored-value cards—a new and rapidly growing class of payment instrument—encompass magnetic stripe cards and "smart cards," closed and open systems, online and offline systems, accountable and unaccountable systems, and a host of other distinctions.

To understand how these payment instruments will translate to an all-electronic environment such as the Internet, and how other new instruments will evolve and flourish in that environment, it is necessary to begin with the obvious but generally overlooked proposition that each of these instruments has a particular set of attributes that distinguishes it from every other payment instrument. An economist who thinks in Darwinian metaphors would hardly find this surprising. Payment systems have been evolving since the first primitive man traded an arrowhead for a leg of venison. As economies have become more complex, we have created new forms of payment. We have been using cash for millennia, checks for centuries, and credit cards for decades. To survive, each of these instruments has had to succeed in a competition with others by offering a particular combination of attributes that either duplicated another instrument with greater efficiency or offered a new combination of attributes that users found attractive.

Attributes of Payment Instruments

Let us consider some of the more important attributes of the three most common payment instruments: cash, checks, and credit cards. The reader should be able to extend this discussion to other payment instruments, such as debit cards, stored-value cards, and traveler's checks.

Timing

The relationship between the time the payer definitively parts with value and the time the payee receives it varies substantially among payment instruments. Payment instruments may be divided into three types: viewed from the payer's perspective, there are those in which the transfer of value is *contemporaneous* with the payment transaction, those in which it takes place *after* the transaction, and those in which it takes place *before* the transaction.

A cash transaction is the most obvious example of the first type. The payer parts with the value of the payment—and the payee receives it—precisely at the time it is made, neither before nor after. A check transaction is probably best categorized in this group as well, although a few days usually pass between the time the consumer "makes the payment" by handing over or mailing a check and the time its value is deducted from his or her account.

In credit card transactions, consumers do not part with value until well after they have used the card to purchase goods or services. It doesn't matter whether they are using the credit line afforded by the card or whether they are using the card as a convenient way to make the purchase and intending to pay the bill as soon as it arrives.

Traveler's checks are probably the oldest and most familiar of the instruments that require consumers to part with money before they actually make a purchase. Travelers generally purchase them in advance of a trip and may not use them for weeks or even months. Stored-value cards are a much newer example. Although they come in a variety of flavors, they all must be purchased ("loaded" with value) in advance. Several even newer instruments, used primarily to make purchases on computer networks, also require the user to part with value before using the instrument.

Finality and Revocability

One of the most significant attributes of a payment instrument is its finality—or, from the other point of view, its revocability. Cash sits at one pole on this scale. A cash payment is final and irrevocable. A disappointed customer may be able to persuade a seller to reverse a transaction and give the money back, but only if the seller is honest or wishes to make the customer happy. Nothing in the nature of cash enables the customer to revoke the transaction. A credit card transaction is near the opposite end of the spectrum of finality. A dissatisfied customer who has paid for a good with a credit card need only return the good and refuse to pay the bill when it arrives. If a loss is suffered, it falls on the merchant, on the merchant's bank, or in some cases on the consumer's bank, all according to a complex set of operating rules administered by the credit card association. A consumer who has paid by check may be able stop payment before the check is presented for payment. Doing so, however, is more difficult than revoking a credit card purchase, and it usually incurs a bank fee. Moreover, the period during which revocation is possible is relatively short.

From the perspective of the consumer, a credit card is obviously the most desirable of these three instruments. A consumer who has a problem with a credit card transaction, whether or not it is related to payment, has considerable leverage in getting it resolved. It is necessary only to refuse to pay until the problem is taken care of. Though the other parties to the transaction are not completely without tools to pressure the consumer, the advantage is clearly on the consumer's side.

Privacy

Another important attribute of a payment instrument is privacy. To be more precise, the attribute of significance is not the privacy of the instrument but the extent to which it alters the quality of the privacy otherwise inherent in the transaction. Privacy advocates sometimes lose sight of the simple fact that the degree of privacy in an Internet transaction more often than not has little to do with the nature of the payment system. If, for example, the transaction involves the purchase of physical goods that must be delivered to a named person at a physical address, whether the payment instrument preserves the anonymity of the buyer is largely irrelevant. It is true that a consumer who is particularly concerned about privacy might disguise his identity by using an alias and taking delivery at a post office box, but few consumers are really so concerned about protecting their privacy that they are prepared to go to such lengths.

Here, too, cash falls at one end of the spectrum. It is anonymous, and it generally leaves no trail that would permit either party to a transaction to reconstruct it. If a cash transaction takes place in the physical world, the record of the transaction will be at most a cash register tape reporting that the merchant received a certain sum at a certain time (and, if there is a sophisticated inventory control system, perhaps a record of what was sold).

Obviously one cannot literally spend cash on the Internet. Providers of Internet payment services have, however, have devised a variety of systems that mimic cash in many respects, including anonymity. The privacy benefits of these systems can, however, be oversold. The use of cash does not *guarantee* the privacy of a transaction, even in the physical world. And the use of a cash-like instrument to make a payment over the Internet will do little to protect the privacy of the purchaser if he is required to provide information that compromises his anonymity. If the purchaser must provide a delivery address, or if he gives the seller a name and an address in order to procure "membership benefits" or take advantage of a discount or some other marketing program, the transaction loses its privacy, and there is no magic about the payment instrument used that can restore it. In the end, the best that can be said about the privacy attributes of any payment instrument is that it does not alter the privacy attributes otherwise inherent in the transaction.

Most payment instruments other than cash preclude anonymity by their very nature. In the physical world, a consumer who wishes to take advantage of the benefits of using a credit card, must, at a minimum, allow the merchant to make a record of the name and the number on the card. The Internet may offer some advantages here. Some systems designed to enable secure credit card transactions on the Internet have been designed so that the merchant is "blinded" from seeing the credit card number. This has significant security advantages for the consumer, as it reduces the risk of being taken advantage of by a fraudulent merchant that has set up a web site solely for the purpose of stealing and misusing credit card numbers. It also provides protection against incautious merchants who store credit card numbers on an insecure computer that may be vulnerable to thieves or hackers.

Checks, also, cannot very well be used anonymously. Generally, a consumer presenting a check in a physical store must generally not only hand over a check with a name, an address, and perhaps even a telephone number printed on it but must usually also present some form of corroborating identification.

Authentication

Although we seldom pay it any attention, it is generally necessary for the participants in a financial transaction to authenticate themselves to each other. Consider, for example, a consumer making a purchase in a store in the "three-dimensional world." One of the steps consumers use to protect against fraud or abuse is to deal with a known, reputable merchant who will stand behind the goods and take them back if they are defective. Thus, the consumer begins the purchase by "authenticating" the merchant, although usually without thinking of it. One does so by walking into a physical store with a familiar sign on the door. Without thinking of it, one has authenticated the merchant and thus created a set of expectations as to how one will be dealt with. Of course this form of authentication is not always perfect (probably no means of authentication ever can be), but it is certainly adequate to meet the practical requirements of the situation.

Unless the consumer pays with cash, the merchant has a similar need to authenticate the consumer. (If payment is to be made in cash, the merchant's only concern is that it is not counterfeit.) If the consumer wants to pay with a credit card, the merchant will ask that she present the card and will swipe it through a point-of-sale terminal to get an authorization for the transaction. If she wants to pay with a check, the merchant will ask for a driver's license or some other form of identification.

A financial transaction on the Internet also requires authentication of both the merchant and the consumer, but the authentication problem obviously assumes a different form.

Vulnerability to Fraud or Loss

Payment instruments also vary considerably in the risk of loss, theft, or fraud they present to the user. If cash is lost or stolen, the consumer can usually figure the amount lost. The loss of a check exposes a consumer to the much lower risk that a dishonest finder is brazen enough to forge a signature and attempt to cash the check. Even if that happens, an alert consumer who reports the forgery will suffer no loss. Loss if a credit card (or acquisition of a credit card number by a thief) presents a greater risk. If one notifies the card's issuer before any misuse of the card, there is generally no loss. If one promptly notifies the issuer of the loss or theft but a thief uses the card before the issuer can invalidate it, federal law limits the consumer's exposure to $50.[2]

One of the most important effects of this attribute of payment instruments is the relationship between the size of a transaction and the instrument used. The general reluctance of consumers to carry large amounts of cash means that most larger transactions are accomplished with a check or a credit card. Indeed, in some contexts payment of a large sum of cash would raise questions about the provenance of the money.[3]

Convenience and Choice of Instrument

Another factor that influences the choice of payment instruments is simple convenience. Cash is currently the instrument of choice for smaller payments, in large part because it is faster and more convenient than any of the alternatives.

Although few of us ever think about it, there are substantial costs associated with the operation of any payment system. The use of cash implies armored cars, the counting and recording of large volumes of bills and coins, losses from "shrinkage," and other costs. Card associations and card issuers operate extensive authorization and processing networks involving dedicated communication lines and large mainframe computers. Merchants must bear the cost of point-of-sale terminals. The processing of checks requires large check-sorting machines and the physical transfer of millions of pieces of paper each business day.

For the most part these costs are hidden from consumers. As a rule, consumers do not bear the costs directly. Banks charge fees for maintaining checking accounts, and a consumer pays a fee of about 1 percent to purchase traveler's checks, but using cash or credit cards appears to be free. Yet, of course, the costs have to be borne by someone. Banks charge many merchants fees for cash handling and check processing. They charge even higher fees (ranging from 1 percent to 4 percent) for processing payment card transactions. Of course, one way or another, the costs incurred by merchants and banks will eventually be passed on to consumers.

Cost and convenience both influence which payment systems consumers use and merchants accept. Why don't we expect to pay for a hamburger at a fast-food restaurant with a credit card? Partly because it would be too slow and inconvenient; partly because the greater cost of a credit card transaction would cut too deeply into the already low profit margin in this business. Why, on the other hand, have gasoline pumps that accept credit cards been deployed so widely in the last few years? They are more convenient for the consumer, and they reduce labor costs for station owners (despite the higher costs of the payment mechanism).

Operation of Payment Systems

Modern payment systems could not function without the efforts of a variety of participants. For cash, the most important participant is probably the US Mint, but banks and armored car services also play important roles.

In the world of checking accounts, there must, of course, be financial institutions—banks, thrifts, and credit unions. But in addition, several institutions, the most important being the Federal Reserve Board, run large clearing operations that sort checks, post each one to the accounts of the bank on which it is drawn and the bank in which it has been deposited, send it (usually physically) to the drawee bank, and provide for settling the net changes in the accounts of the banks.

A typical point-of-sale credit card transaction involves the merchant's bank (the "acquiring bank"), the consumer's bank (the "issuing bank"), a network operated by a credit card association (such as Visa or MasterCard), or a single issuer (such as American Express). The transaction looks something like this, all of it taking place in a few seconds:

• The customer presents a card to the clerk at the point of sale.
• The clerk swipes it through a terminal (which reads the card number stored on the magnetic stripe on the back of the card).
• The clerk enters the amount of the transaction into the terminal.
• The terminal transfers the information about the transaction to the acquiring bank or the credit card processor that is handling the transaction for the bank.
• The acquiring bank (or processor) forwards this information through appropriate credit card network to the issuing bank or its processor.
• The issuing bank or processor checks its records to check that the card has not been reported lost or stolen and that the customer's credit is still good.
• If there is no problem, the issuing bank or processor returns an authorization message through the credit card network to the acquiring bank.
• The authorization message is forwarded to the merchant.

The Role of Trusted Parties

At some point in most payment transactions, one or both parties have parted with something of value without yet receiving what they are expecting in return. For that reason, all payment systems beyond simple barter transactions require a "trusted party" in order to function effectively. The role of the trusted party is to ensure that the transaction will be completed as intended, and thus to eliminate or at least reduce the risk that the payment will not be effected.

In each of the three principal payment systems discussed above, banks play a central role. While they perform a variety of mechanical tasks, their most important role is as the trusted party in the system.

Consider payment by check, for example. Merchants regularly accept checks in payment for goods and services that are delivered before a check has cleared. In so doing, a merchant takes two risks. The first is that the payer's checking account is not bona fide or that the payer has insufficient funds to cover the check. The second is that the bank on which the check is drawn will be unable or unwilling to pay it (in technical terms, will "dishonor" it). Merchants take precautions to protect themselves against the first risk. They usually require identification and make sure that the customer's address is on the check, and they may use remote electronic databases similar to credit reports. Finally, they sometimes ask the bank to verify the validity of the account and the sufficiency of the funds in it. To the extent that they do check with the bank, merchants are obviously trusting it to provide accurate information. The second risk involves a more important aspect of the bank's role as trusted party. A check is simply a "draft"—a form of negotiable instrument drawn on a bank. In theory, the customer could present a draft drawn on anyone. By accepting a check, a merchant is implicitly placing its trust in the bank on which it is drawn to honor the check.

The other side of a check transaction also involves trust. Consumers trust their banks to receive and hold funds, to pay checks promptly when presented, and to maintain an honest and accurate accounting of the funds in checking accounts. In short, without the role played by banks as trusted parties the checking system would not function as we know it.

Banks play an even more important role as trusted parties in credit card transactions. When a merchant accepts a credit card in payment for goods and services, he is relying on the acquiring bank to credit him with the amount of the purchase (less, of course, the applicable discount). In turn, the acquiring bank is relying on the issuing bank to make good the payment, for it is the issuing bank that has granted a line of credit to the consumer and has authorized the transaction. Under the applicable rules, the merchant is paid whether or not the consumer eventually pays his or her credit card bill.[4]

What Rules Govern Payment Systems?

Imprecision and uncertainty are acceptable, indeed inevitable, in many aspects of the world, and even in some aspects of the commercial world. A payment system, however, is not one of those aspects; it could not function without great certainty and precision, and that requires a clear set of rules defining the rights of the participants and affording protection against fraud and overreaching.

In the United States, state law (in particular, the Uniform Commercial Code) forms the skeleton of the body of rules governing the major payment systems. Article 3 of the UCC, for example deals with negotiable instruments, including checks. Article 4 deals with bank deposits, and it forms another part of the body of rules for the checking system. Article 4A, which governs wire transfers through the banking system not involving consumer transactions, is obviously important to electronic payment systems.

The influence of federal law on payment systems results primarily from federal regulation of banks, which affects virtually all banking institutions in the United States to some degree. The Federal Reserve Board's Regulation Z embodies a comprehensive set of rules designed to protect the interests of consumers in credit card transactions.[5] It is likely, in fact, that the use of credit cards would be far less widespread without Regulation Z's limitation of a consumer's liability to $50 in case of the loss of a card. Regulation Z applies as much to the use of a credit card over the Internet as to its use in the physical world.

Another Federal Reserve Board rule of particular significance to electronic payment systems is Regulation E,[6] which governs consumers' electronic fund transfers. Like Regulation Z, it limits a consumer's losses from unauthorized use of a debit card (or some other "access device") to $50 in most cases. And, like Regulation Z, it will almost certainly be a significant factor in promoting consumers' confidence in transferring funds over the Internet.

Finally, some payment systems, especially payment card systems (which include both credit cards and debit cards), depend heavily on systems of "operating rules" developed and maintained by card associations and card issuers. Perhaps the most important aspect of these rules is to determine where the loss falls in case of a failed transaction. Of course, these rules apply to Internet transactions just as to transactions in the physical world.

Payment Systems and Payment Instruments in the Virtual World

To understand electronic payment systems, it is essential to have at least a basic understanding of the underlying technology—not the technology of the Internet (nodes, routers, hubs, TCP/IP, and so on), but the technical architecture of what makes a payment happen over the Internet: what institutions are involved, what messages flow from where to where, and what happens that causes value to move from one place to another.

The Role of Encryption

Virtually all Internet payment systems make use of public-key cryptography. This powerful and well-accepted form of cryptography enables large numbers of people to communicate sensitive information over the Internet, with the sender authenticated and, when desired, with the privacy of the information protected from potential eavesdroppers.[7] Each user has a "public key" and a "private key," so related to each other that a message either signed or encrypted with one key can only be verified or decrypted with the other. Users make their public keys available to the world, but treat their private keys as closely guarded secrets. Under this system, one party to a payment transaction signs a transaction with his private key, and the other party uses the corresponding public key to verify that the sender did not forge the signature. Similarly, when it is desired to communicate information privately, the sender uses the receiver's public key to encrypt the sensitive information. Only the recipient, who holds the corresponding private key, can read it.

Public keys are usually communicated broadly by means of "digital certificates." In the context of financial transactions over the Internet, a digital certificate typically takes the form of a message reading "The holder of this certificate is Jane Doe, she is the rightful owner of credit card number 1234-5678-9012, and her public key for transactions related to this account is the following very long number." The certificate is issued by a "certificate authority" (CA)—an entity willing to act as a trusted party in credit card transactions effected by Jane Doe (usually her bank or some agent authorized by it).

The CA signs the certificate using a digital signature created with the CA's private key. A recipient of the payment message uses the CA's public key to verify that it was indeed the CA that issued the certificate and not some impostor. (The recipient may verify the CA's public key by referring to a certificate issued by a higher-level CA, whose function it is to publish, under a certificate, a table of public keys of lower-level CAs.) Thus, for example, in a credit card transaction, the acquiring bank (or its agent) can examine the certificate presented with a credit card number to verify that the certificate holder is in fact the owner of the credit card (or at least that the CA says that is so).

On the other side of the transaction, certificates enable purchasers to authenticate the merchants with whom they are dealing. This provides the consumer with a digital means of verifying that the merchant is in fact L. L. Bean, and not someone posing as L. L. Bean for the purpose of collecting credit card numbers or checks.

Basic Architecture: Wallets, Cash Registers, and Gateways

Most Internet payment systems involve three basic pieces of software. One runs on the consumer's computer and is often referred to as a "wallet."[8] The second runs on the merchant's computer (or is operated for the merchant by the system operator or a hosting service) and serves as a sort of Internet cash register. The third is a "gateway server" run by the system operator, a bank, or a transaction processor. The three programs exchange data over the Internet. Each provides cryptographic capacity so that the communications can be secure. The wallet operates as a "helper application" for the leading Internet browsers. The programs usually provide some database or other record-keeping capacity to enable the user to track and record transactions. Variations of this basic architecture are, of course, possible, and no two systems function exactly alike.

Credit Transactions

The existing Internet electronic payment systems can be divided into two classes. In the first, the Internet serves primarily as a communication vehicle. These payment systems allow conventional payment instruments to be used conveniently and securely over the Internet, but they do not create new payment instruments. The second class of systems use electronic technology to create a fundamentally new type of payment instrument. These new instruments may resemble conventional ones, but they have no counterpart in the physical world.

The best example of the first class is an Internet credit card system.[9] Credit card transactions in the physical world are already largely electronic, but they take place over dedicated lines and networks other than the Internet. What makes Internet credit card transactions different is that the consumer "visits" the merchant virtually, which creates special problems of security and authentication.

The news media have paid so much attention to security concerns about the Internet that consumers can be forgiven if they have come to believe that any attempt to effect a financial transaction over the Internet could lead to personal bankruptcy. In particular, consumers have been conditioned to believe that sending a credit card number over the Internet exposes them to a serious risk of theft of the card number. This is all, of course, wildly exaggerated nonsense. In fact, a consumer runs a greater risk of theft of a credit card number when she gives her card to a waiter in a restaurant than when she sends it over the Internet.

This is not to say that, without appropriate security precautions, there are no risks in making purchases electronically. There are risks in using *any* payment system. And the risks involved in accomplishing payments virtually do differ somewhat from those involved in making conventional payments. For example, in an Internet credit card transaction the greatest threat is not that an electronically savvy thief will capture a card number as it passes over the Internet. There are two more serious risks. One is thieves who masquerade as Internet merchants for the purpose of collecting and misusing credit card numbers. The second is honest merchants who collect credit card numbers in an insecure computer that is vulnerable to break-ins by electronic thieves.

There is also a third security issue, the burden of which falls on banks. Although they are vulnerable to fraud through the use of stolen credit cards, at least the thief must present the card at the point of sale. Since that is not (yet) possible on the Internet, the risks from stolen card numbers are somewhat higher.

Fortunately, there are effective ways to make the use of credit cards even less vulnerable to fraud on the Internet than in the physical world. The Internet credit card systems are not fundamentally new; they simply allow consumers and merchants to effectuate a conventional credit card payment over the Internet conveniently and securely.

Several secure Internet credit card services already in operation address the security problems cited above. Most use public-key cryptography for secure communication of payment information over the Internet, and some use a form of digital certificates. Visa and MasterCard, with the participation of a variety of other companies, have developed an advanced protocol for Internet payment card transactions. Known as the Secure Electronic Transaction (SET) protocol, it is expected to be widely deployed during 1998 and 1999.

SET is built on an architecture similar to one introduced by CyberCash, Inc. in 1995. It involves communication over the Internet among three of the participants in a credit card transaction: the consumer, the merchant, and the merchant's financial institution or card processor. An SET credit card transaction flows as follows:

· The merchant's computer sends a signed message to the consumer requesting payment for an item the consumer wishes to order.

· The consumer sends a signed message to the merchant containing payment information, including the credit card number. The credit card information is encrypted to keep the merchant from using the information at a later time in a different, unauthorized transaction.

· The merchant's computer reads the payment directions on the message and forwards it to a payment gateway server.

· The gateway server decrypts the message, authenticates the consumer, and forwards a request for authorization to the acquiring bank.

· The transaction is authorized by the issuing bank through the credit card association's conventional messaging service.

· The authorization is communicated to the merchant.

· The consumer is notified that the transaction has been accepted and the goods will be shipped.

Internet "Check" Transactions

At this writing, credit card transactions represent the overwhelming majority of Internet payments. That is not likely always to be the case, however. As we noted above, in the physical world payments by check far outnumber payments by credit card.

The ultimate function of a check is to create a credit to an account of the payee and an equal debit to the checking account of the payer. Although moving paper checks around is still the most-used means of accomplishing this in the physical world, electronic alternatives existed long before the Internet. The most important one for current purposes is the Automated Clearing House (ACH) system operated by the Federal Reserve Board and a few private-sector entities. This system enables bank customers to transfer funds electronically from one bank account to another. The most familiar uses of the ACH system in the realm of consumer payments are direct deposits of wages and salaries in the employees' bank accounts and pre-authorized payments of utility bills.

The ACH system uses batch processing. For reasons beyond the scope of this essay, it cannot be used to effect irrevocable real-time payments. It is, however, well established and relatively low in cost. Accordingly, until other systems are developed, the ACH system is likely to be an integral part of most Internet-based systems for providing electronic "checking" services to consumers.

One model of such a system, now operated by CyberCash, Inc., is as follows:

· The consumer directs that his checking account be "linked" to an electronic "wallet."

· The "linking" is confirmed.

· The consumer directs that money be moved from his checking account to the checking account of a merchant or biller.

· Funds are transferred through the ACH system to the recipient's checking account.

• The recipient is notified that his account has increased by the amount of the funds transferred.

One aspect of this procedure merits special mention, as it requires overcoming one of the greatest barriers to the establishment of a convenient, efficient payment system. Once a checking account is "linked" to an electronic wallet, the user of the wallet has complete freedom to withdraw money from the account. It is essential, therefore, that the operator of the system carefully authenticate the user's right to the account before enabling such access. There are various ways to accomplish this authentication; the first will probably be to use digital certificates issued by the account-holding bank or perhaps by some third party. The issue is a business issue rather than a technical one. The technology for issuing digital certificates is readily available; the difficulty is establishing a set of business relationships that will furnish the necessary incentives to bring a certificate infrastructure into being.

"Digital Cash"

We have been discussing electronic systems that use the Internet to accomplish transactions using existing payment instruments. However, the effect of technology on payments systems does not stop there. Digital communication and modern encryption techniques make it possible to create entirely new forms of payment capable of being used on the Internet.

These systems (often—somewhat inaccurately—referred to as "digital cash"), are of two general types: "account-based" and "token-based." Both serve the purpose of creating "cash-like" payment instruments for use on the Internet, but they are radically different in architecture.

Though both types of system could, in theory, be used for larger payments, they are more likely to be used primarily for payments in the range of $10 and under. Payment instruments designed to be used in this range should have the same attributes for the consumer as cash. As we have already noted, this means that it should be fast, convenient (no forms to fill out, credit card numbers to give, etc.), final, and anonymous.

Enabling consumers to make small payments conveniently and anonymously will eventually enrich the content available on the Internet. It will permit Internet merchants and publishers to sell digital content "by the glass" rather than requiring consumers to pay a hefty subscription fee. Consumers will be able to "pay cash" to purchase an article, a picture, or a database search, to play a game, or to listen to a song.

Account-Based Systems

Account-based systems, sometimes referred to as "notational" systems, are built from elements drawn from the conventional financial system. The most prominent example is CyberCoin®, developed by CyberCash, Inc. The objective of the system is to enable consumers to make relatively small payments (from 25 cents to $10) on the Internet. To use the system, a consumer acquires (free) an Internet wallet and "loads" it with "cash" from a credit card account or a checking account. That, anyway, is how the transaction appears to the consumer. Analogues to familiar objects and transactions in the physical world make comprehension and use much easier for the average user and even for the technologically sophisticated user.

In the "real" world, what happens when a consumer loads a wallet is that money is moved through the ACH system[10] into an agency account maintained by CyberCash in a major bank. Each consumer who has loaded money into a wallet has a sub-account in the agency account. CyberCash, as the operator of the system, maintains these accounts and enables consumers and merchants to move funds in and out of the agency account in "load" and "unload" transactions.

A "load transaction" from a checking account goes as follows; a "load" from a credit card is similar.

• The consumer sends a message to the payments gateway directing that money be moved from his or her checking account to the "wallet."
• The gateway computer directs the bank that holds the agency account to transfer the funds.
• The bank effects an ACH transaction, withdrawing the funds from the consumer's bank and depositing it in the agency account.
• The gateway confirms that the load has been successful.

Internet publishers and other merchants that use this system also have a sub-account in the agency account. When a consumer makes a purchase, CyberCash simply makes a bookkeeping entry, debiting the consumer's sub-account and crediting the merchant's. A purchase transaction using this system goes as follows:

· The consumer orders the digital goods.
· The goods are delivered in encrypted form.
· Payment instructions are sent to the merchant.
· The merchant forwards to the payment instruction to the gateway.
· The gateway checks the authenticity of the payment instruction, debits the consumer's sub-account, credits the merchant's sub-account, and returns a positive acknowledgement.
· The merchant sends an acknowledgment to the consumer and a key with which the previously sent digital goods can be decrypted.

It should be evident that this type of payment system retains and builds on many of the qualities of its more conventional physical-world counterparts. This has a number of advantages. It does not involve the "creation" of money. Because the funds remain in the banking system, it is possible to create an audit trail. This means, among other things, that these systems do not lend themselves to money laundering and other abuses that are concerns for token-based systems. Nevertheless, the system does differ from any payment system in the physical world. And it would be impossible without digital technology.

Token-Based Systems

Because they are designed to be used for essentially the same purposes, token-based systems and account-based systems can be made to appear nearly identical to the user. With some attention to system design, they can be made to have very similar attributes. Under the hood, however, they function quite differently.

In a token-based system, the system operator—usually, but not always a bank or group of banks—issues digital tokens in exchange for value.[11] The tokens, which are created using the techniques of public-key cryptography, are nothing more than very long numbers, but numbers that have been generated through a process that gives them special properties. They are redeemable by the issuer for "real" money at the option of the holder. In effect, then, these tokens are "digital bank notes." Their value depends entirely on the credibility of the promise of redemption. Unlike the value held in the wallet of an account-based system, which represents an undivided interest in an ordinary bank deposit, this form of "digital cash" is in a real sense a new form of money, albeit one that has an ancient (and not altogether untroubled) lineage.

Digital tokens also form the basis of some smart-card payment systems, such as Mondex. Though these systems were initially intended to be used in the physical world as a substitute for cash, it is only a matter of time before they become fully interoperable with the networked world. It is generally anticipated that by 1998 most personal computers will come with smart card readers as standard equipment. This means that it will be possible to transfer digital tokens from a card to a computer, and from one computer to another, via the Internet or another communication link.

Digital tokens can, in fact, be transferred via any form of digital transmission. The Mondex system permits transfers from a card to a hand-held card reader, and thence to another card. With properly equipped telephones, "Mondex value" can be transferred from one card to another via a telephone call.

Digital tokens have a number of interesting characteristics. First, just as physical bank notes (or their modern replacement, currency issued by central banks) can be passed from person to person to effect immediate, anonymous payments, digital tokens can be passed from one computer, card, or other storage medium to another, with the same effect. Likewise, just as lost currency is irreplaceable, digital tokens can be lost forever if the hard disk on which they are stored fails.[12]

Of course, digital tokens differ from cash in a number of ways. For example, they can circulate much faster, and they weigh a lot less. These particular characteristics give law enforcement authorities heartburn, as they have the potential for being used to launder funds. In addition, digital currency of this sort has the potential of reducing the amount of "seignorage" governments can capture through the currency they create. Seignorage is what the government earns when it issues a non-interest-bearing debt instrument—which is what, in effect, currency is. (Viewed from another perspective, it is the interest the government saves when it issues currency to pay for goods and services—or, more likely, to repurchase its own debt—rather than interest-bearing government securities.)

When a private issuer of digital tokens issues a replacement for cash, it captures the seignorage (by taking in interest-free funds in exchange for the tokens), rather than the government. Of course, this is one of the biggest reasons anyone would want to go into this business.

The qualities we have described of these two different versions of "digital cash" are the qualities of their native or "pure" forms. As with most things digital, it is possible to modify these qualities considerably by changing the architecture of the system. For example, while account-based systems by their nature create an audit trail that would make most payment transactions traceable, the system operator can design the system so that its transaction logs are erased or are encrypted. Thus, only the consumer, and not the system operator or a third party, knows where the consumer spent money. Likewise, it is possible to build in an element of traceability.

Special Issues for Electronic Payment Systems

The electronic payment systems of the future will, of course, have to overcome a number of hurdles, some quite similar to their physical-world counterparts and some particular to electronic commerce. Some of these are practical business considerations. Others relate more to concerns of public policy. Among the more important issues are authentication, concerns related to safety and soundness, questions about the effect of digital payments on the money supply, and concerns related to the use of these new systems for money laundering and other criminal purposes.

Authentication
The special problems of authentication in electronic commerce are not insuperable. Internet commerce is growing steadily without the deployment of new techniques of authentication; however, in the absence of more certain means of authenticating the parties to an electronic transaction, there will be more losses from fraud, and payments will therefore be more costly and less efficient than they would otherwise.

The first solution to this problem will be digital certificates. On the horizon are a number of other techniques that have the prospect of making Internet commerce even more secure and reliable than present-day commerce in the physical world. Smart card readers in personal computers will enable a merchant or a bank to know, with a high degree of certainty, that the party on the other end of a communication is the bearer of the card identifying a particular individual and knows the password or personal identification number associated with that card.

A little further over the horizon, biometric identification will eliminate even the possibility that the party at the other end of an Internet communication is using a stolen card. It is still too early to tell whether the winning technology will use fingerprints, voiceprints, iris scans, or something else associated with a difficult-to-forge physical characteristic. What is nearly certain, though, is that at least one and perhaps several inexpensive and easy-to-use means of authenticating individuals over a network will be widely deployed and will lower the risks of fraud below what they are in the physical world today.

Safety and Soundness

A system that requires the consumer to part with value in exchange for digital tokens can function effectively only if consumers and merchants have a high degree of confidence in the redeemability of these tokens. This makes the financial safety and soundness of the issuer a matter of concern.

This problem is, however, not different in principle from the issue of the safety and soundness of a depository institution in the conventional banking system. A check, for example, is worthless if the bank on which it is drawn is unable to honor it. We deal quite satisfactorily with those issues in the paper world through bank regulation and deposit insurance. There is no reason in principle why they cannot be addressed just as satisfactorily in the world of electronic payment. Indeed, as long as the digital tokens are issued by banks, the existing system of bank regulation should be perfectly adequate to address this issue.

Money Laundering

Another set of concerns often expressed by law enforcement authorities is that electronic payment systems will make it easier for drug dealers and other criminals to launder the proceeds of their activities. These concerns have two parts. First, in combating drug trafficking and similar crimes, the authorities rely heavily on making it difficult to convert the cash proceeds from illegal activities into legitimate-appearing deposits in financial institutions (a step often referred to as "placement"). Second, law enforcement authorities are also concerned about transfers of tainted funds within the financial system, especially across international borders. They want to be sure that they can "follow the money" in an investigation by examining the records of financial institutions. Indeed, they have gone beyond that to require that financial institutions file reports with the Financial Crimes Enforcement Network of transfers in excess of $10,000. The authorities have expressed concerns that electronic payment systems will make it easier for criminals to transfer funds without leaving a trail that investigators can follow.

There are only limited bases for these concerns. In the first place, there is nothing in the nature of electronic payment systems that makes placement of tainted cash into the legitimate financial system any easier. It is unlikely that any of the providers of advanced electronic payment systems will go into the business of handling cash; it will be left to banks and other traditional financial institutions that are already subject to reporting and record-keeping rules designed to attack money laundering. The second concern is valid only to the extent that new payment technologies can be used to accomplish untraceable transfers of funds. The account-based systems described above pose no threat to effective law enforcement, since they make use of conventional banking systems and leave the same audit trail as any other transaction effectuated by traditional financial institutions. Token-based systems might pose a legitimate concern if they were to allow anonymous transfers of large amounts of money, especially if those transfers could take place across international borders. No one currently operates a service that would make that possible, and there is no legitimate reason for anyone to do so.

The final concern is that, if the Mondex system or some similar service were to become widely used, it would enable drug dealers to accept payment on the street in digital form by means of card-to-card transfer. In theory, they could then transfer their receipts electronically without leaving an audit trail. Again, however, it appears that these concerns may be more theoretical than real. Stored-value products such as those offered by Mondex are designed primarily as substitutes for cash in consumer transactions. This means that limits on the size and the frequency of transactions could be implemented that would frustrate the use of the products for moving large sums untraceably. It is virtually certain that there will be an easy way to reach an accommodation between the requirements of an effective and useful system and the needs of law enforcement.

The Money Supply

Some have questioned whether electronic payment systems could cause central banks to lose control of the money supply. "What if private institutions issue large volumes of digital currency?" they ask. "Could this not at least weaken the ability of the central bank to limit the amount of money in the system?" Although it is possible to spin out theoretical scenarios in which this could happen, there is no reason for concern in the realm of practical reality. First, it is almost certain that, for the reasons discussed above, the issuers of digital currency will all be depository institutions. The bank regulators will, therefore, have a perfectly good handle, using reserve requirements and other conventional techniques, on the amount of "new currency" they can create. Moreover, the Federal Reserve Board has concluded that the amount of such new money will, for the foreseeable future, be so small as to be of little concern even were it to be issued by non-banks.

Conclusion

No one who is paying any attention would deny that the Internet will change in numerous ways how we accomplish many commercial tasks. It is already doing so. Paying for things is a small but essential part of commerce, one that most of us take for granted except when it comes time to pay the monthly bills. Making it easier to pay for things on the Internet may not revolutionize our lives, but it will make them more convenient in a hundred ways, saving us time and money. It will also vastly expand the potential of the Internet by creating economic incentives for content providers to offer online a host of products and services that are now accessible if at all only in the physical world, usually less conveniently and at higher cost. And it is all inevitable. There are no technical obstacles, only problems of human organization. The only question is how soon we will be able to take full advantage of these new ways of doing things.

Notes

1. See Debt Collection Improvement Act, Pub. L. 104–134, ch. 10 (1996).

2. It can be greater if one waits too long to notify the issuer.

3. The tendency of consumers to carry cash varies from country to country, and in some countries it is less unusual for consumers to settle large transactions in cash.

4. There are exceptions for disputes between the consumer and the merchant as to the quality or proper delivery of the goods.

5. 12 CFR Sec. 226.1 et seq.

6. 12 CFR Sec. 205.1 et seq.

7. For more details, see, e.g., Bruce Schneier, *Applied Cryptography*, second edition (Wiley, 1996).

8. The term was originally coined by CyberCash and has since been widely adopted in the industry. The architecture described is based on that developed by CyberCash, but it now serves as the basis for a number of payment systems.

9. This description would be equally applicable to debit card transactions, at least so long as no PIN is required.

10. As of this writing, CyberCash uses the ACH system to accomplish these transactions. That system has a number of drawbacks, however, the most important being that it does not effect transactions in real time. It is likely that CyberCash and its competitors will develop alternative methods of transferring funds electronically between bank accounts that will improve the efficiency and speed of account-based systems.

11. The leading provider of Internet-oriented token-based systems is Digicash.

12. It is possible to design a system to permit some degree of recoverability of tokens lost in this way.

11

Stars of Good Omen: Satellites in the Global Electronic Marketplace

Irving Goldstein

The ultimate result will be to encourage and facilitate world trade, education, entertainment, and many kinds of professional, political and personal discourses which are essential to healthy human relationships and understanding.
—John F. Kennedy, speaking on the Communications Satellite Act of 1962 and the creation of the International Telecommunications Satellite Organization

In 1965, when the International Telecommunications Satellite Organization (INTELSAT) launched its first satellite, it seemed that the science fiction of Arthur C. Clarke was coming to life.[1] Challenging the limitations of copper wire, the "Early Bird" satellite was able to transmit 240 telephone calls simultaneously, more than doubling the capacity for international telecommunications between Europe and North America. In addition, Early Bird's ability to transmit video meant that live international broadcasts had become a reality, ending the era when newsreels arrived by airplane or ship. Today this may seem a modest beginning, but it was the birth of the INTELSAT global satellite system, a cooperative international venture that would have enormous implications for telecommunications development and global interaction. The world, it seemed, was beginning to shrink.

Since then, the INTELSAT system and an ever-growing number of regional and domestic satellite networks have become integral to the global communications infrastructure. Unfortunately, most of us do not have Clarke's acuity when it comes to predicting the twenty-first century. It is clear, however, that satellites will play an even larger and more diversified role than they do today in the transmission of information in all its forms—voice, video, data, and multimedia.

In the next decade, satellites will be instrumental in bringing greater capacity to the international infrastructure, more service possibilities to consumers, and greater global access to the emerging electronic marketplace.

1998–2008: A Satellite Boom

In the days before submarine fiber-optic cables, INTELSAT satellites carried about 90 percent of international telecommunications traffic, linking the wired national networks together. In the late 1980s, the proliferation of new domestic and international fiber-optic cables began to lead some industry analysts to predict that fiber would all but replace satellites, especially as the medium used to connect the world's computers (and the individuals using them). These analysts were correct to recognize that fiber's development was important and that it might change communications. However, the global electronic market has been evolving in ways that also favor satellite. For the moment, at least, the overall capacity of some fiber cables (that is, a fiber cable's capacity from one major gateway switch to another) can be much larger than that of a single satellite network. Yet to take only this into account when assessing the role of satellites in the marketplace is to ignore some important factors that are fueling a boom in satellite service provision: the relentless growth of communications capacity and the changing patterns of demand for it; the constant advances in satellite transmission technology; the synergy of these advances with technological changes in computer hardware and software; and the inability of fiber cable to reach many parts of the world within the time frame demanded, both because of its point-to-point nature and because of the daunting amount of capital investment it requires.

In the race to provide basic and advanced communications services, operators are continuing to use and to plan satellite systems alongside fiber and other terrestrial networks (wired and wireless). In some geographical areas and for certain services, these technologies are, or will be, direct competitors to one another. However, relative to the interconnected global information infrastructure as a whole, these technologies also play complementary roles, and they are all necessary if a truly global electronic marketplace is to exist. Satellites are helping pull all the pieces together, as they have been doing for 30 years. In the electronic marketplace of the future, they will continue to help compensate for the lesser efficiency of other technologies. Indeed, naysayers have probably buried their old market reports. There is little doubt now that the worldwide satellite communications industry will experience tremendous absolute growth over the next decade, just as terrestrial networks are growing rapidly in many parts of the world.[2]

Improvements in spacecraft and parallel progress in communications technologies have made it easier and less costly to use satellite networks, and improvements in wired telecommunications have led to cost reductions in that area. Communications satellites have practically doubled in transmission power and capacity every 5 years since they were invented. More power (and therefore stronger signals) means that earth station requirements have become more flexible and less onerous in terms of the size, cost, and location of antennas. Today's advanced geostationary satellites have longer lifetimes (at least 12 years), operate in multiple frequency bands, and can have specially shaped, concentrated, and steerable antenna beams. In addition to allowing the unit cost of transmission to fall by about 600 percent since 1965, these improvements have fostered new services and applications in response to great customer demand in both the developed and the developing countries.

Global Demand

A main reason behind the global market's push to develop satellite services is the need of many areas to gain rapid access to communications capabilities, which is not possible if extended wired networks do not exist. This question of global access is also a key to the success of the future electronic marketplace, because the virtual market and the virtual society that are being created will reflect and benefit the true global political economy only if consumption of electronic communications moves beyond its current restriction to high-end users (i.e., those in the developed countries and in certain emerging market capitals). If one of the strengths of the electronic marketplace will be our ability to use the World Wide Web to develop ideas, businesses and partnerships without regard to distance, one of its limitations will be that any group lacking access to that marketplace will be left out—to the detriment of all.

The much decried "information gap" caused by the uneven distribution of access to communications networks really represents a "communications gap" that affects both the network-rich and the network-poor countries (albeit not to the same extent). Those left out are not just "information seekers"; they are also potential consumers, partners, teachers, employees, consultants, and providers of increasingly valuable information about their local and national economies. It is plausible that by 2008 many businesses and associations in network-rich cities such as Boston, Munich, and Singapore may prefer to deal with suppliers and consumers through electronic multimedia. A "communications gap" means that these businesses may miss out on otherwise desirable opportunities simply because they will never "meet" those who lack access to the electronic marketplace at any of the market's stalls. In a world where interdependent international trade, finance, production, and tourism have become commonplace and essential for the success of all "national" economies, global universal access to information and communications networks is crucial—and nobody wants to wait years to get it.

For 30 years, geostationary satellites have enabled telecommunications operators to connect cities and countries to national and international communications networks. Often, satellites have been the sole means of connection to the outside world.[3] This will continue to be the case over the next 10 years in many regions, despite the frenzy about building fiber networks "everywhere." In view of the cost of laying fiber, the reality is that the "global information highway" will not even come close to having truly global and mass participation by 2008 without the use of alternative transmission technologies for both long-distance communications and the "local loop" (i.e., local connections to individual homes and businesses).

In developed countries, where demand for broadband communications will be greatest in the near future, the high cost of laying fiber in the local loop is already deterring some large companies from risking the investment. Efforts are refocusing on adding broadband capabilities to the existing terrestrial infrastructure through less costly innovations, such as cable modems, digital subscriber lines, and wireless terrestrial technologies. In most of the developing countries, however, even the idea of upgrading is impossible, since terrestrial networks are unevenly distributed and often very limited (especially outside large urban areas). For topographical or financial reasons, or because of low population density, the highly developed copper, microwave, and fiber networks taken for granted in the United States and in Europe have not spread throughout many regions of the world. There may be connected pockets or enclaves in these areas, but about 80 percent of the world's people get by with fewer than 10 telephone lines per 100 inhabitants, whereas in the United States there are more than 60 lines per 100 inhabitants. Furthermore, consistent and reliable interconnection of neighboring homes, businesses, and towns often does not exist.[4] China, the most populous nation in the world, is reported to be spending US$350 billion to improve its telecommunications infrastructure between 1998 and 2002. This investment is expected to raise telephone penetration in that country from less than 4 percent to almost 20 percent—a remarkable improvement that nevertheless leaves the majority of the population with little in the way of communications services.

In the next decade, the main goals in most countries will still be more widespread provision of affordable basic telephone, fax, data transmission (including Internet), and broadcast services and the augmentation of reliable and more direct backbone connections to neighboring countries and to the industrialized countries with whom they do most of their business. These goals will be all the more critical in the next century because developing countries are experiencing great population growth, economic development, rising personal incomes, deregulation, and technological progress. These factors are pushing demand ever higher and are highlighting the problem of access to communications. In a few cases, the rate of growth might warrant commercial investment in an extended domestic cable infrastructure (where topography permits). The time it takes to do this is long, however, and satellites will often be chosen as the most cost-effective solution. In many other cases, even investment in copper networks is not viable. In many countries, the actual prospects of extending fiber connections beyond the gateway switches of major cities are dim in the foreseeable future.

A Brighter Future

Because of new and time-tested satellite transmission technologies, terrestrial wireless technologies (such as GSM or DECT) for the local loop, and new intelligent networking possibilities, there are real, tangible prospects that people in rural, remote, and/or developing areas will be able to connect to each other and to the rest of the world on at least a basic level—and on a much larger scale than ever before. Trials of rural telephony via satellite are already planned or carried out in Peru, Indonesia, and Thailand. Further research, network tests, and development of new equipment are still underway, but there is a concerted effort within the communications industry to make investments worthwhile by bring the cost per subscriber "line" down to a level that is commercially viable for regions with lower traffic demand (i.e., regions where recovering the costs of infrastructure and equipment will take longer).

Of course, we cannot expect that most developing countries will reach teledensity levels that rival those of developed countries in just 10 years. Nevertheless, millions of individuals and businesses in heretofore unconnected or underconnected towns and villages will gain at least some access to essential national and even international narrowband voice, data, and Internet services—leapfrogging the traditional wait for wired services. This will be one of the most significant developments in communications over the next decade, although the true impact of these new entrants into the electronic marketplace may only begin to be felt by 2008.

Changing Markets

The boom in satellite services is not solely about extending fiber's reach and bridging the gap in basic communications access between developing and developed countries. The changing composition of communications traffic everywhere means that demand is on the rise in all markets. Communications providers, private businesses, and consumers everywhere are increasingly looking at satellite applications for many types of basic and advanced multimedia services, in addition to the provision of traditional wholesale broadcast and public switched telecommunications services. Demand is increasing for more capacity, flexibility, mobility, and direct access to high-speed private and public networks, in order to support the feature-rich applications of the electronic marketplace being invented every day by the computer and content industries. In other words, "access"—both direct access for consumers and wholesale access for communications providers—is also a major issue in even the most developed economies.

Present geostationary and future non-geostationary satellite systems can support the same range of applications as fiber, with comparable performance and with the ability to operate with high-speed networking technologies, such as frame relay and asynchronous transfer mode (ATM). In fact, when fiber networks break down, satellite networks are used to back them up.[5] Past concerns over latency (i.e., delay caused by the great distance that signals must travel to and from geostationary satellites) have already been resolved or are being dealt with on a service-by-service basis by means of specially developed transmission protocols. Relatively new applications already in use and under constant development include the following:

private network services (e.g., video conferencing, file sharing and transfer, voice and data exchange)
business and community intranets and extranets
distance education
medical diagnostics services
agricultural, mining, and weather networks
video contribution (e.g., satellite news gathering)
video distribution, including direct-to-home services.

These services are the basics of the electronic marketplace. Their constant development and their increased consumption via private networks and the public Internet are pushing up the demand for domestic and global backbone communications capacity. Because the exponential growth of the Internet was not anticipated even a few years ago, congestion, bottlenecks, and quality fluctuations are all too common. By 2008, these delivery problems should be largely resolved thanks to new wired and wireless broadband communications technologies and the addition of dozens of new satellite networks to help meet the demand for long-distance narrowband and broadband service.

A Global Internet

The Internet's traffic configurations are expected to change over the next decade in two ways that will favor satellite solutions. First, geographic dispersion of Internet traffic will increase markedly as the Internet grows farther and farther beyond its current base (which centers on North America). The International Telecommunication Union estimates that the number of Internet users will increase from about 60 million in late 1997 to more than 300 million by 2001, and that dispersion will continue to increase. Whereas today more than 70 percent of the Internet's users are in North America, by the turn of the century North American users are expected to represent only one-third of the total. Many future users will be in developing nations, and they will be employing satellites for at least the international portion of their communications transmissions (through the international gateways of their regular telecommunications provider).

A second expected change in Internet traffic is an increase in the proportion of point-to-multipoint traffic relative to more traditional point-to-point traffic. Point-to-multipoint communications is the transmission of content from one source to an unlimited or specified number of receivers, whereas point-to-point communication occurs when a signal or a group of signals travels directly down a single path from one sender to one receiver. As the costs of computer storage capabilities fall and the geographic dispersion of Internet host computers increases, point-to-multipoint applications for updating Web caches and databases are expected to proliferate. This trend represents a natural expansion opportunity for satellites, in view of their inherent advantage in broadcast quality and their economic advantage in carrying multipoint traffic.

In the remainder of this chapter I will look more closely at changes in satellite technology that are favorable to the development of new systems and service applications. The industry is moving quickly both to provide basic communications on a large scale and to build a whole new broadband infrastructure in outer space. In just a few years, the capacity of satellites will be ten times what it is today. Beyond a few years, who can tell? What we do know is that by 2008 no single application (such as the telephone) and no single transmission technology (such as fiber or satellite) will rule. Moreover, the development of content will no longer be driven by the restrictions of single transmission technologies. Content will be driven more by consumer demand, and we will begin to see end users participating in the segmentation of content and in the choice of which transmission technology to use and when. In some cases, a consumer, a business, or a service provider may choose one form of transmission service over another, from end to end, to meet a particular need. In other cases, one burst of transmitted content may travel through fiber, satellite, and terrestrial wireless systems before reaching its destination. In any case, diversity, flexibility, and the adaptation of different technologies to different applications and customer needs will rule. In a way, it will be like moving in just 10 years from the constrained conventions of classical painting to the unpredictable lines of Picasso.

New Generations, New Frequencies, Lower Costs

Though satellites have been a mainstay of the international communications infrastructure for some time, exciting new developments in satellite transmission technology have emerged over the last 5 or so years as a result of converging improvements in spacecraft and advances in digital technology. In a nutshell, here is what we will see in the next decade:

the construction of more powerful, higher-capacity satellites capable of carrying more signals and high-speed communications traffic

the utilization of previously unused higher frequencies that will allow for the widespread provision of broadband communications

the operation of satellites in lower, non-geostationary orbits, which will allow the use of personal, hand-held, mobile satellite communications devices

improvements in reception technologies that will allow even smaller and cheaper antennas to be employed in homes and offices.

Spurred on by increased deregulation and demand, the transformation of these developments into service applications over the next 10 years will mean that institutions, businesses, and consumers will have an expanded palette of flexible, affordable fixed[6] and mobile narrowband and broadband services to meet their communications needs. Direct satellite links to broadband backbone networks will be available, but so will niche services not on the market today. By 2008, some applications that are currently available but not yet widespread for consumer and business use (e.g., videoconferencing at home, global mobile satellite telephone service, global positioning services, global messaging and tracking services) will become commonplace and even "essential" for some people.

Other current satellite communications services will be enhanced by the addition of full-service, two-way broadband multimedia capabilities that are not yet generally available in any medium; in many countries, though, such additions will probably still be very new by 2008. In the area of mobile satellite services, broadband applications will include personal mobile multimedia access, enhanced services for search and rescue operations in natural disasters or war relief efforts, and better onboard communications for fleets of ships and trucks. In the area of fixed satellite communications, network access services and backbone capacity will grow in order to carry all multimedia applications, including high-definition television broadcasts. And new services combining aspects of fixed and mobile applications will put the service provider's network concerns beyond the concern of the end user.

Getting communications from the local loop to the nearest public telecommunications switch will no longer be seen as so difficult. In many places, narrowband and/or broadband service access will be provided by means of small direct-to-home or direct-to-business antennas. In other areas, the problem of the local loop will be solved by the use of ground-based wireless local loop (WLL) technologies, which will then connect to a satellite network for longer-distance transmissions.[7] People in all countries will have the potential to access a number of global satellite systems in addition to INTELSAT and in addition to any domestic or regional ones. What exactly is chosen in each country will depend on the level of development of other infrastructural options, on the country's policy goals, and on the ability to pay.

Cheaper Bits

Besides the advent of competition, a major reason why all these services are becoming more affordable to many users is the dramatic lowering of the cost that service providers must bear to transmit a bit of digital data via satellite. This lowering of costs is attributable to the combination of more powerful satellites and continual advancements in digital voice and data circuit multiplication and digital video compression. The aforementioned advancements allow a higher number of distinct signals to be packed into the same transponder space, thus decreasing the cost per unit of transmission on any single satellite. For example, by 2008 the newest broadcast TV satellites will be operating more efficiently, employing thousands more watts of power and employing even more advanced compression techniques than the satellites being launched today. Instead of 100 or 200, they will be delivering several times more channels of content to their customers.

A far greater development affecting satellites' capacity and transmission costs will be the introduction of satellites that can operate at higher frequencies than the ones being used now. Higher-frequency satellites should be operating just after the turn of the century, and they will revolutionize the satellite industry in the same way that fiber cable revolutionized wired communications. Whatever level of maximum capacity we might currently attain in the lower frequencies, the switch to higher frequency bands will allow us to surpass that capacity by as much as a full order of magnitude in the next step and eventually even more.

At present, commercial communications satellites operate in several different bands of the higher portion of the radio frequency spectrum. Named decades ago by military engineers, radio frequency bands typically have cryptic and imprecise labels (depending on the book one consults), such as "L band" and "S band" (respectively, the 1–2-gigahertz and 2–4-gigahertz bands, used mostly for mobile communications) or "C band" and "Ku band" (respectively, the 4–8-gigahertz and 12–18-gigahertz bands, used mostly to link fixed or temporarily fixed communications antennas). Utilization of these bands is managed by national regulatory agencies within their territories and coordinated internationally by the International Telecommunication Union.

Since the overall demand for bandwidth is expected to increase, new technology has been developed to deal with the particularities of the previously little-used frequency band called Ka (18–30 gigahertz). Using this higher part of the frequency spectrum, operators will soon be able to offer high-quality, fully interactive, high-bandwidth service on a very large scale. In theory, data rates in the Ka band could range from

16 kilobits per second to 1.2 gigabits per second. It is probable, though, that services will be in the range between 2 and 155 megabits per second, at least in the beginning.

The use of frequencies beyond Ka, also under study, could mean another great leap in the ability of satellites to provide broadband capacity. Although the technology is in its research stages, companies are already racing to make regulatory filings to build very-high-speed broadband systems using the so-called V band (approximately 40–50 gigahertz). It is doubtful that many V-band applications will be ready before 2008, although they may be in the testing stage by that point. The development of these systems will be aimed at the even greater capacity needs of the mature electronic marketplace and information age. The operation of Ka-band broadband service is still being perfected, and the first global broadband Ka-band systems are not expected to be operational until 2001 or 2002.

Satellites operating in the Ku band are excellent for direct-to-home broadcast distribution and for some direct business services. There will be many Ku-band services operating 10 years from now and beyond.[8] Interactivity is limited in the Ku band because there is only enough spectrum available for users to return (uplink) information at about the same rate as today's telephone lines permit. Yet for some applications this is fine. For example, a private retail services network operator might find this appropriate for quickly and cheaply broadcasting new catalogue information from its headquarters to its outlets across a region or a country on a weekly basis, including pictures or video graphics of the products and appropriate ordering software for specialized needs. A return communications path would only be needed for the remote outlet to place orders with the headquarters office, which could be done efficiently with a low-bit-rate service. Ka-band, broadband interactive service would be required, however, if employees at the outlets were to have greater multimedia requirements, such as placing customized orders based on real-time modifications of catalogue information or the ability to perform real-time collaborations on joint design projects. In these cases, a true two-way, broadband, Ka-band connection would be necessary. It would allow designers to share their work on screen and to discuss and implement changes "face to face" in real time.

The Ka band is already being used in Japan for trunk transportation of domestic telecommunications services via satellite. There are also several test satellites operating, such as NASA's Advanced Communications Technology Satellite, launched in 1993 to test Ka-band service and the use of onboard digital processing and switching of telecommunications signals. Though onboard processing and switching are neither required by nor restricted to Ka-band satellites, they are inherent to several of the commercial multimedia Ka-band satellite systems that will be in orbit starting around 2002.

Unlike the lower radio frequencies, the relatively wide Ka band is able to offer enormous amounts of unused bandwidth for commercial communications applications. In addition, the bandwidth per unit coverage of a typical Ka-band satellite will be much larger than those of the Ku-band and C-band satellites in use today. In contrast with a small number of active beams covering a large geographical area (and therefore limiting the total regional capacity of the satellite to the bandwidth available in those beams), Ka-band multi-spot antennas allow a high level of frequency reuse. Ka coverage can be split into many cells, each covering a much smaller geographic area than the larger beams available in the Ku band or in the C band. This means that about the same number of bits can be carried simultaneously to each cell as are carried in one beam using the other frequencies. This is similar to the principle used for terrestrial cellular telephony, but applied to space. When signals are uplinked to the satellite, onboard processors receive them, determine where they should go, then switch them to the appropriate "cell" for downlinking.

Inter-Satellite Links

Onboard processing and switching also facilitate inter-satellite links, which will be another standard feature of certain satellite systems by 2008. When communications signals are able to travel from one satellite to another, the expense and the inconvenience of intermediate hubs or gateways are eliminated. Otherwise, intermediate "hops" are necessary to directly connect a sender and a receiver via satellite when their antennas are not pointed toward the same satellite. Today, satellites operate largely as "bent pipes": a signal is beamed from one antenna (a ground station) up to a satellite and is then transmitted back down to another ground station within its coverage area. In the future, satellites will be more intelligent and will be able to act like telecommunications switches in the sky, allowing direct user-to-user satellite communications. With today's communications offerings, the "bent pipe" scenario rarely causes a problem, since telecommunications signals involving satellites are usually transmitted via a combination of satellite and standard terrestrial networks, depending on the location and who is providing the long-distance service. Consequently, pure satellite communications from user to user have been rare until now—at least in the domain of fixed telecommunications.

Inter-satellite links are a prerequisite for the operation of the new low-Earth-orbit (LEO) and medium-Earth-orbit (MEO) systems, which will soon offer global mobile personal communications and more options for both narrowband and broadband wireless services. Today's commercial communications satellites (including those of INTELSAT) are in geosynchronous orbit about 36,000 kilometers from Earth. At this distance, they orbit above the equator at the same speed as the planet rotates. From Earth they appear stationary, and antennas can be permanently fixed in their direction. At this distance, the satellites' beams can cover up to 42 percent of Earth's surface; this maximizes the number of connectable antennas in one satellite coverage area (called a "footprint") and minimizes the number of "hops" required between satellites and ground terminals. This is what has made global satellite communications via satellite possible until now.

For example, in order for a telephone call or a television broadcast to reach the opposite side of the world via geostationary satellite transmission, the maximum number of hops it would need to make is two. Because MEOs and LEOs orbit Earth at a much lower altitude (about 10,000 km and 700–1400 km, respectively), the coverage area for each satellite at any particular time is much smaller than that of a GEO. A similar round-the-world transmission would require multiple hops if it were not for inter-satellite links, which will allow transmissions to travel from satellite to satellite until they reach the one in the appropriate coverage area where the downlink portion of the transmission may be completed.

Some future GEO systems may also make use of inter-satellite links for east-west connectivity between regional landmass satellites. They are crucial, however, to the success of the LEO/MEO systems. Inter-satellite links will also allow the development of entirely new applications, such as inter-orbit linking between different satellite networks (e.g. GEO to LEO) or space-based communications with very low-orbiting data-gathering satellites and devices. For example, communications satellites will have the ability to track and locate smaller data-gathering satellites and then broadcast the collected information down to Earth at very low cost.

Some data-gathering applications are already in operation and will become widespread in the United States and other countries fairly soon. One example is precision farming, in which a satellite can monitor and communicate crop growth patterns in the fields so that farmers can recognize weak areas and treat them regularly. Environmental monitoring in general will probably be a major application of data-gathering technology; however, other uses will also become common, such as satellite tracking of traffic. Satellite tracking may also be used in sporting events.

Bandwidth on Demand

Onboard processing is important for the future of many services in the electronic marketplace because it will also allow easier access to bandwidth on demand. Rather than lease satellite capacity (transponder space) and keep it reserved at all times, users will be able to pay for the amount of bandwidth they use, charged either by the length of time it is needed or by the number of bits transmitted. Such on-demand capability, quite new in the satellite services industry, will be the norm for many types of services 10 years from now. Further, on-demand capacity will be available at varying bandwidths to accommodate the needs of various applications, ranging from just 64 kilobits per second (what a normal voice circuit or a narrowband Internet connection requires) to at least 10 megabits per second.

On-demand capability of another type is already possible for narrowband geostationary voice and data applications in the C band and the Ku band. Here a ground-based processing technology called demand-assigned multiple access (DAMA) is used. The development of DAMA has been a major step in making fixed satellite voice services more flexible and affordable, especially for developing countries with low traffic requirements.[9] Over the next several years, DAMA equipment will be installed in many unconnected locations where the demand for connection to the national or international networks is too low to warrant the permanent lease of transponder space. DAMA technology allows satellite capacity to be efficiently shared and charged on the basis of capacity actually used. In addition, it allows countries to provide relatively low-cost direct voice and data connections to correspondents without having to use (and pay for) third-country transit. By 2008, on-demand fixed networks (which are much cheaper in the long run than on-demand mobile satellite services) will be commonplace in the developing countries, and they will have been largely responsible for the expansion of rural access to basic telecommunications, including Internet services.

The future availability of onboard processing will improve fixed and on-demand services and will allow more applications to be developed because it will eliminate the need for network commands to be communicated through a hub (where the processor is located). Onboard processing will thus facilitate the further development of full mesh fixed service networks in which each participant can directly and easily communicate with all the others. On-demand access using onboard processing is obviously crucial for personal mobile services via satellite, whether for narrowband telephony or broadband multimedia service. In all cases, onboard processing will help satellite service options mirror those of terrestrial wired and wireless networks.

Shrinking Antennas

Aside from the lower transmission cost per bit and the availability of on-demand service, the falling prices of antennas are making satellite communications more affordable for all potential users, whether they be service providers or individual consumers. More powerful satellites and higher frequencies are allowing the development of ever-smaller antennas. (At higher frequencies, wavelengths are smaller and so the receiving terminal can be made smaller.) In the next 10 years, "fixed" geostationary satellite services such as private business networks and direct-to-home (DTH) interactive services will use small two-way antennas ranging from about 60 centimeters to a meter wide, depending on the service and the frequency used (Ku or Ka). Antennas for these higher frequency bands will continue to become cheaper as the services become more widely consumed and as economies of scale enable manufacturers to enter the mainstream of consumer electronics. This is already happening for the slightly larger business VSAT[10] antennas in use with the C and Ku bands today and for the small one-way "receive" antennas used in many countries for direct-to-home television and Internet service. (The return path for the "interactive" direct-to-home services available today is usually a telephone line, but this will not be the case for long.)

Of course, the smaller antennas become, the less expensive they are to transport and install. In addition, the standardization of approval processes in different countries and the deregulation of telecommunications equipment markets are making it faster and easier to buy and/or install this equipment in many regions. This too should facilitate the greater production and utilization of all types of satellite antenna terminals, which will in turn bring prices down even further. And although many of these terminals will be purchased and used in the developed countries, those who will benefit most from their mass commoditization are in the developing countries; for them, the purchase of antenna equipment can mean the difference between some communications and none at all.

The same trend to smaller terminals is happening in mobile satellite communications. Consider, for example, the antennas used for geostationary mobile telephone and data services, such as those traditionally provided to ships and coastal areas by the International Mobile Satellite Organization (INMARSAT). Power increases in INMARSAT satellites have helped reduce the size of mobile satellite telephone and data units from that of a large briefcase to that of a small laptop computer (with the antenna built into the lid). The telephones and data units that will be used for personal mobile communications via the planned LEO and MEO systems will be even smaller. Because LEO and MEO satellites will orbit much lower than GEOs, their signals will be much stronger when they reach Earth than those of the GEOs. This means that the antennas required to capture their signals will be as little as 3 centimeters in length, making hand-held satellite telephones a reality.

System Architectures—GEOs, MEOs, LEOs

Before looking more closely at the service applications of the next decade, it is worth noting a few additional points about the GEO, MEO, and LEO systems that are already in operation or that will begin operation over the next few years.[11] Because LEOs and MEOs are new types of systems, there have been misconceptions about the novelty of some of the services they will provide. Many of the misconceptions are due to confusion between the importance of the satellite system's architecture and the importance of more general advances in satellite technology as it applies to all three systems. There will be some service differentiation, much of it based on the fact that LEOs and MEOs will have stronger signals and thus expand the possibilities for direct mobile satellite services. Stronger signals do not necessarily equate to greater bandwidth, however. All three types of systems are capable of carrying narrow or broadband signals, and all three of them will be doing so in the near future.

In the meantime, the first generation of LEOs are narrowband satellites offering simple voice and/or data services. For example, the US-based company Iridium is due to begin offering direct satellite telephone service by the autumn of 1998. This system and similar competing ones have been receiving an inordinate amount of attention because they are the first to put LEO systems to the test and because the idea of global roaming with a simple mobile satellite handset is very appealing. Yet these systems and direct satellite telephony represent only the tip of the iceberg of the new range of consumer services that will be available via GEO, MEO, and LEO systems within 5 to 10 years (in addition to increased wholesale trunk services for telecommunications operators and broadcasters). Moreover, direct satellite telephony may not even be a main application of LEOs in the longer run. It really is more of a niche service for business users, since the per-minute costs will be high relative to the expanding ground-based wireless systems. Some of the other early narrowband LEO applications, such as mobile low-speed data, global positioning, and paging services, will become more mainstream. By 2008, however, many of these services may be integrated or even absorbed into the greater broadband satellite systems now being planned, even if some of the market niches and specialized services remain distinct. Many of the companies that are launching early LEO systems are also planning broadband LEO, MEO, and/or GEO systems, to follow a few years later.

With all three orbital architectures taken into account, it is expected that at least 1000 commercial communications satellites will be in operation by 2008. (There are about 200 today.) The bulk of these will be LEOs and MEOs, because those systems require the highest minimum number of satellites to ensure an operational system and global coverage (since the satellites are not "stationary" and the individual footprints of each satellite are small). New-generation GEO systems will be operating, too—many of them in the Ka band and perhaps some in the V band. Indeed, at least half of the planned worldwide investment in satellite systems over the next few years is going toward GEOs.[12] Moreover, the early regulatory filings with the US Federal Communications Commission for V-band frequency allocations show that potential operators are, so far, concentrating on geostationary service in that frequency, sometimes as a complement to Ka-band LEO service.[13]

In all, there should be a number of global broadband service providers in 2008, plus many regional and domestic systems, offering fully interactive services that can match what is available on end-to-end fiber networks. Some of these providers will use a single type of orbital system; others may use interconnected, hybrid orbital architectures (e.g., LEO plus GEO) to provide service flexibility and to lower the initial investment and operational costs of pure LEO systems (which are more expensive to launch and which require more sophisticated network controls). The first full Ka-band systems should be in operation by 2001 or 2002, although these may not yet have full onboard processing and switching and so the capacity potential will not yet be optimized.

Of course, to end users the system architecture usually will not matter, and most consumers will not be concerned with how far their signals are traveling (or, indeed, whether they are traveling by fiber or by satellite).

What they will judge are price and service quality. GEOs, MEOs, and LEOs will perform many comparable service functions, ranging from regular voice transmission to video telephony to high-speed data transmission and tele-education services, within the same frequency levels. The different systems will also be complementary, however, with areas of specialty based on different characteristics. Because antenna size is an issue for some services, particularly for mobile communications, LEO systems will tend to dominate in the field of personal mobile satellite services. At the same time, many "fixed" applications via geostationary satellite may be cheaper, simply because the satellites are cheaper to launch and operate in the long run.

On the one hand, GEO systems, owing to their wide coverage, will continue to be the most suitable and cost-effective medium for delay-insensitive fixed broadcast and multicast services, such as video distribution to cable companies and multimedia distribution to private business networks and direct-to-home subscribers. In addition, GEOs operating in the Ku and C bands will continue to be suitable for certain relatively lower-cost, lower-speed data services for business and home, such as home banking and credit card verification at the point of sale. On the other hand, LEO/MEO systems, with their near-to-Earth, multi-spot coverage of small areas, will be better suited to highly delay-sensitive point-to-point services (in addition to mobile voice and multimedia services), such as interactive data transfer and the highest-resolution videoconferencing required for services such as remote surgery.

Most applications are not as delay sensitive as remote surgery, however, so there will still be strong competition between different types of broadband systems. GEOs have been carrying Internet traffic ever since the Internet was invented. For higher-speed, interactive, packet-switched traffic (the basis of the future Internet), it is true that the 250-millisecond propagation delay that is inherent to geostationary satellite communications becomes problematic if it is not accommodated. This is because the transmission of packet-switched traffic is slowed as a result of the dynamic between the propagation delay and preexisting Internet protocols (which require the end terminal to acknowledge receipt of content packets during the course of the transmission). Internet protocol enhancements have been developed to handle this problem by controlling the flow of the content packets. This has minimized delay to a level that goes undetected by users of the most common Internet applications.

Successful comparisons to terrestrial fiber have been carried out (using frame relay and ATM technology in each case), and commercial ATM satellite services via GEO are actually available today. Moreover, new "fast byte" data communication protocols have been defined and developed by INTELSAT engineers and standardized by the International Telecommunications Union. These completely eliminate the effects of satellite round-trip propagation delay, and they will form the basis for the development of new, efficient circuit switched telematic applications and high-speed multimedia services. What all this means is that GEOs will be competing with "fiber-like" LEOs in the Internet market for everything but very specific applications.

Operating in the Electronic Marketplace

In view of the importance of the Internet, intranets, and extranets in the new electronic marketplace, the kind of flexibility and competition just described will help ensure that service providers and end users can get the most out of computer hardware and software advances—which generally tend to be ahead of developments in the communications infrastructure. The great efforts behind the development of new protocols and entirely new satellite systems to support the Internet's needs underscore how integrated satellites are, and must be, in the overall information infrastructure. People will be using GEOs, MEOs, or LEOs to get their Internet-based multimedia and other business done. Service providers are realizing that, though fiber-optic cables often have advantages for high-traffic areas and trunk routes, satellites may offer more economical choices, especially for low- and medium-traffic routes. In addition, satellites can add special value to certain applications because of their broadcast and multicast capabilities and their ability to provide both symmetric and asymmetric service, creating efficiencies according to users' needs. (With asymmetric service, the bandwidth purchased in each direction can be different—e.g., broadband downlink and narrowband uplink.)

Owing to the evolutionary nature of the market, there is a high degree of uncertainty associated with projections about multimedia (defined here as the content of a communications channel that simultaneously delivers digital voice and data, sound, and full-motion video). However, on the basis of the numbers and the growth rates of customers who are expected to be early adopters of multimedia, such as current multichannel and DTH subscribers, Internet users, and subscribers to online services, it appears that the potential is large in both business and consumer areas. With the assistance of satellites, that customer base should expand to even the most isolated communities as the benefits of new business applications, tele-education, and telemedicine become more widely appreciated.

In the provision of future Internet-based multimedia services, satellites will help alleviate congestion by connecting the primary international network service providers using high-speed trunk routing and Internet backhaul services. In addition, Internet Service Providers (ISPs), large corporations, and other entities will increasingly use satellites to meet requirements for direct high-speed links to a backbone point of presence, bypassing investment in direct fiber links to owners' premises. However, for very large capacity requirements (e.g., above 45 megabits per second) fiber cable may be more competitive, depending on the location. At the same time, the choice will also depend on other transmission needs and on what new operations might be possible. And, just as ISPs may connect directly to fiber backbones via satellite, businesses and specialized networks will increasingly turn to satellites for direct connection to their ISPs and for connections between local-area networks in different corporate locations.

Multicasting

One of the determining factors for both ISPs and private businesses in choosing transmission options will be whether it is possible to exploit the potential of multicasting. The need for and the utility of point-to-multipoint communications capability are rising. Multicasting will have many uses in private business and education networks. As Internet host computers become more widely dispersed, multicasting will become an integral part of ISP business operations and will play a crucial role in keeping the "information" part of the electronic marketplace up to date and globally accessible at local transmission rates. Multicasting makes it possible to broadcast sets of information of any kind exclusively to specific recipients whose "addresses" are keyed in at the broadcast source. This is a highly efficient way to reach subsets of servers and people and to create virtual communities in private networks and on the Internet at large.

In a way, multicasting is already being done on the wired Internet: news-distribution companies and advertisers are sending "cookies" to online users. On the wired system, however, multipoint traffic is transmitted at a great cost to network capacity, since the same messages must be sent down many telephone lines in order to reach the intended recipients. This creates bottlenecks and contributes to the congestion currently experienced on the wired networks. Fiber and copper networks are inherently point-to-point transmission media, so multicasting is naturally more limited and difficult over them than it is via satellite, and it requires additional equipment at greater costs. With the spread of VSAT and DTH services, satellite multicasting will enable information providers to send their content only once, to specified addresses, and still reach any number of people located in the satellite's footprint. This is a much more efficient use of bandwidth, aside from being a cheaper solution for the sender.

Thus, the development of multicasting is playing a major part in the transformation of the Internet from a "pull" environment to a "push" environment. The effects of push technologies are already becoming apparent, and they will change the dynamics of the Internet—creating new business models that will facilitate the opening of emerging markets. This will help turn the Web into a real commercial tool, with information, advertisement, and sales channels tailored to specific audiences.

The "push" environment will also affect the business operations of the ISPs and major content providers who will be using satellite multicasting to regularly update databases and multiple local servers around the world. The establishment of local and regional caches or mirror sites will continue to grow, fostered by the multicasting of content from "parent" or affiliated organizations. With an increased number of servers in use around the world and the ability to mix tailored international content with local and regional content, the accessibility and thus the utility of Internet content will be tremendously improved everywhere. Improved utility will lead to greater use and participation, which of course will then lead to greater innovation and adaptation to local needs. Because most Internet servers have been located in industrialized countries, the greatest impact may be felt in developing countries.

Direct Business Networks

The recent growth of C-band and Ku-band VSAT services for business networks has been fueled by and has contributed to unprecedented growth in domestic, regional, and international business communications. This is undoubtedly part of the greater pattern of globalization. VSAT's growth has been greatest in Asia and in Latin America, where terrestrial networks are less abundant than in North America or Europe. Almost every major multinational company operating in multiple locations has some requirement for private networking between decentralized offices and the head office. When this requirement includes remote, offshore locations, satellites are the only answer. When the requirement includes multiple disparate locations, satellites are often the best answer, especially with the advent of multicasting capabilities.

When direct Ka-band multimedia services become available to businesses and homes, they may overtake the use of certain C-band and Ku-band VSAT services. This will take some time, however, because broadband communications will not be required by everyone immediately (especially in the developing countries) and because in many areas people will hang onto their VSAT terminals and services for at least a few years. In any case, the increasing popularity of VSATs today will set the tone for the electronic marketplace of 2008, particularly on the supply side. Because satellites are naturally suited to connecting geographically dispersed sites, more and more businesses are exploring the utility of national and international VSAT networks to economically send identical sets of content to multiple locations (affiliates or other organizations). Businesses are learning that they can perform remote software upgrades (thus saving the time and expense of having technicians visit each site) and that they can broadcast and multicast sales information, training materials, videos, and even music to customers visiting their remote premises. With VSATs, businesses can send financial information for instant verification. They can also have basic voice telephony, video-conferencing, and file sharing. As full two-way broadband capability becomes available, businesses will discover how to combine it with other technologies and how to adapt it to their needs. One interesting application now under development is a remote mining operation in Northern Canada in which mining equipment can be controlled via a remote satellite connection.

Typical examples of companies taking advantage of satellite technology are the oil and gas companies Chevron and Shell, which use VSAT antennas to connecting remote oil drilling sites and to connect service stations. In the media industry, national newspapers in several countries have decentralized their printing locations and now send each news edition to different parts of the country via satellite in order to cut down on shipping costs. The government of India has used satellite technology successfully to promote the exportation of software to companies in the United States and elsewhere. In the United States , the retail industry is the main user of VSATs, with retail outlets performing point-of-sale processing and communicating financial and stock information back to warehouses and head offices. The financial sector is a another heavy users of VSAT technology; indeed, it is the main user in some countries. Everywhere, all kinds of companies are finding satellite business networks to be a relatively cheap and efficient way to do business, especially as the number of locations increases. In short, satellite networks are becoming integral parts of enterprise data networks and of the burgeoning electronic marketplace.

This change in how information is delivered and spread goes hand in hand with the fact that companies are starting to externalize data and to get away from the information hoarding that came naturally in the era of mainframe technology. This externalization of data and even of business processes is what we see on the World Wide Web. In North America, a point is being reached where even the smallest company needs to have a virtual presence on the Web in order to affirm that it exists in the real world. Moreover, the static home page is already being surpassed, and companies are increasingly converting their standard business processes into electronic format so that people with whom they do business (not just customers) can deal with the company at their own convenience.

This externalization of business processes is one of the ideas behind electronic data interchange (EDI), a well-established, standardized, text-based electronic messaging system used internationally for ordering, stocking, transport, and invoicing between large establishments such as supermarket chains and their various suppliers. With the digitalization of telecommunications and the increasingly widespread use of machine-readable product bar codes, whole supply chains are being transformed.

For users of EDI who are connected via satellite, multicast capabilities will further enhance the range of available applications and the efficiencies that can be gained. For example, the main "purchaser" in a supply chain could use multicast technology to send out instant information and requests to subsets of suppliers, such as all the growers and shippers of fresh produce in a supermarket supply system. Beyond invoicing and stocking, satellite multicasting could efficiently keep all members of the chain up to date on all matters that affect their business. With multicasting the head office of a retail chain could go beyond merely sending electronic catalogues to all the outlets; it could tailor the catalogues to regional needs so that not all stores would be receiving the same information. Satellites, by virtue of their inherent broadcast capability, are the perfect transmission medium for all such applications, and as more businesses become more familiar with them more new applications will be developed.

Remote and Developing Areas

The spread of VSAT technology is also a key to connecting rural areas and much of the developing world to basic voice and data services in the next few years. Other enhanced business and social applications will be added whenever possible. Multinational companies and international hotel chains are installing such systems in developing countries for their own use, which may or may not benefit the community at large (except insofar as it facilitates business, jobs, and so on). The addition of DAMA technology to VSAT terminals is making it feasible for town administrations, schools, hospitals, and other institutions to purchase and use antenna equipment to provide a range of affordable fixed communications applications that can be shared among the members of a community. Though the purchase of one VSAT would not increase the teledensity of a town by much, it could change life in the town by bringing its leaders into closer contact with neighbors and the world. Initially, VSATs will be installed in many areas purely to provide a local pay telephone connection because that is all that the citizens can afford to use.[14]

Although telephones in homes may continue to be rare, individuals and local businesses in the more dynamic towns could have an opportunity to tap into Web resources and create a virtual presence there, in addition to making plain old telephone calls. Businessmen, teachers, doctors, functionaries, and community workers could eventually initiate participation in a wider virtual community (even if only text-based at the beginning) and thus build connections with peers and associations in other towns that also have VSAT connections.

In a way, this is similar to the early days of telecommunications in developed countries, when each town may have had only one or two telephones to be shared by everyone. The existence of the Internet, multicasting technologies, and the global electronic marketplace will make the impact of these local communications centers even greater, however. Though we should not expect miracles, direct access to even the smallest amounts of information can lead to innovation and can have dramatic effects, if it is the right information—such as world commodity prices for farmers who would otherwise have to trust the word of middlemen who purchase their harvests. In effect, the availability of affordable, on-demand satellite services means that generalized low teledensity in a region no longer has to mean that the region is absent from the modern economy and the electronic marketplace. The potential is enormous ,and it will be interesting to see how things will have changed in certain areas by 2008.

Health and Education

Another area in which satellites will have a major impact over the next decade is the electronic health and education marketplace. Like most other aspects of information age, services is this area are not exclusive to any transmission medium. However, their development will be closely tied to the use of satellites, particularly in the field of education. In both developed and developing countries, satellites operating in the Ku and Ka bands will offer unique and economical capabilities to address multipoint educational gatherings, either through real-time videoconferencing or through multicasting of course materials, tests, and other types of content.

Attempts to create tele-education systems have been around for some time, primarily in the form of correspondence courses and broadcast television but also in the form of videoconferencing. There have been some successes, but in the past bandwidth constraints have pushed the cost of quality videoconferencing out of reach for most users. The situation has changed now, however, and the future introduction of Ka-band services will make larger education programs even more feasible. In the industrialized world, where traditional education is already widely available, tele-education via satellite will probably be used mostly in business and higher education niches rather than to replace any significant portion of traditional education. Though DTH services will certainly tempt some people to take courses at home, regular tele-education services will be used mostly by companies having multiple offices and significant training needs.

As with other services, the greatest beneficiaries of distance education via satellite will be people in remote areas and in developing countries. Often, areas without access to fiber networks and perhaps without qualified teachers, libraries, and course materials will find satellite transmission to be the most feasible way to bring in information and expertise.[15] This applies not only to developing countries but also to countries (such as Canada and Australia) that have a large land mass but a relatively small, dispersed population. Perhaps pointing the way, these countries are taking satellite services seriously and are currently undertaking policies to ensure that by 2008 no community is without access to essential training courses and specialized medical advice.

Direct-to-Home Services

Many homes around the world, particularly in Europe but increasingly in Asia, Latin America, and the United States, already have direct-to-home television antennas. These small antennas, currently operating with

Ku-band satellites, generally offer only broadcast television and radio reception, although they may allow some narrowband return options. Asia is one of the fastest-growing regions for DTH; it is projected that the Asia-Pacific DTH market will reach more than 35 million homes by 2008, compared to under 10 million just a few years ago. DTH is growing everywhere, especially as equipment prices and regulatory prohibitions fall. In many less developed areas, DTH antennas may not make it into homes in the near future for financial reasons; however, they may well be put into local gathering places for the community to share, just as VSATs may provide shared telecommunications services.

When the use of the Ka band becomes a reality, DTH service will expand to include full, interactive multimedia services, and the distinctions between direct satellite "business services" and direct-to-home services will become less clear. In fact, bringing these multimedia connections and capabilities into the home will probably lead more people to work at home. Ten years ago, people were beginning to talk about "teleworking," and it was often thought that by now many workplaces would be more decentralized than they have become. Multimedia capability should really bring this revolution about by 2008, however, because home videoconferencing will make "meetings" possible and will provide closer interaction than remote voice and text-based electronic communications have done for us until now.

Conclusion

The pace of technological change being what it is, it is always a risky business to forecast what the world will look like 10 or 20 years hence. Arthur C. Clarke was a visionary because as early as 1945 he understood the great possibilities of communications satellites. But even Clarke did not foresee the invention and proliferation of the microprocessor and the subsequent innovations that would flow from the convergence of computer and communications technologies.

Keeping his story in mind, I have outlined technological and service developments which are underway now and which are likely to come into mass global commercial use by 2008, rather than trying to predict technology developments that may not affect the global market by that year. Perhaps it is easier to comfortably take this approach when one is in the satellite industry, where product development cycles are relatively long. But the subject of this book is the electronic marketplace of 2008, and the most important aspect of markets is that they are essentially meetingplaces where people interact, socialize, teach, learn, and do business. Issues of global access and the attainment of mass participation are important, therefore, because they touch on the question of who is present under the market's roof, which is at least as important to that market's future development as is the mode of interaction (virtual or physical).

Very often, ideas and technology are ripe for the creation of some new and important invention but our minds and societies are not ready for it. At other times, many different influences converge, and the pace of innovation and the spread of ideas seem to increase. Although regulatory, economic, and physical barriers to the flourishing of a truly global electronic marketplace do exist, it seems that we are in a time of innovation, a juncture at which people all over the world are beginning to embrace change on an unprecedented scale. The development of global telecommunications has been very important in helping us reach this juncture. The new global electronic marketplace will help take us beyond, thanks in major part to the still-visionary concept of satellite communications.

Notes

1. Arthur C. Clarke, best known for the novel *2001: A Space Odyssey* and its sequels, is considered to be the "grandfather" of the geostationary satellite, even though he was not its developer.

2. It is estimated by various sources that global commercial and non-commercial revenues for satellite services will reach almost US$40 billion by the end of 1998 and almost US$60 billion by the end of 2000. Continued outstanding growth can only be expected in view of the dozens of new market entrants and the great number of new satellite networks that are in the pipeline.

3. Nearly all countries use satellites to fulfill at least part of their international telecommunications needs, in addition to using copper and fiber cable and some terrestrial wireless systems. More than 50 countries still rely exclusively on INTELSAT to communicate with the rest of the world.

4. President Nelson Mandela of South Africa brought this into sharp perspective in 1995. Addressing an audience at the ITU's Telecom '95 event, he said that

there were more telephones in Manhattan than in all of sub-Saharan Africa. The comparison would still be a good one today, and it is still true that almost 80 percent of the people in the world have never used a telephone.

5. Unlike cables, satellites are not subject to natural disaster, and they have extremely high reliability. Satellites are routinely used for "cable restoration" services—i.e. backup services when cable fails or breaks for natural or unnatural reasons. It generally takes a week to repair a broken submarine cable. For broken terrestrial cables the time depends on the circumstance.

6. Fixed satellite services have been defined by the International Telecommunication Union for regulation purposes as services to antennas or user terminals that are not mobile at the time of service (unlike ships, for example), even if they are transportable when not in service. In practice, the lines between fixed and mobile services are becoming blurrier as mobile technologies and applications develop.

7. Though narrowband WLL technologies are now mature, WLL technologies for economical fixed broadband services will likely be possible before 2008, perhaps using higher-frequency versions of wireless cable technologies such as the Local Multipoint Distribution System (LMDS) and the earlier Multichannel Multipoint Distribution System (MMDS).

8. The lifespan of Ku-band satellites being launched now and in the next few years could be more than 15 years.

9. INTELSAT first introduced this capability in order to address the low-traffic needs of many of its developing country members. Global DAMA capabilities have been available since mid 1997. Some other organizations and companies have also developed DAMA services.

10. VSAT—the acronym for "very small aperture terminal"—has a specific connotation in the engineering world. In the commercial world it usually denotes any "small" antenna under about 5 meters.

11. There are dozens of national, regional, and international GEO satellite systems in operation today for telecommunications and broadcast services. In addition, at least one "little" LEO global messaging company was already operating at the time of this writing: the US-based Orbcom Global LP.

12. According to a number of market study groups, including HSBC Washington Analysis.

13. The FCC registered these filings in late 1997. See "Satellite Companies Flood FCC with Applications" (*TR Daily*, September 26, 1997) and "FCC Inundated with New Satellite Applications" (ibid., October 10, 1997). *TR Daily* is published by Telecommunications Reports International, Inc.

14. Current scenarios of rural telephony development view the installment of a pay telephone connected to a VSAT and a DAMA processor as a first step. The next step would be the addition of wireless local loop connections, giving a number of customers wireless access to the connectivity provided by the VSAT. Within 10 years, thousands more communities should be connected using this kind of technology combination.

15. Large tele-education projects, such as the African Virtual University, are now in their early stages. The AVU is a World Bank project begun in 1996; its pilot phase was sponsored in part by INTELSAT. Using VSATs, it links more than ten African capitals to several European and American universities, and it includes access to electronic libraries. The network offers significant improvement in the range of choices and opportunities for higher education in these African cities. As the VSAT network is gradually extended beyond the capitals, secondary schools will also be able to participate.

About the Authors

Les Alberthal has, since 1987, been chairman of the board and chief executive officer of EDS, one of the world's largest systems integration companies. He is also an active member of the World Economic Forum, co-chairman of the Global Information Infrastructure Commission, and a member of the board of directors of the JASON Foundation for Education. He holds a BBA from the University of Texas.

William D. Bandt is corporate executive vice president of the Entergy Corporation, one of the largest energy providers in the United States. He is responsible for retail services. Previously he was corporate senior vice president of UtiliCorp United and president of UtiliCorp Holding. He has been managing director of a venture capital firm specializing in high-tech investments, director of international business development at United Technologies, and director of strategic planning at Northrop. He holds an MBA from the University of Southern California, an MA in mathematical statistics and economics from the University of Iowa, and a BA in computer science, math, and economics from Texas A&M University. He served as a captain in the US Air Force Systems Command.

Robert J. Bonometti is president of the Strategic Technology Decisions consulting practice of MGB Enterprises LLC. Previously, he was executive director of technology strategy at Bell Atlantic Corporation, responsible for business planning and analysis for advanced technologies, including Internet and multimedia data networking technologies. He served in the White House Office of Science and Technology Policy from 1993 to 1995, and before that at the Advanced Research Projects Agency.

At the White House he was a founding member of the Committee on Information and Communications under the National Science and Technology Council. A licensed professional engineer in electrical engineering, he has taught university courses in science, engineering, and business. He holds PhD and MS degrees in physics from the Massachusetts Institute of Technology and an MBA from Long Island University.

David Braunschvig is a managing director at Lazard Frères & Co. LLC in New York, where he advises governments and corporations on transactions and technology. In addition to his ongoing work as an advisor in the fields of information technology, Internet services, and "new media," he has advised the Mexican government on the privatization of its national satellite system. Before joining Lazard Frères he was a director at Coopers & Lybrand, where he co-founded the company's strategy consulting practice and was responsible for international assignments in telecommunications and technology. Previously he was a consultant at Arthur D. Little and a fellow at Harvard University's John F. Kennedy School of Government and at MIT's Media Lab. He has served on Vice President Gore's National Information Infrastructure Advisory Council. He holds a doctorate in operations research and computer science from the University of Paris and an MPA from the Kennedy School.

Stephen D. Crocker is a founder of CyberCash, Inc., the pioneer company in enabling secure Internet payments. As the company's senior vice president for development, he is responsible for security architecture and for the design and implementation of server systems. He is also a member of the Internet Architecture Board. Previously a vice president at Trusted Information Systems, a program manager in the Advanced Research Projects Agency, a senior researcher at the USC Information Services Institute, and an area director for security for the Internet Engineering Task Force, he holds a PhD in computer science from the University of California at Los Angeles. He is known as one of the creators of the Internet.

Walter Forbes was the original investor in CUC International, the multi-billion-dollar leader in the field of electronic shopping. He has served as

CUC's chief executive officer since 1976. As a venture capitalist, he has started numerous companies. He holds an MBA from Harvard University and both a master's and a bachelor's degree in journalism from Northwestern University.

Denos C. Gazis is president of Gazis Associates, a consulting firm that applies computer and communications technologies to intelligent transportation systems and specialized intelligent agents to various business problems. During his 30 years at IBM, he served that corporation as director of general sciences, assistant director of computer sciences, and assistant director of the Department of System Technology and Science, and also as a member of the Research Review Board. His books concern traffic science and the theory of vibrations of solids. He has been a visiting professor at Yale University. In 1959 he received the Lanchester Prize of the Operations Research Society and Johns Hopkins University for his pioneering contributions to traffic science, and in 1996 he received the Lifetime Achievement Award of the Institute For Operations Research and Management Sciences. He holds a PhD in engineering sciences from Columbia University, an MS in engineering mechanics from Stanford University, and first degrees from the Polytechnic in Athens.

Daniel E. Geer Jr. is vice president of CertCo, LLC, which enables banks, corporations, and public institutions to conduct secure high-value transactions worldwide. Previously director of engineering at Open Market, Inc., he has also worked as a technical director at Digital Equipment Corporation. As the manager of systems development for MIT's Project Athena, he was responsible for the technical development of "X," Kerberos, and all other aspects of the Project Athena Network Services System. He serves as vice president of USENIX, the UNIX and advanced computing systems professional and technical association. He is the author of *Web Security Sourcebook*. He holds a Doctor of Science degree in biostatistics from Harvard University and a BS in electrical engineering and computer science from the Massachusetts Institute of Technology.

Irving Goldstein is director general and chief executive officer of the International Telecommunications Satellite Organization, a commercial consortium of more than 140 countries which owns and operates a global system of satellites. Previously he was chairman and chief executive officer of the Communications Satellite Corporation. He is a director of Computer Associates International, Inc., and chairman emeritus of the Board of Trustees of the Queens College Foundation. A graduate of Queens College of the City University of New York, he holds a law degree from New York University.

Edward D. Horowitz is executive vice president for advanced development at Citicorp and its principal subsidiary, Citibank, with global responsibility for incorporating electronic interactive delivery into product lines and customer distribution systems. Before joining Citibank in 1997, he was senior vice president for technology at Viacom and chairman and chief executive officer of Viacom Interactive Media. From 1974 to 1989 he held senior management positions with Home Box Office. A member of the Global Information Infrastructure Commission, a director of the Ariel Corporation, a member of the executive committee of the Montreux Television Symposium, and a visiting scholar at MIT's Media Lab, he holds an MBA from the Columbia University School of Business and a BS from the City College of New York.

Daniel P. Keegan is a partner in Price Waterhouse LLP, where he has worked for 30 years, consulting with the largest US corporations on problems of financial planning and control. Over the last few years he has concentrated on advising company leaders on subjects such as corporate measurements, cost management, and product pricing, as well as helping companies strengthen their internal procedures. He has published a number of articles on these topics. He holds an MBA in Operations Research from the University of Pittsburgh and a BA in economics from John Carroll University.

Derek Leebaert is a founder of Linguateq, Inc., a data interoperability software company that sells interface management systems to the communications industries. He also teaches the economics of innovation at

Georgetown University and advises corporations on technology management and on adopting new information products and services to leverage
computerized infrastructures. Previously chief economist at the Information Industry Technology Council and a postdoctoral fellow at Harvard
University's Center for Science and International Affairs, he is an occasional consultant to the Department of Defense. A founding editor of
The International Economy and of the *Journal of Policy Analysis and
Management,* he has edited two previous volumes published by The MIT
Press: *Technology 2001* and *The Future of Software.* He holds a D.Phil.
in Economics from Oxford University.

Raymond W. Smith has been chairman and chief executive officer of Bell
Atlantic Corporation since 1989. He previously held the titles of president and vice chairman. He serves on the US House of Representatives'
Advisory Board for Renewing US Science Policy and also on the advisory
boards of the Business Roundtable and the Library of Congress. Known
as a writer, playwright, and theatrical director, he was appointed to the
President's Committee on the Arts and Humanities in 1995. He holds a
BS in industrial and electrical engineering from Carnegie-Mellon University and an MBA from the University of Pittsburgh.

Russell B. Stevenson Jr. is senior vice president and general counsel of
CyberCash, Inc. Before coming to CyberCash he practiced corporate and
securities law in Washington. From 1971 to 1981 he was a member of
the law faculty at George Washington University, where he taught corporations, securities regulation, international business transactions, and
international economic development. During that time he also was a
visiting faculty member at Cornell Law School and at the University of
Paris II (Sorbonne). From 1981 to 1984 he served as deputy general
counsel of the US Securities and Exchange Commission. The author of
two books on corporate law, he has also written numerous articles on
securities law and corporate law. He has also lectured frequently on these
and related topics, and he has been active in the Business Law Section of
the American Bar Association, the District of Columbia Bar, and the

International Law Association. A member of the bars of the District of Columbia and the United States Supreme Court, he holds a BME degree from Cornell University and a JD from Harvard Law School.

Patrick E. White is a managing director at Arthur D. Little & Co. Previously he was vice president for advanced technologies at Bell Atlantic and assistant vice president of network architecture and analysis research at Bellcore. A frequent author on topics ranging from software engineering to ISDN and high-speed communications systems, he edits papers on telephone switching systems for the Institute of Electrical and Electronics Engineers. He holds a PhD in electrical engineering and computer science from Northwestern University.

Index